Political Institutions under Dictatorship

Often dismissed as window dressing, nominally democratic institutions, such as legislatures and political parties, play an important role in non-democratic regimes. In a comprehensive cross-national study of all non-democratic states from 1946 to 2002 that examines the political uses of these institutions by dictators, Jennifer Gandhi finds that legislative and partisan institutions are an important component in the operation and survival of authoritarian regimes. She examines how and why these institutions are useful to dictatorships in maintaining power. In their efforts to neutralize threats to their power and to solicit cooperation from society, autocratic leaders use these institutions to organize concessions to potential opposition. The use of legislatures and parties to co-opt opposition results in significant institutional effects on policies and outcomes under dictatorship.

Jennifer Gandhi is an assistant professor in the Department of Political Science at Emory University. She received her PhD in comparative politics and political economy from New York University in 2004. Her research interests include the political institutions dictators use to maintain power and the strategies the opposition may adopt in response. Her work has appeared in *Economics and Politics* and *Comparative Political Studies*.

Political Institutions under Dictatorship

JENNIFER GANDHI

Emory University

CAMBRIDGE
UNIVERSITY PRESS

CAMBRIDGE UNIVERSITY PRESS
Cambridge, New York, Melbourne, Madrid, Cape Town, Singapore,
São Paulo, Delhi, Dubai, Tokyo, Mexico City

Cambridge University Press
32 Avenue of the Americas, New York, NY 10013-2473, USA

www.cambridge.org
Information on this title: www.cambridge.org/9780521155717

First published 2008
First paperback edition 2010

A catalog record for this publication is available from the British Library.

Library of Congress Cataloging in Publication Data

Gandhi, Jennifer, 1975–
Political institutions under dictatorship / Jennifer Gandhi.
  p. cm.
Includes bibliographical references and index.
ISBN 978-0-521-89795-2 (hardback)
1. Dictatorship – History – 20th century. 2. Dictatorship – Case studies.
3. Political parties. 4. Legislative bodies. I. Title.
JC495.G36   2008
321.9–dc22   2008025515

ISBN   978-0-521-89795-2 Hardback
ISBN   978-0-521-15571-7 Paperback

Permission to reprint material is gratefully acknowledged. Portions of Chapter 3 appear
in Gandhi, Jennifer, and Adam Przeworski, "Cooperation, Cooptation, and Rebellion
under Dictatorship," 2006, Economics and Politics 18, 1: 1–26; portions of Chapter 5
appear in Gandhi, Jennifer, "Dictatorial Institutions and Their Impact on Economic
Growth," forthcoming, European Journal of Sociology; and portions of Chapter 6
appear in Gandhi, Jennifer, and Adam Przeworski, "Authoritarian Institutions and the
Survival of Autocrats," 2007, Comparative Political Studies 40, 11: 1279–1301.

To my parents and Neil

Contents

List of Tables and Figures

FIGURES

Acknowledgments

My intellectual debts are many, but first and foremost are my dues to Adam Przeworski. From him, I have learned much, but the lessons that stay with me are the ones he taught by example: to aspire to ask big questions and to embrace the process of retooling in order to answer those questions. I thank others from whom I have learned valuable lessons: Bernard Manin for his carefulness, John Roemer for his clarity, and Stephen Holmes for his boldness. In addition, my thanks to Leonard Wantchekon, Youssef Cohen, Jonathan Nagler, and Kanchan Chandra for their encouragement at various stages in the process.

My time in New York was enriched by a cohort in graduate school that spanned many years and countries. I thank the members of the Thursday group who provided much criticism, made easier to swallow with much laughter: Suzy Fry, Matt Golder, Sona Nadenichek Golder, Wonik Kim, Covadonga Meseguer, and Sebastian Saiegh. Wonik and Sebas, in particular, were loyal companions who provided advice that made me a better scholar and, often, a better person. I am grateful to Carmela Lutmar and Jeff Lax for their support. José Cheibub and Jim Vreeland deserve special thanks for their suggestions on my work and their counsel on becoming a scholar in one's own right. Finally, I consider myself lucky to have been part of the melting pot that came together in the Department of Politics at New York University: My thanks to Despina Alexiadou, Tamar Asadurian, Dulce Manzano, and Julio Ríos Figueroa.

Since graduate school, the political science department at Emory University has provided a supportive environment. I thank members of the Political Economy Workshop and, in addition, Dan Reiter, Tom Remington, and Jeff Staton for their feedback on my work. For their encouragement and advice, I am in debt to Cliff Carrubba, David Davis, Rick Doner, and Alex Hicks. My thanks to Amy Liu and Jeffrey Kucik for their research assistance. In addition, the Stanford Comparative Politics Workshop, Jason Brownlee, Bill Keech, and Beatriz Magaloni provided helpful feedback on either parts of or the whole manuscript. Finally, my thanks to Eric Crahan at Cambridge University Press for his heartening interest in the project and his steady guidance in its completion.

Through this experience, I learned that writing a book is at times a gratifying experience and, at other times, an excruciating one. I owe many thanks to Michael Owens, Maisha Fisher, Tavishi Bhasin, Leslie Davis, and Ravish Bhasin for helping me remember that the tempest should stay in the teapot. I also thank Joanne Fox-Przeworski for her endless hospitality and kindness.

Life in New York was a formative moment in no small part due to three people without whom my life would have been all that much poorer. A constant companion since graduate school, Melissa Schwartzberg always has shown a generosity of spirit in all things that helped me complete this book and so much more. In addition, I thank Carol Hsu and Carissa Montgomery, the best of friends who always forgave my absences and allowed me to pick up our friendship wherever it left off. I am grateful to the three of them for their enduring support and for making me feel at home whenever I am back in the city.

Finally, I thank Neil for his patience with an itinerant sister and his willingness to close the gap as we grow older. His sincerity and sense of humor help me keep things in perspective. In addition, heartfelt thanks to my parents, Josephine and Niranjan, for encouraging us to do the best we can in all things and for indulging me my intellectual curiosities. This book is dedicated to the three of them.

Introduction

Why do nondemocratic rulers govern with democratic institutions, such as legislatures and political parties? One view is that these institutions under dictatorship are mere shams. Scholars and policy-makers alike have pronounced the irrelevance of formal institutions under dictatorship. In discussing the role of political institutions on regime change, Gasiorowski (1995: 883) writes: "Huntington's (1968) argument about the importance of institutionalization also applies under authoritarian regimes, but consociationalism, party system structure, electoral rules, and the type of executive system are largely irrelevant and therefore presumably have little effect...." A USAID report (n.d.: 1), in describing communist regimes in Eastern Europe and Central Asia, states more bluntly: "Elections were a sham. Parliaments had no real power. Basic democratic freedoms – free speech, the freedom to assembly and organize, the right to form independent parties did not exist." The conclusion is clear: nominally democratic institutions constitute mere window dressing that dictators can point to as evidence of their democratic credentials.

Yet those who encourage the formation of these institutions in the interests of promoting democracy imply another view. As Jeane Kirkpatrick (1979: 37) observed: "democratic governments have come into being slowly, after extended prior experience with more limited forms of participation during which leaders have reluctantly grown accustomed to tolerating dissent and opposition...." As a result, nongovernmental organizations, such as the National Democracy Initiative for International Affairs (NDI), provide countries with ". . . assistance in building their democratic structures. These include: national legislatures and local governments that function with openness and competence; broad-based political parties that are vehicles for public policy debates; and nonpartisan civic organizations that promote democratic values and citizen participation."[1]

In this view, semiautonomous parties should provide political leaders and followers the opportunity to learn and practice the "civic culture." Electoral contests and legislative debates should enable opposition forces to make progress, even if incremental, in liberalizing the regime. The hope, of course, is that liberalization sets the stage for democratic transitions, even if with disappointment; we have witnessed enough instances in which this has not been the case. But if this anticipated sequence of events motivates encouragement of elections, parties, and assemblies under nondemocratic rule, then it must be the case that we believe these institutions serve as more than mere ornamentation. Mere drapery cannot sow the seeds of destruction of dictatorships.

The variation in dictatorial institutions is immense. During the post–World War II period, the proportion of nondemocratic regimes with legislatures varies from 60 to 88 percent. Legislatures are ubiquitous in party dictatorships, but less so under military rule and monarchy. More heterogeneity exists in the number of political parties tolerated by authoritarian regimes, whether they are allowed simply to legally exist or also to obtain seats within the legislature. The share of dictatorships in any given year that has banned parties ranges from 8 to 25 percent. Although the majority of nondemocracies have allowed for multiple political parties to exist (58 percent, counting by country-year observations), only in half of these cases are parties other than the one organized by the regime permitted to obtain seats within a legislative body.

The aggregate patterns are a reflection of some infamous examples. Communist dictatorships always have been organized around the regime party or a front in which auxiliary parties are forced to join alongside in an assembly. Lenin's invention was copied by other authoritarian incumbents, such as William Tubman of Liberia and

---

[1] http://www.ndi.org/about/about.asp.

Rafael Trujillo of the Dominican Republic, even if they did not import the ideological trappings. Other nondemocratic rulers, such as Mohammed Mahathir in Malaysia and Anastasio Samoza in Nicaragua, allowed for the formation of multiple parties that participated within legislatures. Still other dictators, such as Idi Amin in Uganda and Augusto Pinochet in Chile, banned legislatures and parties upon seizing power. Incumbents also may change their institutional arrangements like musical chairs. King Hussein, for example, closed and reopened the Jordanian parliament four times. What becomes apparent is that the institutional variation in dictatorships is bounded by neither geographic nor temporal considerations.

The two views of nominally democratic institutions under dictatorship, then, appear contradictory. One says that legislatures and political parties are nothing more than window dressing with little expected effects for policies or outcomes, whereas, in another view, these institutions are meaningful precursors for greater liberalization if not more dramatic democratic change. Yet neither view can account for the variation in the behavior of authoritarian rulers and their institutional choices. If these institutions are costless window dressing that provides reputational benefits on the international stage, why do not all dictators have them? In turn, if these institutions have the potential to undermine autocratic rule, why would any incumbent create or tolerate them? Whether nondemocratic rulers should either promote or shun these institutions, their behaviors should be consistent.

If parties do not compete and legislatures do not represent under dictatorship, what is the purpose of these institutions? Are there systematic reasons for why some nondemocratic rulers govern with these institutions, whereas others do not? Furthermore, if institutions are the product of conscious choices, do they have effects on policies and outcomes under dictatorship?

0.1 THE ARGUMENT

Dictators face two basic problems of governance. First, as rulers who hold power without the legitimacy of having been chosen by their citizens, they must prevent attempts to undermine their legitimacy and usurp power. In other words, they must thwart challenges to their rule. Second, autocrats also must solicit the cooperation of those they rule. Even if their interests lie only in accumulating wealth and power, incumbents will have more to amass if their countries are affluent and orderly. Internal prosperity can be generated only if citizens contribute their capital and their labor to productive activities. Autocrats, in other words, need compliance and cooperation.

Yet the severity of the problems of ensuring compliance and generating cooperation vary across authoritarian incumbents. The degree to which they face serious threats to their rule depends on the strength of the potential opposition within society. Incumbents have more to fear from a united, broad-based resistance movement. When the opposition is weak – whether due to an unpopular ideology or collective action problems – rulers have less need to manage outside groups. Similarly, the degree to which dictators must solicit cooperation from citizens to generate prosperity and rents for themselves differs. If rulers have access to external sources of revenue, for example, they may rely less on the cooperation of domestic groups for the creation of wealth.

To both thwart rebellion and solicit cooperation, dictators must make concessions to outside groups. Concessions may come in the form of rents; the dictator may agree to distribute some of his spoils to certain segments of society as a solution to these two problems of governance. Yet the potential opposition may demand more, and incumbents may have to make policy concessions as well.

To organize policy compromises, dictators need nominally democratic institutions. Legislatures and parties serve as a forum in which the regime and opposition can announce their policy preferences and forge agreements. For the potential opposition, assemblies and parties provide an institutionalized channel through which they can affect decision-making even if in limited policy realms. For incumbents, these institutions are a way in which opposition demands can be contained and answered without appearing weak. If authoritarian leaders face a weak opposition and need little cooperation, they will not need to make concessions and, therefore, will not need institutions. But if they must impede opposition mobilization and solicit outside cooperation, rulers may need to make policy concessions, in which case they need institutions to organize these compromises.

As a forum through which dictators can make policy concessions, nominally democratic institutions are instruments of co-optation. As such, they determine the way in which political life is organized in dictatorships and, consequently, affect the policies and outcomes that are produced. Legislatures and parties facilitate policy concessions that result in policy differences across differently organized authoritarian regimes. Variations in policy translate into differences in economic outcomes. But assuming that incumbents are able to observe with some accuracy the conditions that dictate the choice to institutionalize and then choose their institutions as a strategic response to these conditions, we should observe no significant differences in tenure on the basis of institutions. These are the claims to be elaborated and empirically assessed for all post–World War II dictatorships. Considered together, they not only demonstrate that institutions have effects in dictatorships but also account for the institutional variation across nondemocratic regimes.

0.2 THE STUDY OF INSTITUTIONS IN DICTATORSHIPS

The focus on institutions that long has pervaded the study of democracies is now resurgent in the study of dictatorships. Traditional classifications have recognized – even if implicitly – that dictatorial regimes differ in their organization and bases of support. Arendt (1951) and Friedrich and Brzezinski (1965) highlighted the features of totalitarianism, whereas Linz (1970: 254) argued for distinguishing authoritarian regimes because they have "... distinctive ways in which they resolve problems common to all political systems...." Because institutions are precisely those procedures and structures by which actors try to resolve a variety of political problems, we can understand Linz's distinction as one founded on institutionalist criteria.

Moving beyond the distinction between totalitarian and authoritarian regimes, comparative politics scholars have identified a number of important types of nondemocratic regimes. The communist totalitarian state eventually evolved into posttotalitarianism (Linz and Stepan 1996), whereas various forms of personalist rule have been identified as sultanism (Chehabi and Linz 1998) or neopatrimonialism (Bratton and Van de Walle 1997). The prevalence of military regimes throughout the developing world stimulated the study of these regimes: their emergence and their organization (e.g., Barros 2002, Finer 1988, Nordlinger 1977, Stepan 1971) as well as their effects on policies and outcomes (e.g., Biglaiser 2002, Remmer 1978, Zuk and Thompson

1982). O'Donnell (1979) identified an important subtype of military regimes in bureaucratic-authoritarianism (see also Collier 1980, Im 1987). Even monarchy, as a subtype of nondemocratic regimes, persists in the contemporary world.

Within these categorizations is an understanding that institutions matter under nondemocratic rule, but which institutions matter depends on the subtype of nondemocratic regime. The literature on bureaucratic-authoritarianism and military regimes in general focuses on the importance of the armed forces, whereas the study of monarchies emphasizes their dynastic structure (Herb 1999). Studies of personalist regimes focus on the nature of executive power that allows for dictatorial leaders to exert tight control. Although these works emphasize important institutional features for each nondemocratic subtype, none of them focus on the role of nominally democratic institutions, such as legislatures and political parties. These institutions are assumed to play a marginal role in these types of nondemocratic regimes.

The exception is the voluminous literature that surrounds the single-party state. Many initial studies of regime parties focused on their description and categorization, providing useful intuitions about the origins and functions of regime parties (Collier 1982, Huntington 1970, Michels 1949, Tucker 1961, Zolberg 1969). More recent work, such as that by Geddes (1999), Slater (2003), Smith (2005), Magaloni (2006), and Brownlee (2007), builds on their insights, making prominent again the study of hegemonic or dominant parties. From this work, we have acquired a better understanding of the origins of regime parties and their maintenance, especially through their combination with other institutions such as elections.[2]

In tandem with theoretical development and the accumulation of evidence from specific countries and regions, the compilation of

---

[2] Elections under dictatorship are another nominally democratic institution under significant inquiry. Hermet et al. (1978) examine the institution in detail as do more recent works that investigate "hybrid regimes" (Diamond 2002), "competitive authoritarianism" (Levitsky and Way 2002), and "electoral authoritarianism" (Schedler 2006), as well as how nondemocratic incumbents shape electoral rules (Lust-Okar and Jamal 2002), perpetuate electoral fraud (Lehoucq 2003, Schedler 2002), and manipulate the economy (Blaydes 2006, Magaloni 2006) to win electoral contests and remain in power. Although these elections are another example of nominally democratic institutions under dictatorship, I do not cover them here because they may serve different roles from those of dictatorial legislatures and parties.

cross-national data on nondemocratic states allows us to determine whether more general statements about the genesis, functioning, and effects of these regimes are supported by evidence. In this regard, Geddes' (1999) categorization of personalist, party, and military regimes and her use of this classification to examine theories regarding the survival of dictatorships and the likelihood of democratic transitions have been path breaking. Her collection of data on dictatorships allows for cross-national empirical tests that often better fit our theories than those based on older regime measures, such as Polity or Freedom House. The result has been a burgeoning of quantitative research on the effects of dictatorial types and institutions on outcomes such as war (Lai and Slater 2006, Peceny et al. 2002), repression (Vreeland 2008), and economic development (Wright 2008).

This work follows contemporary trends in both the emphasis on institutions and the use of various methods to examine the institutionalist account. Yet the argument advanced here and the data used to assess it differ from previous work in a number of important respects. First, a common assumption is that rents are the only means by which dictators build political coalitions. Spoils certainly constitute a significant share of dictatorial concessions, but in this account, policy compromises take center stage because there is no reason to believe that policy is not an important second dimension over which the potential opposition and incumbents may want to bargain. Second, although the idea that rulers trade concessions for broadened political support is not new, the claim that dictatorial legislatures and parties play a significant role in this exchange is novel. As discussed earlier, these institutions frequently have been dismissed as insignificant window dressing. Finally, the claims about the emergence and effects of these institutions are assessed using new cross-national time-series data on the legislative and partisan arrangements of all nondemocratic regimes from 1946 to 2002.

0.3 PLAN OF THE BOOK

Chapter 1 commences with a brief sketch of our historical understanding of dictatorship, demonstrating how an institutionalized form of rule in ancient Rome devolved into contemporary forms of dictatorship that frequently are thought to operate without institutional constraints. Yet looking more carefully, we see that in reality dictatorships vary in their institutional structures as illustrated by the different types of dictatorships (e.g., military, civilian, and monarchy) and their nominally democratic institutions (e.g., legislatures and parties). In this opening chapter, I provide an overview of this variation using data from 1946 to 2002 on all dictatorships around the world. Because ultimately the goal is to understand the role of nominally democratic institutions in dictatorships, the focus in this chapter is on providing a systematic picture of the variation in legislative and partisan arrangements.

After a description of the institutional forms under dictatorship, the following two chapters are intended to provide an explanation for the variance. In other words, the question to be answered is: What accounts for the differences in legislative and partisan arrangements across dictatorships? I argue that dictators face two basic problems of governance: first, the need to obtain cooperation from some segments of society and, second, the need to neutralize potential opposition. Dictators can solve these problems by using nominally democratic institutions to share the spoils of power and to make policy concessions. Policy compromises, in particular, require an institutional forum in which demands can be revealed and agreements can be hammered out. Chapter 2 uses three case studies – the ruling family of Kuwait, the monarchy of Morocco after independence, and the military dictatorship of General Rodriguez Lara in Ecuador – to illustrate the logic and plausibility of these arguments. Even though the cases are very different – in historical, cultural, and political contexts – they demonstrate the logic of institutionalization. The cases are not intended as tests of the theory but simply as illustrations of the plausibility of these arguments.

The intuition provided from the cases is used to construct the formal argument elaborated in Chapter 3. The model relates institutional strategies of dictators to the conditions they face, predicting that the number of legislative parties should increase in the dictator's need for cooperation and in the strength of the opposition. A statistical test of this prediction for all the countries for which the requisite data are available between 1946 and 2002 shows this is the case. When dictators need to build support within society, they use legislatures and parties as instruments of co-optation.

For dictatorial institutions to effectively encapsulate the potential opposition, they must offer groups within society some real decision-making power even if in very limited policy realms. Without the hope of policy concessions, the potential opposition has few incentives to participate in nominally democratic institutions. In addition, the crafting of policy compromises requires an arena in which negotiations can occur and deals can be hammered out. Legislatures and parties under dictatorships serve this purpose. As a consequence, institutionalized dictatorships should exhibit differences in policies from their noninstitutionalized counterparts. Chapter 4 provides a quantitative analysis of this observable implication derived from the theory elaborated in the previous chapters. An examination of both civil liberties and government spending for all dictatorships during the postwar period shows that institutions have an effect on government policies about which citizens can form reasonably unified preferences. As such, institutionalized dictatorships are forced to institute more liberal policies regarding citizens' rights to speak freely and to organize collectively as workers and to spend less on the military. Yet the effect of institutions on other types of spending is mixed, likely due to the heterogeneity of preferences citizens may have over distributive goods.

If institutions influence policies under dictatorship, do they also have an impact on outcomes? In Chapter 5, I take up this question, looking specifically at the impact of dictatorial institutions on economic growth. In previous chapters, I argue that legislatures and parties help dictators build their bases of support in part by allowing for some policy concessions to the potential opposition. As a result, these institutions foster greater cooperation between the regime and outside groups, reducing the potential for political instability. In addition, institutions serve as a conduit of information between the two sides. Finally, the willingness of rulers to play the institutional game indicates a measure of policy predictability. For all of these reasons – political stability, greater information, and policy predictability – institutionalized dictatorships are expected to have higher economic growth than noninstitutionalized regimes. A statistical analysis of all dictatorships during the postwar period shows that institutions, in fact, have a positive effect on economic growth.

The last observable implication concerns the political survival of autocrats. In Chapters 2 and 3, I argue that authoritarian rulers choose to operate with legislatures and parties only when conditions dictate that they must. As a result, depending on how badly dictators need cooperation and the strength of the potential opposition, their degree of institutionalization varies. Yet because dictators formulate their institutional strategies as a best response to the conditions they face, those rulers who choose to rule with institutions should not survive significantly longer than those who govern without them. Chapter 6 provides details of this argument along with an event history analysis of the 558 dictators of the postwar period. The results confirm that nominally democratic institutions do not have a statistically significant impact on their survival in power.

The book closes with a brief conclusion that summarizes the arguments and findings of the previous chapters and addresses whether the presence of legislatures and parties in dictatorships renders these regimes "more democratic." I argue against such a view because these institutions are instruments of co-optation for authoritarian regimes, offering little in the way of representation and accountability to participants and ordinary citizens. In addition, because dictators retain the power to alter and eliminate assemblies and parties, institutionalized dictatorships remain closer in spirit to their noninstitutionalized counterparts than to democracies. Nominally democratic institutions under dictatorship do matter but in ways that differ from their counterparts in democracies. This distinction has implications for our understanding of these regimes and for scholars and policy-makers who would encourage the creation of these institutions for the purpose of facilitating democratic transitions.

1

The World of Dictatorial Institutions

1.1 INTRODUCTION

The contrast between democracy and dictatorship – in structures, policies, and performance – has been the object of intense scrutiny. Yet little consensus exists over the definition of regime type. What cases qualify as "democracies"? Which cases constitute the universe of "dictatorships"? The latter question is easy to answer when we encounter the ferocity of a Joseph Stalin or a Pol Pot. No one would quarrel with labeling their regimes as dictatorships. But other regimes are more controversial. For almost seven decades, a new president in Mexico was elected every six years. Nevertheless, the same party's candidate always won. Or consider Singapore, where Lee Kuan Yew crushed political competition for over thirty years. Yet continuous measures of regime type rate him somewhere in between "most autocratic" and "most democratic."

Part of the problem is that dictatorial rulers are quite inventive in how they organize their rule. Decision-making power is concentrated in everything from juntas to politburos to family councils, for example. Yet the institutional inventiveness of dictators is most apparent when they govern with nominally democratic institutions, such as legislatures and political parties. Dictators frequently govern with legislatures, some of which have formal law-making powers, whereas others serve only to "advise and counsel." Membership to assemblies

1

may be by appointment or by election. In elections, candidates may use party labels or may be forced to run as independents. Party identification may mean little if political space is monopolized by a single party. But many dictatorships allow for multiple parties, picking and choosing the types of parties to ban. Of course, some dictators rule without any such institutions. The institutional diversity, however, makes it difficult to identify a consistent set of criteria by which to define and classify dictatorships.

The other reason for the confusion is that the historical usage of the term *dictatorship* originated in ancient Rome, where it was identified with very clear and specific institutional traits – in sharp contrast to contemporary usage. Over time, however, the understanding of what constitutes dictatorship evolved due to political manipulations of the term. As a result, a regime type that originally was well-defined by its rules became known as a regime type characterized by the absence of rules.

What are dictatorships? Who are dictators? In what ways do they organize their rule using nominally democratic institutions? The answers to these questions are mired in contemporary controversies. To grasp the source of these disagreements, it is necessary to track the historical understanding of this regime type. This chapter, then, begins with a brief account of this historical evolution as a means to understanding contemporary debates over what constitutes dictatorship. I adopt a minimalist definition of dictatorship to identify the post–World War II sample of cases to study. To impose a minimal amount of meaningful order on the dictatorial zoo, I classify dictators into three types: monarchical, military, and civilian. Finally, the chapter shows the institutional diversity of dictatorships in the various ways they combine nominally democratic legislatures and political parties. From this chapter, which delineates the universe of cases for analysis and highlights the empirical patterns to be explained, a systematic study of the emergence and effects of dictatorial institutions can proceed.

1.2 WHAT IS DICTATORSHIP?

Defining dictatorship should be simple: it is obviously the opposite of democracy. At least, titles such as *The Social Origins of Dictatorship and Democracy* and *The Economic Origins of Dictatorship and*

Democracy would have us believe.[1] Yet defining dictatorship is not a trivial matter. Its conception has evolved from an institutional device used in ancient Rome to a system of rule that in modern times is frequently associated with the absence of institutions and constraints. The transformation of its meaning was the result of several distinct moments when the original term was contorted and twisted for political ends. The result, by the mid-twentieth century, was a negative definition of dictatorship that defined this form of rule by the absence of attributes associated with democracy. Yet the neglect of institutional forms in nondemocratic regimes is not justified, as will be demonstrated by a description of the post–World War II sample of dictatorships. Authoritarian regimes vary widely in their institutional arrangements, and the task for the remainder of the book will be to examine the reasons for and the effects of this variance.

1.2.1 Historical Usage

In contemporary usage, the terms *tyranny* and *dictatorship* maintain close association. Yet this was not always the case. Although tyranny was recognized as a type of regime since Aristotle, it initially was not linked to the concept of dictatorship. For one, the term *dictatorship*, originating in ancient Rome, postdates Aristotle. For two, in its original conception, dictatorship had a very distinct and specific meaning: rule by a leader who was selected by the Consul in Rome to govern during periods of emergency when external war or internal rebellion threatened the existence of the polity.[2] The term of the dictator was to last no more than six months, and he could not remain in power after the Consul that appointed him stepped down.[3] During his term, the dictator was authorized to use whatever power was deemed necessary to deal with the crisis at hand with the goal of restoring the old constitutional order.

Within such a concise description of the institution are several aspects worthy of highlighting. First, regular institutions of the state, such

---

[1] Moore's (1966) classic work has been followed by Acemoglu and Robinson (2006).

[2] The following description of dictatorship during the Roman period relies on the account of Nicolet (2004).

[3] Initially, limits on the term of the dictator were unspecified; he was to abdicate power as soon as the task for which he was appointed was completed.

as magistrates or the Senate, determined whether the situation at hand required the nomination of a dictator for a resolution. Yet those who decided on the necessity of a dictatorship were not allowed to nominate themselves for the position. Second, the position of dictator was explicitly designed to be occupied by one man; collective leadership might stymie attempts to resolve the crisis. Third, the dictatorship had a broad range of power but not the authority to abolish other state institutions. Fourth, the dictator was never chosen by the people.[4] Finally, the goal of dictatorial rule was restoration of the old political order.

Within these institutional parameters, seventy-six dictatorships existed in Rome from 501 to 202 B.C. The majority of dictatorships during this period were engaged in either military campaigns against foreign powers or attempts at domestic reconciliation but not in repression of sedition. As a consequence, dictatorship was not associated with brutal or repressive rule.

Sulla, a Roman general who refused to accept his dismissal and went on to march on Rome, revived the institution of dictatorship in 82 B.C. in an attempt to legitimate his rule. Significant differences, however, existed between traditional dictatorships and Sulla's regime. For one, because Sulla obtained power only after his armies conquered Rome and massacred his enemies, his regime marks the first time that a dictatorship was established by the use of military force. The excessive brutality that Sulla used to neutralize his opponents led to an association of dictatorship with terror. Moreover, in contrast to past dictators whose tenures were understood to be limited given the nature of the problem to be addressed, Sulla's dictatorship involved the complete placement of power – military, executive, legislative, judicial – in one man to remake the political order. The notion of dictatorship to restore a previous political order was over.

Oddly enough, however, Sulla still adhered to the term limitations attached to the title of dictator. In fact, after a short period, he stepped down from power and returned to private life. It was not until January 44 B.C., when Caesar accepted the title of "dictator for life," that the temporariness of dictatorial power was abandoned.[5]

---

[4] With one exception in 211 B.C. Yet the decision to allow for popular participation was very controversial within the Senate. See Nicolet (2004) for more details.

[5] Caesar initially had accepted dictatorial terms of one and ten years (Nicolet 2004).

That the concept of dictatorship was already corrupted by Sulla and Caesar was often forgotten by later advocates. In *The Discourses*, Machiavelli (Book I, Chapter XXXIV; 1950: 203) lauded the Roman invention, observing: " . . . truly, of all the institutions of Rome, this one deserves to be counted amongst those to which she was most indebted for her greatness and dominion." The reason was simply because processes of collective decision-making and even laws themselves may be inflexible and, hence, ill-suited instruments for resolving crises. In a similar vein, Rousseau (Book IV, Chapter VI; 1987: 217) remarked approvingly, " . . . a supreme leader is named who silences all the laws and briefly suspends the sovereign authority. In such a case, the general will is not in doubt, and it is evident that the first intention of the people is that the state should not perish." For defenders of both absolutist and liberal states, then, dictatorship constituted a solution due to its decisiveness. But its temporary nature was equally important for otherwise, " . . . once the pressing need has passed, the dictatorship becomes tyrannical or needless" (Book IV, Chapter VI; 1987: 218).

Aside from these mentions, however, dictatorship received scant reference. In the nineteenth century, for example, the term was used during only two periods: between 1789 and 1815 in reference to France and briefly after 1852 to denote the Second Empire. What is noteworthy about the use of the term in the former period is how dictatorship no longer referred to rule by just one man but to rule by a group. In October 1793, the French National Convention suspended the constitution of the same year and established a provisional government that served as a dictatorship of a revolutionary group: the Committee of Public Health. Another feature of the original Roman conception – rule by one man – was changed yet again.

It was only a matter of time, then, that the term *dictatorship* was used to refer to not just a group but to an entire class. The term resurfaced after 1917, when Lenin and his comrades used the phrase "dictatorship of the proletariat" in self-congratulatory terms. Yet in just a few years, the term *dictatorship* was imbued with pejorative connotations as liberal opponents of the Fascist Italian and Nazi regimes used the label to describe what they were fighting against: "a highly oppressive and arbitrary form of rule, established by force or intimidation, enabling a person or group to monopolize political power without any constitutional limits, thus destroying representative government, political rights, and any organized opposition" (Baehr and Richter 2004: 25). Following these trends, the Socialist International did its own about-face in 1933, using "dictatorship" as a negative description of the Soviet regime as well. In any case, the employment of the term in reference to both the self-proclaimed dictatorship of the proletariat in Russia and the fascist dictatorship in Italy were deviations from the original Roman conception. The fascists were never committed to any temporary notion of power; and although the dictatorship of the proletariat was to be temporary in nature, as a fundamental step in the transformation from capitalism to socialism, it would obviously not aim for restoration of the old order.

Events of the interwar period were important in that they precipitated an attempt to save the original notion of dictatorship.[6] Attempting to save the notion of exceptional power and to counter the Bolshevik use of the term, Carl Schmitt distinguished commissarial from sovereign dictatorship. Commissarial dictatorship conforms to the original Roman concept of dictatorship. With sovereign dictatorship, Schmitt collapses the distinction between normal and exceptional times, claiming that the dictator has authority to restore the preconstitutional will of the people, even if it means altering the constitution itself. At the time, Schmitt was writing to justify giving dictatorial powers to Germany's *reichspresident* to deal with escalating economic and social crises. Schmitt's conception of sovereign dictatorship is important because it cements an important alignment of theory and practice in the understanding of the term: this type of dictatorship may be neither temporary nor restorative of the prior constitutional order.

The positive connotation of dictatorship, however, was never to take hold. As Baehr and Richter (2004: 26) observe: "well into the 1940s, in liberal, constitutional states, dictatorship continued to be used as the polar opposite of democracy in countless books, as well as in political discourse." During and immediately after the war, because democracy was thought to embody all that was good, its antithesis, by definition, was negative.

The emphasis on the distinction between democracy and dictatorship is similarly a twentieth-century phenomenon. Regime distinctions historically have been threefold since Aristotle first distinguished

---

[6] This discussion is from McCormick (2004).

regimes by number of rulers. The distinction among monarchy, aristocracy, and democracy collapsed in two ways. Machiavelli was the first to distinguish between government of the one versus government of the assembly (whether of the few or the many), thereby setting monarchy apart from other forms of regime. Bobbio (1989) attributes the second collapse of the threefold regime distinction to Hans Kelsen, who claimed distinctions on the basis of number to be superficial. Instead, Kelsen proposed distinguishing on the presence or absence of political freedom: "Politically free is he who is subject to a legal order in the creation of which he participated" (Kelsen 1945: 284). The crucial distinction, then, is between autonomy and heteronomy: democratic forms of government are those in which laws are made by the same people to whom they apply (i.e., autonomous norms), whereas in autocratic states, lawmakers differ from those to whom the law is addressed (i.e., heteronomous norms). As a result, "it is now more precise to distinguish between two types of constitution, instead of three: democracy and autocracy" (Quoted in Bobbio 1989: 137).

With this dichotomy, contemporary focus fell on the task of defining democracy, leaving dictatorship as the residual category, defined only in terms of what it is not. Dictatorships are regimes without competitive elections, without rule of law, without political and civil rights, without regular alternation in power. These attributes may well characterize dictatorships relative to democracies, but such definitions emphasizing the relative absence of traits also masks significant heterogeneity in the organization of these regimes.

1.2.2 Contemporary Controversies

Dictatorships are defined here as regimes in which rulers acquire power by means other than competitive elections.[7] Leaders may come to power by a coup d'état, a palace putsch, or a revolution. They may take power themselves or be installed by military or foreign powers. The critical distinction is that they do not accede to power by

---

[7] Except when the ruler first entered power by election and then consolidated his power at the expense of democracy. In these cases (e.g., Marcos in the Philippines, Park in South Korea, Fujimori in Peru), the leader's reign is considered a dictatorship from the beginning of his elected term.

a "competitive struggle for people's votes" (Schumpeter 1976). This conception of dictatorship, although not an advancement toward a positive definition, is useful for both practical and conceptual reasons. These reasons are discussed in turn.

The above definition of dictatorship is a minimal one, focusing on the procedural rather than substantive aspects of the regime type. The purpose of a minimalist definition is primarily for analytical clarity. Definitions of regime type that incorporate a number of attributes suffer from a number of problems. First, and most important, a multiplicity of attributes makes verifying causal connections more difficult. Consider, for example, Linz's (1970) four defining elements of authoritarianism: limited political pluralism, distinctive mentalities rather than a guiding ideology, little political mobilization, and a leader who exercises power predictably even if within ill-defined limits. If authoritarianism is defined on the basis of these four dimensions and we were to find a relationship between authoritarianism and economic development, what then should we conclude about the causal story behind the observed relationship? Is it the limited political mobilization or the predictable leadership or some combination of these factors that causes the observed patterns? With dictatorships distinguished in this way, we hardly can say.

Second, broad definitions can entail substantive notions that either generate tautologies or limit the applicability of the concept produced. Evans's (1989) distinction between "developmentalist" and "predatory" states already hints at the type of development outcomes they will generate. Not surprisingly, bureaucratic-authoritarian regimes will pursue exclusionary policies because they are defined, in part, by the fact that this is what they do (O'Donnell 1979). Even if we were to discover that these regimes, in fact, pursue inclusive policies, we would be able to do nothing more than comment on the validity of the label's criteria.

Third, although not a problem inherent to broad-based definitions, a strong correlation seems to exist between the number of attributes and the amorphousness of these concepts. "Distinctive mentalities," for example, is difficult to measure or even identify.

Finally, by appending more and more attributes to a definition of dictatorship, we run the risk of creating an empty set or, at the very least, neglecting the most important distinctions among regimes.

Mexico, for example, in spite of nearly a century of the Institutional Revolutionary Party (PRI) dominance, was thought to be a case of a dictatorship with qualifications. Yet the variety of dictatorships based on other dimensions (e.g., freedoms and rights, civilian control of the military) should not cloud the central distinction that is common to all dictatorships and sets them apart from democracies – the absence of competitive elections.

The reasons for using minimalist criteria do not constitute a justification for the substance of the criteria. In fact, the focus on elections as the distinguishing feature between democracy and dictatorship is not uncontroversial.[8] Given a minimalist approach, then, why focus on elections?

First, the focus on elections is compatible with most of the theoretical issues that animate empirical research on political regimes. The prospect of acceding to power by regular, contested elections is thought to produce incentives for political actors that are different from those produced by irregular, nonelective methods of selection. Different incentives will lead to different behavior (e.g., policies) that then should produce different outcomes. Consider the impact of regime type on economic development, for example. According to arguments made famous by Locke and later the framers of the U.S. constitution, democracy was believed to be detrimental to political order and economic development because elections without suffrage restrictions would enable the poor to elect demagogues who would seize and redistribute the assets of the propertied classes.[9] More recent arguments, in contrast, claim that dictatorships are bad for development because without electoral constraints, dictators are free to extract rents and substitute the provision of private goods for public ones. In either case, elections are the reason why political actors are expected to behave differently and produce different outcomes in democracy and dictatorship.[10]

---

[8] For some background on this debate, see Cheibub and Gandhi (2004), Collier and Adcock (1999), Diamond (2002), and Munck and Verkuilen (2002).

[9] The argument was repackaged in the twentieth century with the fear that democratic governments would capitulate to demands for consumption (rather than investment) made by workers who, of course, were also voters (de Schweinitz 1964, O'Donnell 1979).

[10] Elections also feature prominently in arguments about the relationship between regime type and education (Brown 1999, Brown and Hunter 2004, Habibi 1994),

Second, distinguishing regime type on the basis of elections reminds us that even if dictators have other nominally democratic institutions, such as legislatures and parties, they are still dictators. Political life is organized fundamentally differently in systems in which leaders are chosen by competitive elections and in systems where they are not. As Przeworski (1991) explains, democracy is distinct from dictatorship as a political system in which no actor can control outcomes with certainty, either by altering chances *ex ante* or overturning outcomes *ex post*. The most tangible signifier of this uncertainty are competitive elections because the result is "an *instruction* what the winners and the losers should and should not do: the winners should move into a White or Pink House or perhaps even a *palacio* . . . The losers should not move into the House and should accept getting not more than whatever is left" (Przeworski 1999: 45). This point is revisited and elaborated in the Conclusion because it has implications for how we think about dictatorial parties and legislatures and whether their presence makes some authoritarian regimes "more democratic" than others.

I use Przeworski et al.'s (2000) dichotomous classification that distinguishes regimes by electoral criteria. The resulting sample encompasses 140 countries that experienced dictatorship at some point during the period 1946 to 2002, or 4,607 country-year observations. In Figure 1.1, all countries that have been ruled by dictators at some point during the postwar period are shaded. During the 1970s, 75 percent of all countries were dictatorships. By the mid-1990s, that percentage had fallen to around 50 percent.

In most cases, the identification of dictatorships is uncontroversial in that the most prominent cross-national regime classifications agree. The correlations among Freedom House, Polity, and Przeworski et al. (2000) range from 88 to 95 percent. Even though Przeworski et al. (2000) is a dichotomous measure, its correlation with both Freedom House and Polity are high because these continuous measures have bimodal distributions. Once the easy cases at the extremes of the distribution (e.g., North Korea, Iran, Sweden, and Great Britain) are excluded, however, the correlations become significantly weaker: for example, only 0.75 between Polity and Freedom House. The difficulty appears

economic reforms (Haggard and Kaufman 1995, Hellman 1998), interstate war (Fearon 1994, Reiter and Stam 1998), and many other things.

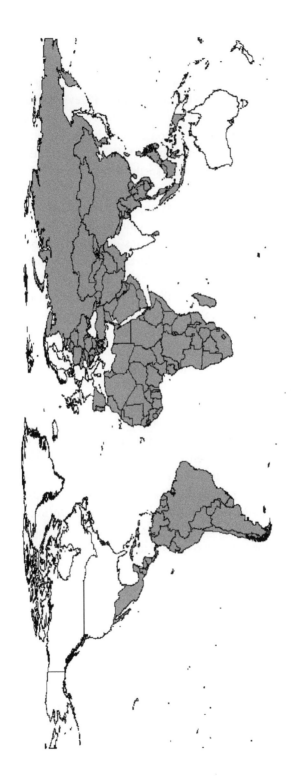

FIGURE 1.1. Dictatorships in the world, 1946–2002.

with cases such as Mexico, Botswana, Malaysia, and other countries that populate the middle of the distribution. Przeworski et al. (2000), however, determine the regime type of countries on the basis of clear and observable criteria that are consistent with the minimalist, procedural definition of regimes used here.[11] Table 1.1 provides the list of countries and years of dictatorial spells by region.

During the 1946–2002 period, the sub-Saharan African region constitutes the largest portion of the sample with over 1,800 country-year units. Eighty-seven percent of these country-years were under dictatorship. The proportion of observations under nondemocratic rule is similarly high in the Middle East/North Africa (87 percent), Eastern Europe/former Soviet Union (74 percent), and Asia (68 percent). The Latin American sample has a smaller proportion of dictatorial country-years (38 percent) due to numerous transitions between democratic and authoritarian rule. Finally, only 7 percent of Western European country-years are included in the dictatorial sample because authoritarianism was confined to southern Europe during this fifty-six-year period.

Within regions, high variance in number of dictatorial spells and in duration of authoritarian rule also exists among countries. Some countries, such as Jordan and the People's Republic of China, have been dictatorships since their respective dates of independence. Other countries have had smaller, but multiple, authoritarian spells, such as Argentina with four periods or Ghana with three. Still other countries have had very limited experience with dictatorship. During the postwar period, Costa Rica, for example, was a dictatorship for only 18 months after José Figueres' seizure of power in May 1948. The average length of a dictatorial spell, however, is long (40 years).[12]

1.3   WHO ARE THE DICTATORS?

After determining the sample of dictatorial regimes, the next step is to identify the effective head of government. Effective heads of

---

[11] A regime is a dictatorship if it fails to meet at least one of the following four rules: (1) the chief executive must be elected; (2) the legislature must be elected; (3) there must be more than one political party competing in elections; and (4) an alternation in power must have taken place. For more details, see Przeworski et al. (2000).

[12] Lengths of spells are not left-hand censored.

TABLE 1.1. *Countries under Dictatorship, 1946–2002 (in Alphabetical Order by Region)*

Country	Years under Dictatorship
Africa	
Angola	1975–2002
Benin	1960–1990
Botswana	1966–2002
Burkina Faso	1960–2002
Burundi	1962–92; 1996–2002
Cameroon	1960–2002
Cape Verde Island	1975–1990
Central African Republic	1960–1992
Chad	1960–2002
Comoro Island	1975–1989; 1995–2002
Congo	1960–1991; 1997–2002
Djibouti	1977–2002
Equatorial Guinea	1968–2002
Eritrea	1993–2002
Ethiopia	1946–2002
Gabon	1960–2002
Gambia	1965–2002
Ghana	1957–1968; 1972–1978; 1981–1992
Guinea	1958–2002
Guinea-Bissau	1974–1999
Ivory Coast	1960–1999
Kenya	1963–1997
Lesotho	1966–1992
Liberia	1946–2002
Madagascar	1960–1992
Malawi	1964–1993
Mali	1960–1991
Mauritania	1960–2002
Mozambique	1975–2002
Niger	1960–1992; 1996–1999
Nigeria	1966–1978; 1983–98
Rwanda	1962–2002
Sao Tome and Principe	1975–1990
Senegal	1960–1999
Seychelles	1976–2002
Sierra Leone	1967–1995; 1997
Somalia	1969–2002
Somaliland	1991–2002
South Africa	1946–1993

(continued)

TABLE 1.1 *(continued)*

Country	Years under Dictatorship
Sudan	1958–1964; 1969–1985; 1989–2002
Swaziland	1968–2002
Tanzania	1961–2002
Togo	1960–2002
Uganda	1962–1979; 1985–2002
Zaire	1960–2002
Zambia	1964–1990
Zimbabwe	1965–2002
Middle East	
Algeria	1962–2002
Bahrain	1971–2002
Egypt	1946–2002
Iran	1946–2002
Iraq	1946–2002
Jordan	1946–2002
Kuwait	1961–2002
Lebanon	1975–2002
Libya	1952–2002
Morocco	1956–2002
Oman	1951–2002
Qatar	1971–2002
Saudi Arabia	1946–2002
Syria	1946–2002
Tunisia	1956–2002
Turkey	1946–1960; 1980–1982
United Arab Emirates	1971–2002
Yemen	1990–2002
Yemen Arab Republic	1967–1989
Yemen PDR	1967–1989
Asia	
Bangladesh	1971–1990
Bhutan	1971–2002
Brunei	1984–2002
Cambodia	1953–2002
China	1946–2002
Fiji	1970–2002
Indonesia	1946–1998
Korea, North	1948–2002
Korea, South	1948–1959; 1961–1987
Laos	1959–2002
Malaysia	1957–2002
Maldives	1965–2002
Mongolia	1946–1991

TABLE 1.1 *(continued)*

Country	Years under Dictatorship
Myanmar	1958–1959; 1962–2002
Nepal	1946–1990; 2002
Pakistan	1956–1971; 1977–1987; 1999–2002
Philippines	1965–1985
Samoa	1962–2002
Singapore	1965–2002
Sri Lanka	1977–1988
Taiwan	1949–1995
Thailand	1946–1974; 1976–1982; 1991
Tonga	1970–2002
Vietnam	1976–2002
South and Central America	
Argentina	1955–1957; 1962; 1966–1972; 1976–1982
Bolivia	1946–1978; 1980–1981
Brazil	1964–1978
Chile	1973–1989
Colombia	1949–1957
Costa Rica	1948
Cuba	1952–2002
Dominican Republic	1946–1965
Ecuador	1946–1947; 1963–1978; 2000–2002
El Salvador	1946–1983
Grenada	1979–1983
Guatemala	1954–1957; 1963–1965; 1982–1985
Guyana	1966–1991
Haiti	1946–1993
Honduras	1946–1956; 1963–1970; 1972–1981
Mexico	1946–1999
Nicaragua	1946–1983
Panama	1946–1948; 1951; 1968–1988
Paraguay	1946–2002
Peru	1948–1955; 1962; 1968–1979; 1990–2000
Suriname	1980–1987; 1990
Uruguay	1973–1984
Venezuela	1948–1958
Eastern Europe and former Soviet Union	
Afghanistan	1946–2002
Albania	1946–1991
Azerbaijan	1991–2002
Belarus	1991–2002

(continued)

TABLE 1.1 *(continued)*

Country	Years under Dictatorship
Bosnia-Herzegovina	1991–2002
Bulgaria	1946–1989
Czechoslovakia	1946–1989
Georgia	1991–2002
Germany, East	1949–1989
Hungary	1946–1989
Kazakhstan	1991–2002
Kyrgyzstan	1991–2002
Moldova	1991–1995
Poland	1946–1988
Romania	1946–1989
Serbia and Montenegro	1991–2002
Tajikistan	1991–2002
Turkmenistan	1991–2002
Uzbekistan	1991–2002
U.S.S.R.	1946–1990
Yugoslavia	1946–1990
Western Europe	
Cyprus	1960–1982
Greece	1967–1973
Portugal	1946–1975
Spain	1946–1976

government constitute the focus because we are concerned with the effects of institutional features of dictatorial regimes on policies and outcomes, and decisions about the regime's institutional features and its policies are made only by those who truly have authority. Under democracies, identifying the effective head of government is usually straightforward: prime ministers lead parliamentary regimes, whereas presidents are at the helm in presidential systems.[13] Under dictatorship, the task is considerably more difficult. Why?

One reason is that in dictatorships, the head of government goes by many different titles. Under dictatorship, the chief executive often bears the title of "president." In monarchies, the dictator is known as the

---

[13] Even in democracies, exceptions do exist. The effective head of government in France, for example, depends on the partisan identities of the president and the prime minister. Or in South Africa, the effective head of government bears the title of "president" even though he is head of a parliamentary system.

"king" or the "emir." But other dictators have assumed more creative titles: "Chairman of the State Law and Order Restoration Council,"[14] "Leader of the Revolution,"[15] or simply "spiritual leader."[16]

Semantics aside, identifying the effective head of government within a dictatorship is difficult because dictatorships frequently have multiple executive figures – both nominal and effective. In communist regimes, for example, a prime minister, a chairman of the council of state (i.e., a president), and a general-secretary of the Communist Party nominally constitute the authorities, yet the prime minister and president are not effectively in charge. An extreme example makes the point: Liu Shaoqi remained president of communist China even as he was dragged from his home by Red Guards and forced to make a "self-criticism" during the Cultural Revolution (Short 2000, Salisbury 1992).[17] In communist regimes, in fact, the general-secretary of the party is the effective head of government.

Even more difficult are noncommunist cases in which the nominal and effective heads differ because an *éminence grise* lurks behind the scenes. The military may be in charge, but unwilling to assume power directly. In this case, a civilian is propped up as president, as occurred in Algeria under Abdelaziz Bouteflika, in Uruguay under Juan Bordaberry Arocena and Aparisio Mendez Manfredini, and in Fiji under Ratu Sir Kamisese Mara. In addition, there are rare cases in which a long-lasting dictator rotates nominal heads of government even as he retains ultimate power. Rafael Trujillo was the effective head even though he made his son, Hector, president of the Dominican Republic in 1952. Similarly, Anastacio Samoza Garcia ruled Nicaragua for nineteen years but allowed Victor Roman y Reyes to assume the presidency for a three-year interlude in the 1940s.

Finally, for some countries, their political histories are largely about fighting over who is the effective head of government. From its independence to 1970, politics in Cambodia largely centered around the struggles between the monarch and the prime minister over how much

---

[14] The official title of the leader of the Burmese junta since 1981.
[15] Muammar al-Quaddafi's official title since 1979, adopted ten years after seizing power.
[16] The title "*rahbar*" was first adopted by Khomeini in 1980. The position is distinct from that of president.
[17] Mao stripped Liu of his presidential position before having him killed in 1969.

power each of them should have. Pakistan has witnessed a similar type of political tug-o-war between the president and the prime minister. In these cases, the nominal head of government may not be the effective head of government.

Given the diversity in leadership arrangements, constructing rules by which the effective head of government can be identified becomes especially crucial in avoiding ad hoc judgments. Here the effective head of government is identified as (1) general-secretaries of the communist party in communist dictatorships, except in the case of Deng Xiaoping in China;[18] (2) king or presidents in noncommunist dictatorships, except in the cases of Singapore, Malaysia, Cambodia, Laos, and Myanmar, where the effective head sometimes bears the title of "prime minister," and (3) another individual or the institutionalized military if sources agree that the nominal head of government is not effectively in charge.[19]

The first two rules are relatively uncontroversial and successfully classify the vast majority of the cases within the postwar sample. In approximately 270 country-year observations, the effective head of government differs from the nominal one for the reasons discussed earlier. The classification of these cases depends on the relative subjectivity of the sources employed, but I have used a consistent set of sources to capture these hard cases.

Dictators do not appear one per year so that each one will neatly fit the data matrix of country-year observations. Political instability is often found in dictatorships so that in any given year, there may be multiple changes in the effective head of government.[20] In 100 country-year observations, the effective head changes more than once. These heads in the middle of the year may be in power for as short a period as five days, as in the case of Leon Cantave in Haiti. No matter how short their tenures, their appearance is recorded because *ex ante* we could not have known how long they would remain in power.[21]

---

[18] Deng never held the official title of general-secretary.

[19] These sources are primarily Banks (various years) and Lentz (1994).

[20] One interesting conceptual question that is not tackled here is whether we can properly talk about a "regime" when the chief executive changes so often. Noteworthy cases include Comoros in 1995, which experienced four changes in heads, or Bolivia in 1979, when power changed hands three times. Such instability, however, occurs in only a small handful of cases.

[21] For this same reason, "interim" and "acting" leaders who survive for longer than one year also are included in the sample (in contrast to Bienen and Van de Walle (1991).

Because the unit of observation is country-year, however, the effective head to consider is that of December 31.

Finally, excluded are dictatorships that were ruled under collective leadership: Yugoslavia after the death of Marshall Tito in 1980 until the disintegration of the state in 1990, Bosnia-Herzegovina from 1998 to 2002, and Somalia under the five-chairmen National Salvation Council from 1997 to 1999. Under collective leadership, it is impossible to assign responsibility for decisions to a particular leader, and for this reason, these observations are not included.

The sample of dictators, then, includes 558 dictators in 140 countries from 1946 to 2002. Some countries, such as Equatorial Guinea and Oman, have undergone a single leadership change, whereas other states have witnessed much more executive volatility. Haiti, for example, from 1946 until the transition to democracy in 1994, was governed by 19 chief executives with some lasting in power for mere days.

Among the dictators, themselves, their backgrounds and tenures vary widely. Ernesto Zedillo, a Western-educated economist and last of a long line of Mexican leaders who came to power under more or less orderly rules of succession under the PRI, seems to share little with Iran's Ayatollah Khomeini, a religious cleric who led a revolution to unseat a king. Similarly, Ferdinand Marcos, who initially won elections and later clung to power in the Philippines for two decades, seems incomparable to Pol Pot, who presided over the Khmer Rouge's killing fields in Cambodia for three years. Even dictators want to believe they are unique. As Imelda Marcos, wife of Ferdinand and first lady of the Philippines, quipped: "At least, when they opened my closets, they found shoes, not skeletons."[22] These examples highlight the diversity of dictators and raise the question: Is it possible to impose order on such a heterogeneous group of rulers?

I distinguish here on the basis of three types of dictators: monarchs, military rulers, and civilian dictators. Why these particular types? For one, monarchy historically has been treated as a separate regime type. Moreover, among other nondemocratic rulers, those who originate from the armed forces are often treated as distinct from their civilian counterparts. Tradition, in and of itself, is not a sufficient reason to

---

One cannot distinguish *ex ante* the cases in which heads attempted to consolidate power and failed from cases in which heads did not try to do so.

[22] Quoted from Diaz (2004).

TABLE 1.2. *Replacement of Dictators by Type*

Type of Current Dictator	Type of Successor				
	Monarch	Military	Civilian	Democrat	Total
Monarch	24	6	4	1	35
Military	0	100	46	58	204
Civilian	2	60	158	33	253
Total	26	166	208	92	492

rely on such distinctions. Yet there are important substantive reasons for distinguishing these types.

First, these distinctions signify the unique types of threats to dictators and the institutional methods by which they deal with them and organize their rule. Although discontent with dictatorship can come from any segment of society, members of the ruling elite usually constitute the first major threat to the dictator. Dictators, in fact, are frequently deposed by a fellow member of the regime. As a member of the ruling elite, the usurper is in a privileged position to acquire the force and support he needs to successfully depose the incumbent. So it is not surprising that, as Table 1.2 shows, when dictators are replaced by other dictators, they usually fall to a ruler of the same type.

To mitigate the threat posed by elites, dictators frequently establish inner sanctums where real decisions are made and potential rivals are kept under close scrutiny. The setup of these inner sanctums depends on the type of dictator because the source of the threat and the means by which the dictator can deal with it depends on his type. As a result, monarchs rely on family and kin networks along with consultative councils; military rulers contain key rivals from the armed forces within juntas; and civilian dictators usually create a smaller body within a regime party – a political bureau – to co-opt potential rivals. Because real decision-making power lies within these small institutions, they generally indicate to whom dictators may be responsible and how power is organized within the regime. These elite institutions produce different incentives and constraints on dictators that, in turn, should have an impact on their decisions and performance.

As will be shown in the following chapter, one of the ways in which these distinctions will reveal themselves as important is in their impact on the decision of dictators to govern with other types of institutions – namely legislatures and political parties. Moreover, because the focus of this study is on the institutional structure of dictatorships, it seems fitting to incorporate another institutional distinction among these regimes. Finally, distinction of these types is possible through clear observable criteria. The justification and criteria for identifying each type of dictator is discussed in succeeding sections.

1.3.1 Monarchs

Monarchy has always been treated as a type apart from other forms of nondemocratic rule. One reason for this separate treatment may be that early regime classifications distinguished on the basis of number of those who rule. Aristotle, for example, distinguished monarchy as rule by one (as opposed to the few or the many) to promote the good life. As mentioned earlier, Machiavelli was among those who perpetuated the distinction between monarchy and other forms of government even as regime classifications became increasingly dichotomous.

Historical accounts of absolutist monarchical power only cemented the distinction, yet they also pointed to the inherent drawbacks of rule by one. Freedom from all constraints opened up the possibility of myopic, unpredictable, and unstable behavior on the part of monarchs that was detrimental to their interests along with those of their subjects. When French kings, for example, continued to engage in various forms of expropriation to fund wars and lavish lifestyles, their subjects suffered. Eventually, his subjects modified their behavior in response to the state's predatory actions.

As a result, the virtues of binding or constraining one's own powers became apparent. Jean Bodin, a staunch royalist of the sixteenth century, counselled his king to share power with others and accept limits on his own will, if only to secure obedience. Bodin observed: "The less the power of the sovereign is (the true marks of majesty thereunto still reserved) the more it is assured" (quoted in Holmes 1995: 115, Bodin, Book IV, Chapter 6: 517).[23] Hence, it is in the king's

---

[23] While liberal thinkers espoused constraints on absolute sovereigns, Bodin's thoughts on the subject are notable not only because they predate liberal thought but also because they are deployed for proroyalist purposes. On the importance of Bodin on this point, see Holmes (1995).

interest to accept various constraints on his power: laws of nature, laws of succession, immemorial customs, a prohibition on taxation without consultation, independent magistracies, and even parliamentary prerogatives.

It is questionable, however, whether European monarchs took to heart the lessons of Bodin and others. Although kings established constitutions along with parliaments and judicial bodies, the extent to which they intended these institutions to serve as a form of self-binding is unclear. The reason for the ambiguity lies in the fact that although the British and French kings may have learned the hard way (by being overthrown and beheaded) that they would have to cede real power to these institutions, most monarchs fought to preserve their discretionary powers in the face of parliamentary challenges.[24] Parliamentary responsibility developed only after several years of wrangling between monarchs and assemblies and often was codified only much later (von Beyme 2000). As the early European examples illustrate, for at least a notable period, constitutions did not necessarily imply constraints on the sovereign or constitutionalism.

Contemporary monarchs in the Middle East evinced the same resistance to constraints on their authority. Faced with a variety of fiscal crises or political independence, monarchs in the region tried to rationalize their rule by establishing constitutions, parliaments, and political parties. The 1925 Iraqi constitution, for example, allowed the king to choose the prime minister but clearly established ministerial responsibility to the parliament. Similar provisions were included in the Kuwaiti constitution and the 1923 Egyptian constitution; under the latter document, the opposition Wafd Party was able to garner impressive parliamentary majorities. Yet like their early European counterparts, these monarchs had no intention of relinquishing authority to their institutional creations. Unlike their predecessors, they had the brute power to insure that such devolution of power would not happen. In Egypt, the monarch fundamentally violated the constitution of 1923 three times in its first seven years of operation (Brown 2002: 39). Similarly, "[O]n paper, Iraq's parliament was as powerful as any that has existed in the Arab world. Yet on no occasion did a single

---

[24] North and Thomas (1973) and other literature in political science of this ilk overstate the generality of the British and French cases.

government, or even a single minister, fall because of a parliamentary vote of no confidence" (Brown 2002: 45).

The price for these monarchs, however, seems to have been accepting constraints of a different kind. Rather than constitutions and assemblies, constraints came in the form of dynastic families. Rulers of contemporary monarchies had to accept kin as holders of important government positions, as legitimate recipients of state revenues, and as participants in decision-making at all levels. Khalifa in Qatar, for example, reshuffled his cabinet in 1992 so that his closest family members would serve as his ministers: his sons were Ministers of Defense, Finance and Petroleum, Interior, and Finance, Economy, and Trade; his grandson was in charge of State for Defense Affairs; and his nephews were in Public Health and Islamic Affairs (Herb 1999: 123). Similarly, in Saudi Arabia, King Fahd appointed his six full brothers – with Fahd, nicknamed the "Sudairi Seven" – to major posts in the government.

Family members play a crucial role in making decisions on important matters, as seen with the issue of succession. In Kuwait, for example, succession alternates between two branches of the Sabah family, but "the most basic rule of the succession is that family 'elects' the ruler by consensus, based on the perception by family leaders of their own best interests" (Herb 1999: 80). In Oman, the next in line must be a male descendant from the al-Said family but must also be chosen by a family council. Saudi succession became resolved by a more consensual process after King Faysal established the Higher Committee of Princes as an advisory council to the king on issues of succession. The Committee's composition was designed to rally the entire family, and the Committee was even given the authority to supervise the succession in the event of Faysal's death (Bligh 1984: 88).

Certainly rules of succession have not always been followed. As the list of post–World War II monarchs and how they left power in Table 1.3 shows, natural death is one way in which monarchs leave power but so is assassination or deposal at the hands of other family members.

Yet even when the rules of succession are broken, it typically happens with the blessing of key family members. Faysal did not depose Sa'ud, his father's designated heir, until he received the support of other Saudi princes. That support was quickly extended due to Sa'ud's

TABLE 1.3. *Postwar Monarchs and Their Exit from Power (Alphabetical by Country within Each Category)*

Exit from Power	Monarch (Country: Year of Exit)
Natural death	Isa (Bahrain: 1999)
	Dorji (Bhutan: 1972)
	Hussein (Jordan: 1999)
	Abdullah (Kuwait: 1965)
	Sabah (Kuwait: 1977)
	Muhammad V (Morocco: 1961)
	Hassan II (Morocco: 1999)
	Tribhuwan (Nepal: 1955)
	Mahendra (Nepal: 1955)
	Tamasese (Samoa: 1963)
	Ibn Saud (Saudi Arabia: 1982)
	Sobhuza II (Swaziland: 1982)
Resignation	Abdullah (Iraq: 1953)
	Naif (Jordan: 1951)
	Dzeliwe (Swaziland: 1986)
	Ntombi (Swaziland: 1986)
Assassination	Abdullah (Jordan: 1951)
	Faysal (Saudi Arabia: 1975)
Deposal by family member	Zahir Shah (Afganistan: 1973)
	Mwambusta IV (Burundi: 1966)
	Talal (Jordan: 1952)
	Said (Oman: 1970)
	Ahmad (Qatar: 1972)
	Khalifah (Qatar: 1995)
	Saud (Saudi Arabia: 1964)
Deposal by outsiders (including military or civilian dictators and transitions to democracy)	Ntare V (Burundi: 1966)
	Sihanouk (Cambodia: 1955)
	Faruq I (Egypt: 1952)
	Haile Selassie (Ethiopia: 1974)
	Reza Pahlavi (Iran: 1979)
	Faisal II (Iraq: 1958)
	Idris I (Libya: 1969)
	Farid Didi (Maldives: 1986)
	Birendra (Nepal: 1991)

Note: Table from Gandhi and Schwartzberg (2004).

incompetence. Nevertheless, Faysal had to obtain it. While vacationing in Switzerland, Khalifa of Qatar was deposed in 1995 by his own son, who had rallied the support of his kin. The main threat to monarchs, then, originates from family members who are the only people legitimately qualified to succeed them.

Bodin's original point – that constraints can be empowering and necessary for political survival – may not have been entirely lost on monarchs. Herb (1999) convincingly argues that in the Middle East, only those monarchs who successfully transformed from traditional monarchies based on the king's supremacy to dynastic monarchies in which the family as a whole is the locus of power have been able to survive. The installation of a dynastic structure saved monarchies in Bahrain, Kuwait, Qatar, and Saudi Arabia from threats of revolution and continue to make regime change unlikely (even apart from the effects of oil). In contrast, monarchies that failed to adapt and maintained absolute monarchism without familial constraints, as in Egypt, Iraq, and Libya, fell to revolutionary dictatorships. The transformation to dynastic monarchy meant that kings would no longer be as powerful vis-à-vis their family members. But given the alternative that came with the failure to transform – the complete end of monarchical rule – it was a price worth paying for most monarchs. Monarchs are not constrained by parliaments or courts but rather by family factions and kin networks. Hence, rule by one has become rule by family.

1.3.2 Military Dictators

As Sulla's march on Rome shows, the use of armies and force in seizing power has a long history. In fact, all extralegal seizures of power require force even if the threat is implicit. In addition, nonmilitary leaders sometimes employ just as much violence as the military in usurping power. Consequently, the use of violence or coup d'états in taking power is not what distinguishes military dictatorship from other forms of nondemocratic rule.

What constitutes military rule is the fact that the armed forces are the institution through which rulers govern. Just as contemporary monarchs must co-opt family members and, in turn, use them to consolidate their rule, military dictators must neutralize the threats posed by their closest colleagues and harness their cooperation to govern.

Within military regimes, then, the junta is the locus of decision-making power. For generals who take power on behalf of the institutionalized military, their juntas typically are small and include heads of the various service branches. For members, sometimes lower ranked, who seize power in a factional coup, their juntas tend to be larger based on their need to attract members to their cause. After the 1966 coup in Ghana, for example, the selection of junta members was extended in stages as the need to consolidate support within the armed forces arose. Immediately after the coup, the National Redemption Council announced six members; the following day, it expanded to nine only to be followed by the addition of two more members four days later. Still two weeks later, six additional officers were added (Welch 1974: 136–138). Indeed, Finer (1988: 260) reports that in contrast to most Latin American juntas that are composed of the three or four heads of the service branches, by the 1980s, juntas outside the region, organized by middle-ranking officers, on average had eleven members.

The preexisting organizational structure of the armed forces can be harnessed for the purposes of governance. In Indonesia, for example, a fifth of the parliament's seats were reserved for members of the armed forces, and a soldier was stationed in each of Indonesia's thousands of villages, serving as the military's representative (Brooker 1995). The Argentine *Processo* is perhaps the most striking use of military hierarchy in governance. Prior to the 1976 coup, the four service branches agreed to a detailed power-sharing agreement in an attempt to prevent dominance by the army. According to the agreement, legislation underwent review by various subcommittees within each service branch before it was considered by members of the junta. In this way, decisions reflected a deliberative process within the armed forces that incorporated the opinions of its most important constituencies (Fontana 1987).

Military dictatorship as a regime type, then, cannot have existed prior to the professionalization of the armed forces that occurred at varying times throughout the developing world. In Latin America, for example, after independence from Spain, it was more proper to speak of armed factions led by *caudillos* than modern military organizations. The establishment of a modern military began as early as 1840 in Brazil and as late as 1896 in Peru with the creation of academies for officer training (Rouquié 1987). The introduction of European instruction (which in some cases lasted until the end of World War II) and of compulsory military service led to the creation of "new" armies by the early 1900s.

Professionalization of the military created an institution distinct from the rest of society. During the era of *caudillos* in Latin America, a career in the military was unattractive. As a result, recruitment became more and more internalized, which in turn increased the separation of the military from civilian elites and contributed to their esprit de corps under formal military education. As Rouquié (1987: 104) observes, the end result was that "The combination of isolation from society as a whole and the cohesion and prestige of the group produces a haughty, closed quality in military life, a proud withdrawal into the institutions that limits one's horizon at the same time that it produces a consciousness of having an important role to play. The professionalized officers of the new armies direct their loyalties to the institution of the military while believing they are serving the state."

The professionalization of the military conformed to the plans of civilian elites who wanted to curtail the power of *caudillos* and to rationalize the state's monopoly on violence. At the same time, civilian elites wanted to be able to call on the military as an arbiter or a problem-solver during times of crisis. As the *poder moderador*, "the military is repeatedly called into politics to be the moderator of political activity, but is denied the right systematically to attempt to direct changes within the political system. The military task in the moderator model is essentially the conservative task of systems maintenance" (Stepan 1971: 63). Concretely, this meant that when the military intervened, it was restricted to the removal of the chief executive and to handing power to alternative civilian forces. As a temporary form of rule designed to restore the old political order, the military came to serve the functions of dictatorship, as understood according to the original Roman conception.

Unforeseen by the civilian elites who advocated military professionalization, however, was that the creation of an autonomous military above civilian parties provided it with the means to intervene on its own in politics. No matter how extensive their interventions increasingly became, the military continued to perceive them as "a sort of internal adjustment. The military coup d'état, then, is only an intervention of the state within itself, producing a rupture in which by a sort of metonymy the part is taken for the whole" (Rouquié 1987: 104).

Military intervention that exceeded the norm of *poder moderador* soon became common.

Latin America's experience of distinguishing between the soldier and the citizen, however, was not universal. In many developing countries, professionalization of the military occurred to some extent during the colonial period as European rulers sought to reinforce their control over distant lands. After independence, the armed forces, having already been molded as a profession, became "a model of development and a microcosm of the state with tentacles reaching, through compulsory military service, to all groups in society" (Khuri and Obermeyer 1974: 62). The socialization process stressed the integration of the military into society rather than its maintenance as an institution apart. If members of the armed forces were not just soldiers, but also citizens, they would lead the way in helping to modernize the societies they shared with their fellow compatriots. In this task, the military was uniquely qualified to lead because it was the first sector to utilize imported technology (i.e., earlier than industry or agriculture), to employ meritocratic standards in recruitment and promotion, to regularly provide for the basic needs of its members (e.g., literacy, food, shelter), and to offer programs associated with the modern welfare state (e.g., insurance, pensions, family benefits). The armed forces came to be seen as leaders in modernization that would transform traditional societies into well-organized ones that could provide for citizens as well as the military did for its own.

Seen as either separate or integral to civilian society, as either temporary solutions to crisis or long-term forces for change, the armed forces came to occupy a special role in which they could claim to stand for the "national interest." As the Argentine junta that took power in 1976 proclaimed: "Since all constitutional mechanisms have been exhausted ... and since the impossibility of recovery through normal processes has been irrefutably demonstrated, the armed forces must put an end to the situation which has burdened the nation and compromised its future" (quoted in Loveman and Davies 1989: 196). Similar words have been proclaimed by men in uniform throughout the developing world to justify their interventions.

Yet the military's claim of "national interest" justifiably has been treated with a great deal of skepticism. Many other types of interests may motivate the actions of the armed forces. As any other organization, the military has its own institutional or corporatist interests that include the establishment of autonomy and the amassment of resources. In addition, the composition of the armed forces may be dominated by particular social groups, resulting from rulers' attempts to insure support from crucial constituencies. Colonial rulers, for example, staffed their armies with members of ethnic and racial minorities in the belief that minority groups would prove loyal out of fear of an independent state in which the majority would dominate. Having inherited such divide-and-rule tactics, contemporary leaders in developing countries continue to use them. The result is that members of the armed forces, if originating from particular social classes or groups, may continue to identify and behave in the sectoral interests of these groups. And of course, some military rulers act in only their personal interests.

Several comparative studies of military regimes attempt to infer these interests from observed actions. Finer (1988) and Nordlinger (1977) suggest that coups by the armed forces are motivated by class or corporatist interests. Yet little evidence that military governments are more committed to the welfare of the armed forces in terms of their size and expenditures exists (Stepan 1971, Zuk and Thompson 1982). In general, military rulers seem to behave very similarly to their nonmilitary counterparts, casting doubt on whether they have unique interests (Remmer 1978).

1.3.3 Civilian Dictators

In addition to monarchs and military rulers are civilian dictators. Theirs is a peculiar situation because, unlike monarchs and military dictators, civilian rulers do not have a ready-made organization on which to rely. Unlike monarchs, civilian dictators typically do not rule with an extensive kin network although there are some cases of civilian dictators who manage to impose their choice of familial successor. Before the father-and-son duos of Kim Il Song and Kim Jong Il in North Korea and Hafez and Bashir Assad in Syria, there were the Somozas of Nicaragua and the Duvaliers of Haiti. Yet these dictatorial fathers and sons are different from monarchs in that they have been unable to insure dynastic succession beyond one generation. This, in part, may be due to their lack of extensive family and kin networks by which they can control rivals within the ruling elite and the populace as a whole.

Nor can civilian rulers appeal to the armed forces as easily as military rulers, who as active members of the armed forces can rely on the institution's hierarchy and norms of comradery. Civilian leaders, in contrast, are often the subject of military contempt particularly when the armed forces are imbued with a sense of mission. In this context, the question of why men with guns obey men without guns looms large. One possibility is that the military may want to stay out of power to maintain institutional cohesion, particularly if politicization and factionalization have been a problem historically (Brooker 2000).

To counteract their precarious position, civilian dictators must have their own type of organization, as observed by Lenin when he claimed "that only the political party of the working class, i.e., the Communist Party, is capable of uniting, training and organizing a vanguard of the proletariat and of the whole mass of the working people that alone will be capable of . . . guiding all the united activities of the whole of the proletariat, i.e., of leading it politically, and through it, the whole mass of the working people. Without this the dictatorship of the proletariat is impossible" (Lenin 1921). The genius of Lenin's innovation included its combination of both charismatic and rational authority in that it combined " . . . the full personal devotion of members to the party with effective impersonal, peer group control over this devotion by enforced and unquestioned obedience to hierarchy" (Kamiński 1992: 143).

As an instrument by which the dictatorship can penetrate and control society, regime parties are also useful in maintaining civilian control over the military. The official handbook of the Soviet army stated that the military was expected to " . . . always approach problems in such a manner that the interests of the Party and government, the interests of communism, are given priority. . . ." (quoted in Kolkowicz 1967: 90). To insure military compliance, the commissar system, or a political hierarchy that mirrored the military one and that reported directly to the Central Committee made civilian control over the military possible because political agents of the party were directly involved in indoctrinating military units, encouraging self-criticism, and reporting political infractions to the *prokuratura* and secret police.[25] The

---

[25] The commissar system was introduced in 1918 to supervise and guarantee the political loyalty of officers from the old imperial army. Once these veterans were replaced, the commissar system was the subject of great controversy but ultimately maintained in large measure due to Stalin's support (Kolkowicz 1967).

military was never given autonomy to determine admission to or promotions within the officer corps. In addition, in the Soviet Union, no military officer ever served as Central Committee secretary. Indeed, at the highest levels, civilian leaders did not communicate with their military counterparts, largely leaving them in the dark. At the strategic arms limitation talks in the 1970s, for example, military and civilian representatives from the Soviet Union did not possess the same information, leading to embarrassing factual errors during negotiations with other states (Colton 1979: 253). Nevertheless, the party's efforts guaranteed civilian control over the armed forces.

The use of a single party to govern was widely emulated by civilian dictators throughout the developing world. Postindependence, single parties emerged in 60 percent of sub-Saharan African states. In some countries, such as Angola and the Ivory Coast, regime parties emerged immediately after independence. In other states, such as Gabon and Zaire, consolidation took a few years. Two arguments, somewhat contradictory, were given for the necessity of single parties in developing countries. Some arguments echoed those originally made by Lenin, claiming that a single party was necessary to overcome traditional cleavages and help "leaders of a more modern social force [in] confronting a more backward social force" (Huntington 1970: 12). Alternatively, the European experience demonstrated that political parties were a reflection of social cleavages, particularly those based on class. Because class was not the dominant cleavage within African societies, there was no need for more than one party. As Madeira Keita of Mali explained: "there is no fundamental opposition among us" and therefore, why was "there any reason to remain divided and split into parties that fought one another"? (quoted in Huntington 1970: 10).

1.3.4 Operationalization of Dictatorial Types

Royal, military, and civilian rule are three distinct forms of nondemocracy. The following rules classify the sample of postwar dictators into these three types:

Rule 1. *The ruler is a monarch if he, first, bears the title of "king" or "emir" and, second, is the successor or predecessor of rulers from the same family.*

Most monarchs are identified by the first rule. The title of "king," for example, is bestowed to only those members of the Hashemite dynasty in Jordan or of the Saud family in Saudi Arabia who are deemed the rightful successor by birth. For these cases, the second rule is redundant.

The second rule is for slightly more complicated cases in which the title of "king" has been taken more recently. In two instances during the postwar period, a member of the armed forces seized power and declared himself king. If he succeeded in passing power to a family member, as did Reza Khan to his son, Mohammad Reza Pahlavi, in Iran, both members are considered to be monarchs. If, however, the ruler fails in his succession plans, he is not considered to be a monarch. Jean-Bedel Bokassa of the Central African Republic falls into the latter category. A colonel in the army, he seized power in 1966, declared himself emperor, and planned to have his son succeed him. His dynastic plans collapsed, however, once he was deposed in 1979. This rule highlights an important point about modern-day monarchs. In considering whether a ruler is a "rightful successor," I look only at whether the ruler belongs to the current family in power. I do not determine whether that family or individual has historically well-founded claims to the throne because contemporary monarchs rule in countries that often were carved by colonial powers without reference to historical claims or social considerations. British colonial authorities created the Transjordan state, for example, and installed Abdullah, a member of the Hashemite family, on its throne. Because he was succeeded by a family member, both Abdullah and his successors are considered monarchs.

Rule 2. *The effective head of government is a military ruler if he is or was a member of the institutionalized military prior to taking power.*[26]

Even if retired from service, the shedding of his uniform does not eliminate his military status. Attempts to appear more palatable to

---

[26] Leaders who served in the armed forces during World War II, but then left, are an exception. Because almost all able-bodied men at the time either volunteered or were drafted, membership in the military during only this period does not count towards one's type. This exception mostly affects those communist rulers of Eastern Europe who fought in World War II.

voters who are more accustomed to civilian rule do not erase their connections and access to the armed forces.

Not included as military dictators are those rulers who come to power as heads of guerilla movements. Successful insurgency leaders, such as Fidel Castro in Cuba, Yoweri Musaveni in Uganda, and Paul Kagame in Rwanda, are considered to be civilian rather than military rulers for three reasons. First, although insurgencies are violent, not all members are involved in the fighting. Members of the civilian, political arm of the movement may not have participated in armed or paramilitary actions to come to power. In addition, some guerilla leaders, once they take power, never assume a formal military role. Castro, for example, was head of the guerilla movement that removed Fulgencio Batista. He became leader of the country but not of the armed forces. His brother, Raoul, occupied that position. So although Castro wore fatigues, he technically never belonged to the military. Finally, and most importantly, having never been a member of the armed forces, these leaders do not answer to that institution. And because the constraints and support offered by the armed forces to one of their members in power is the main reason for distinguishing military from nonmilitary leaders, guerilla leaders do not fall into this category.

Rule 3. If dictators do not qualify as either monarchs or military rulers by these two rules, they are considered civilian dictators.

The sample of dictators from 1946 to 2002, then, includes forty-nine monarchs (674 country-years), 228 military rulers (1,578 country-years), and 281 civilian dictators (2,336 country-years). Table 1.4 provides the number of dictators and country-year observations for each type of dictator by region.

The table shows that most contemporary monarchs govern in the Middle East and North Africa. Military dictators dominate in Latin America and the Caribbean, whereas almost all communist and post-communist rulers in Eastern Europe and the former Soviet Union are civilian.[27] As a side note, the proportion of country-years under Communist Party rule is around 15 percent. These cases include not just the

---

[27] The exceptions are Enver Hoxha in Albania and Wojciech Jaruzelski in Poland.

TABLE 1.4. *Types of Dictators by Region*

Region	Types of Dictators			
	Monarch	Military	Civilian	Total
Sub-Saharan Africa	6 (67)	73 (604)	95 (951)	174 (1622)
Middle East/ North Africa	29 (419)	31 (249)	19 (155)	79 (823)
Asia	12 (171)	36 (305)	51 (432)	99 (908)
Latin America/ Caribbean	0 (0)	82 (335)	48 (247)	130 (582)
Eastern Europe/ ex-U.S.S.R	2 (17)	2 (47)	61 (498)	65 (562)
Western Europe	0 (0)	4 (38)	7 (53)	11 (91)
Total	49 (674)	228 (1578)	281 (2336)	558 (4588)

Note: Listed by number of dictators over number of country-year observations in parentheses.

countries of the Eastern Bloc but also communist regimes in developing states, such as Cuba, North Korea, and Vietnam. Finally, civilian and military dictatorships are more evenly balanced in all other regions, including sub-Saharan Africa, Asia, and Western Europe.

1.4 NOMINALLY DEMOCRATIC INSTITUTIONS

By now, it should be evident that dictators do not rule alone. They govern with institutions that are particular to their type. They may even have nominally democratic institutions, such as legislatures and political parties. Here I provide descriptive patterns to demonstrate the institutional variation among these regimes – for which an explanation is provided in the following chapters.

1.4.1 Legislatures

Legislatures are defined here as a body with formal, but solely, legislative powers. As defined, legislatures under dictatorship do not include (1) juntas because they fuse executive and legislative powers and

TABLE 1.5. *Legislatures under Dictatorship by Method of Selection*

Region	Dictatorial Legislatures			
	None	Appointed	Elected	Total
Sub-Saharan Africa	403	82	1140	1625
Middle East/ North Africa	353	56	402	811
Asia	150	106	652	908
Latin America/ Caribbean	195	6	380	581
Eastern Europe/ ex-U.S.S.R	23	9	543	575
Western Europe	7	31	53	91
Total	1131	290	3170	4591

Note: Listed in country-year units of observation.

(2) consultative councils because, lacking formal legislative power, they are authorized to provide only advice and council to the ruler.

The manner in which these legislatures are selected and organized varies considerably. Legislators may be appointed by the regime, as they were in Ethiopia under the early years of Haile Selassie or at various points under Sukarno in Indonesia. Or they may be elected directly by citizens. Dictators may allow for part of the assembly to be filled by election while keeping a proportion of seats under appointment. Even when elections are allowed, candidates must often be approved by government-controlled bodies. In Iran, for example, the Guardian Council, a conservative body of clerics, vets all candidates for elected office who are also required to run for office as independents. Table 1.5 shows the distribution of legislative arrangements by method of selection of members across regions.

Table 1.5 shows that in most dictatorships that permit legislatures, election is the primary method of selection. In 69 percent of cases in which a dictatorial legislature exists, elections determine its membership. In each region, well over the majority of dictatorial legislatures are selected by election. In states with a communist legacy, almost all legislatures are elected whereas the region that displays the most heterogeneity in legislative arrangements is the Middle East and North Africa.

Even when candidates are allowed to adopt partisan labels, however, a common method of maintaining control is to force parties to join a regime-supportive front. A front is constituted by a single electoral list presented to voters even if parties are allowed to maintain their identities within the legislature. In 636 country-years, fronts were formed. Fronts are common in most, but not all, communist countries and elsewhere, such as Madagascar and Syria.

The proportion of dictatorships that have legislatures and that are selected by either election or appointment has remained fairly stable across time. Figure 1.2 shows the share of dictatorships each year that have no legislature, an appointed body, and an elected legislature.

Elected legislatures have been overwhelmingly popular each year among dictators and the percentage of appointed legislatures each year is fairly stable. There is slight variation in the mid-1970s: almost 40 percent of all dictatorships disbanded assemblies during this peak of deinstitutionalization. Otherwise, conspicuous waves of liberalization are absent.

1.4.2   Political Parties

Political parties are defined here by their *de jure* existence. Hence, if the regime formally bans political parties, they are considered nonexistent even if some may still operate underground. Dictators sometimes enter power, inheriting a system in which all parties have been banned. Yet it is more common for dictatorial rulers to close parties for a short period upon first entering power or to deal with emergencies during their tenures. Less common are the cases of rulers, such as Bokassa in the Central African Republic and the Argentine military during the *Proceso*, who ban parties during their entire rule.

Alternatively, the regime may create its own single party. As discussed earlier, Lenin's invention provided a tool for civilian dictators to control both the military and their rivals within the ruling elite. The single party, however, also serves to mobilize and supervise the masses. Little wonder, then, that so many authoritarian rulers in the developing world sought to emulate this institutional design.

The regime party may contain "groupings" or "factions," but they are not enough to constitute a multiparty system. In addition, when multiple political parties are allowed but are all forced to join a "front"

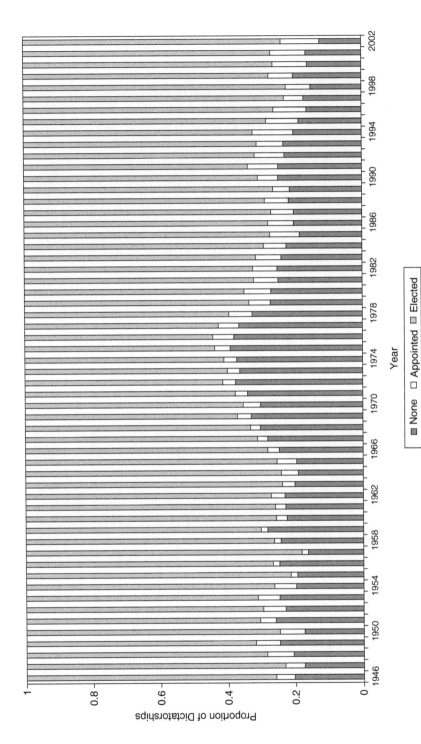

FIGURE 1.2. Dictatorial legislatures by year and method of selection.

with the regime party, the arrangement is considered to be a single party. There may be other parties outside of the hegemonic one, but they are not independent enough to resist the regime's demands that they stand together on electoral lists. For citizens, then, the alternatives are curtailed.

In other cases, autonomous parties are able to stand apart from any front. Dictatorships with multiple political parties range from Brazil in which the regime created official "government" and "opposition" parties to Algeria where the Islamic party, the Front Islamique du Salut (FIS), exerted its independence so strongly that voters almost gave it the majority of seats in 1991 legislative elections. These cases may appear to be qualitatively different so that their combination within one category appears objectionable: a party created by the regime is not the same as a challenger that emerges from the outside. Yet the independence of these parties is a matter of degree that is difficult to classify *ex ante*. Although FIS emerged independently, for example, it ultimately was shut down by the military government. Conversely, while Brazil's two legislative parties were set up by the military regime, they both ended up challenging it. Because *ex ante* judgment of which cases of multiple parties exhibit true autonomy are ad hoc, it is better to rely on observables to determine whether the effects of these parties on outcomes can lead to inferences on how independent they truly are.

Because rules or norms generally do not exist for how dictators should organize political life, authoritarian regimes exhibit a plethora of institutional arrangements. Legislative candidates may be forced to run as nonpartisan agents if the regime allows for a legislature, but no political parties. Or they may be forced to stand as representatives of the regime party if more independent groupings are not allowed. Alternatively, many dictators have allowed for autonomous organization from the regime in the form of an official "opposition" party or several groupings. Table 1.6 shows again by region the distribution of party arrangements.

Party systems in dictatorships exhibit much more variation across regions than legislatures. The dominance of a single party state is apparent not just in communist Eastern Europe but also in sub-Saharan Africa. Dictatorial regimes in Latin America are much more likely to allow multiple parties to operate; in some cases, these parties are

TABLE 1.6. *Number of Dictatorial Political Parties*

Region	Dictatorial Parties			
	None	Single	Multiple	Total
Sub-Saharan Africa	256	555	788	1599
Middle East/ North Africa	369	85	369	823
Asia	168	99	641	908
Latin America/ Caribbean	51	66	455	572
Eastern Europe/ ex-U.S.S.R	31	172	375	578
Western Europe	7	31	53	91
Total	882	1008	2681	4571

Note: Listed in country-year units of observation.

newly formed, but at other times, they are parties that operated during previously democratic periods. In Asia, single-party and multiple-party regimes are almost equally present. Finally, the Middle East and North Africa is the only region in which dictatorships are most likely to ban parties completely.

Variation in the number of parties is also evident across time. Figure 1.3 shows the proportion of dictatorships each year that have no, one, or many parties. After World War II, the percentage of dictatorships without parties drifted upwards at the expense of multiparty regimes. Yet allowing more autonomous groupings became more common after the fall of communism in the early 1990s. The proportion of dictatorships with a single party alone fell precipitously, whereas multiparty regimes predominated.

1.5 CONCLUSION

The historical lineage of dictatorship is long. The institution, originating in ancient Rome, initially had positive connotations – an efficient and effective means by which polities could deal with internal and external threats. In exceptional times, elites would choose one man capable of taking necessary actions to restore the political status quo.

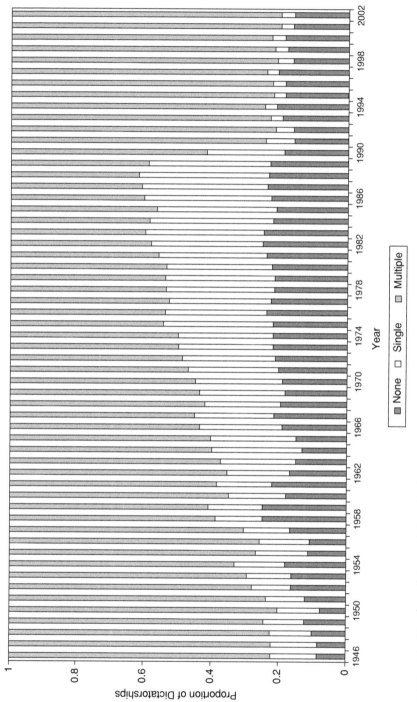

FIGURE 1.3. Number of dictatorial parties by year.

When the problem at hand was resolved, the dictator would step down, having completed his mission.

Over time, however, the term *dictatorship* was used to describe (by self-conscious protagonists and others) institutional arrangements that differed considerably from the original conception. The alterations to the original institution were manifold, and they began occurring as early as Rome. Dictators began appealing to the masses. Dictatorship evolved from the rule of one man to the rule of a directorate, a group, and eventually, a class. Dictatorships adopted revolutionary aims instead of conservation of the old political order. The biggest change of all was that dictatorship ceased to be temporary rule. And although this change occurred as early as Rome, it is the defining feature of these regimes in the contemporary world. Dictators do not submit to the process of competitive elections, introducing the possibility that their terms may be indefinite and their power unlimited. On this dimension, all dictators are the same.

Yet dictatorships do differ in their institutional apparatus. Dictators have a first line of defense to organize their rule and co-opt their closest rivals. The exact form of this first institutional trench depends on the type of dictator. Monarchs rely on extensive kin networks, whereas military rulers can take advantage of the hierarchy and norms of the armed forces. Civilian dictators, without a ready-made organization, must resort to regime parties. Dictators also vary in their choice of nominally democratic institutions – namely legislatures and political parties. As the next two chapters will show, this institutional variation cuts across types of dictators and serves a purpose: legislatures and parties are instruments of co-optation that nondemocratic rulers can use to address some basic problems of governance.

2

Three Illustrative Cases

2.1 INTRODUCTION

The aggregate numbers show that nondemocratic regimes display significant heterogeneity. The variation in institutions and the reasons for it come into sharper focus by examining some specific cases. First, consider Kuwait. Beginning in the early 1900s, merchants were active in the political life of the kingdom. They rebelled against the emir's unilateral imposition of taxes and demanded greater participation in decision-making alongside the Sabah ruling family. Dependent on the merchants for revenues, the emir steadily granted concessions, culminating in a parliament in 1938. The institution, however, did not last. As Kuwaiti rulers were able to disentangle themselves from the merchants through steadily increasing oil revenues and to consolidate and distribute power within their family, they were able to cease concessions to the merchants who eventually, themselves, were co-opted.

The kings of Morocco, however, were not able to avoid making concessions to outside groups. After independence from France in 1956, they sought the cooperation of their citizens in state-building because they had little recourse to external revenues. In addition, a secular, nationalist party that had gained popularity for its leading role in the independence movement foiled the monarchs' designs to consolidate absolutist power. As a result, nominally democratic institutions emerged with the king forced to contend with parliaments containing parties that did not always follow his will. Yet institutionalization seemed to have been the lesser of two evils because opposition demands could not otherwise be contained.

The perils of not institutionalizing become clear in the case of Ecuador. Upon seizing power in 1972, the military junta dissolved the legislature and banned all political parties. Initial support for the coup quickly dissolved as entrepreneurial elites became disgruntled over their exclusion from decision-making. When the regime responded with more repression, business organizations took the lead in mobilizing other segments of society to oppose military rule. Under mounting popular pressure, authoritarian incumbents were forced to step down. Had it made concessions through institutional channels, the opposition may have been appeased and the junta would not have had to cede power so quickly.

These three cases differ in historical period, regional context, regime type, and many other factors. Yet they all portray basic dilemmas of governance that autocrats face. Authoritarian rulers, even if their intention is simply to amass power and rents, must ensure order and a measure of prosperity within their domain (Olson 1993). In Kuwait, the Sabah family was consolidating its rule in the shadow of British protection while in Morocco, Mohammad V and his son were trying to lead a newly independent state. In both cases, the incumbents were forced to engage in state-building projects to propel their respective countries into the modern era. In contrast, by the time the military regime came to power in Ecuador, the country had already been independent for almost 150 years. Yet the junta also found itself occupied by similar tasks as it attempted to shift Ecuador's development strategy and build the necessary infrastructure and administrative apparatus to deal with newly discovered resources.

In the midst of dealing with these critical tasks, authoritarian leaders also tried to consolidate their rule by neutralizing potential opposition. In Kuwait and in Ecuador, organized opposition initially came from the entrepreneurial class as its members increasingly became disenchanted with their exclusion from policy-making. In Morocco, opposition was organized within a more encompassing nationalist movement that, after independence, demanded a constitutional rather than an absolutist monarchy.

The problems of governance facing rulers in the three cases were similar in nature although not in degree. As a result, the degree of policy concessions and institutionalization varied, leading to differing consequences. In Kuwait, the discovery of oil alleviated the need to make policy concessions via institutions. But in Morocco, the dearth of external revenues made the need for instruments of cooptation all the more acute. As a result, the monarchy accommodated a full panoply of nominally democratic institutions that survive to this day. Ecuador's generals were in a similar position, yet they refused to adopt institutions and, hence, failed to successfully co-opt the opposition. Consequently, the junta's demise came swiftly.

This chapter contains the details of these three cases: the conditions facing nondemocratic rulers, their institutional response to these conditions, and the consequences of their decisions. These narratives are not intended to be definitive histories but rather a set of stylized facts about the conditions under which dictators rule and their decisions to govern with and without legislative and partisan institutions. These qualitative snapshots provide some intuitions about why dictators govern with these institutions: assemblies and parties are effective tools in securing cooperation from outsiders and neutralizing potential opposition. As such, they have consequences for their policies and their survival.

2.2 KUWAIT: STRENGTH WITHOUT INSTITUTIONS

2.2.1 Sabah Consolidation of Power

Kuwait City was established as early as 716 A.D., yet modern Kuwait was not founded until the early eighteenth century when a tribe from the Najd, the Anaiza, migrated to the Gulf shores. After more tribes from the Najd had drifted over, they collectively came to be known as Bani Utub. The Bani Utub consisted of three principal family branches: the al-Sabah, who were designated with the task of ruling; the al-Khalifa, who dominated commercial activities; and the al-Jalahimas, who were responsible for maritime affairs. In the 1760s, as a result of internal disputes, the al-Khalifa migrated southeast to become rulers of what came to be known as Qatar, and the al-Jalahimas followed soon after.[1] Their departures left the al-Sabah clan firmly in charge so

---

[1] It is unclear whether the al-Khalifa migrated due to internal disputes or for greater economic opportunities since after their departure to Qatar, Kuwait maintained friendly relations with Qatar and other neighboring states.

that throughout the nineteenth century, internal politics were stable (Crystal 1990).

The situation confronting Kuwait outside of its borders was less secure. It was largely independent but vulnerable to the strategies and actions of surrounding powers. To the east, the al-Sauds were a rising power on the Arabian Peninsula. Their ascendancy induced Kuwait to look for protection from either the Ottomans or the British. Kuwait paid tribute to nominal Ottoman authority in Iraq, but its ties to Basra were mostly commercial rather than political. Preoccupied with preserving an increasingly overstretched empire, Ottoman leaders allowed the Kuwaiti ruling family significant autonomy in directing internal affairs. As a result, Kuwait remained a largely autonomous outpost (Ismael 1993: 42).[2]

Kuwaiti contact with the British empire occurred as early as 1775, when the Persian siege of Basra forced East India Company personnel to reroute their mail through Kuwait (Crystal 1990: 22). British interest developed as colonial authorities realized that Kuwait constituted the first line of defense of Britain's East Indian empire against any encroachment by other colonial powers from the west. Throughout the nineteenth century, however, contact remained friendly but limited. Ottoman authorities had made it clear that they would not tolerate the penetration of other external powers in the area, and Kuwaiti rulers had no intention of disrupting their lucrative commercial and political ties with Basra.

While Muhammad was emir, Kuwait remained in the Ottoman camp, rebuffing British overtures. Britain found an ally, however, in Muhammad's brother, Mubarak, who aspired to be emir. In 1896, Mubarak ascended to the throne after killing his brother. While Britain's role in the coup was never proven, it was certainly true that Mubarak distrusted the Ottomans due to their support for his brother. As a result, Mubarak reoriented Kuwait's foreign policy, signing a secret agreement in 1899 making Kuwait a British protectorate. Five years later, Britain installed its first Political Agent. Yet the Agent did not have the formal status of advisor, and although his advice was taken seriously, it was not always followed. Under the terms of the

---

[2] In 1871, Kuwait did become an administrative unit of the Ottoman empire. Yet the *de facto* autonomy of the Sabah family in domestic affairs remained.

treaty, Britain's official jurisdiction in internal affairs remained extremely limited.

The arrangement left Mubarak significant freedom in determining domestic policy, which he used to build the apparatus necessary for governing a modern state. To raise revenues, he established a series of new taxes: an import tax, a pearling tax, a house tax, a pilgrimage tax, and customs taxes (Moore 2004: 34). To handle the new revenues from the levies on trade, Mubarak created a new customs administration. In addition, under Mubarak, both public and private provision of social services began. In 1911, the emir allowed the Arabian Mission of the Reformed Church in America to build a hospital and open a day school for boys and a night school for men, teaching English and typing. Graduates of the latter went on to serve as heads of Kuwait's first public works, health, and customs departments. Foreign provision of these services also spurred domestic groups, both the Sunni merchants and the Shias, to open their own schools and clinics.

These actions taken to build the Kuwaiti state also helped Mubarak consolidate his own rule. The additional taxes and regulations allowed Mubarak to exercise more control over a greater share of the wealth generated by trade. The emir also redistributed some of the revenues collected from the new taxes to build a potential base of support among middle and smaller merchants. Finally, the provision of social services improved the lives of the wider citizenry. As for the British, Mubarak secured their support for his designated heir to the throne.

2.2.2 Merchants and the Push for Institutions

Many of Mubarak's actions, however, came at the expense of the interests of the larger merchant families. With the best natural harbor in the Gulf and its proximity to the caravan trade to Aleppo and Baghdad, Kuwait was the home of several families who built their fortune in trading horses, wood, coffee, spices, and pearls. Pearling also had become a major industry due to the pearl banks that extended down the Arabian Gulf coast. Division of labor quickly developed, distinguishing the divers from the ropepullers, the captains, and the merchants. The proceeds from pearling and trading were then divided on the basis of occupation.

Many of the emir's new taxes were aimed directly at the merchants' commercial activities, and the last straw came when Mubarak attempted to institute a ban on diving for the season. The response of leading pearl merchants was to decamp for Bahrain and Basra. Because these merchants had established and controlled the division of labor associated with pearling, once they left, their entire work force, including smaller merchants, divers, and ship crews, left as well. The labor pool associated with pearling was estimated at half the population of Kuwait (Ismael 1993: 58). In addition, the revenues from pearling and trade that constituted most of Kuwait's economic activity prior to the discovery of oil were no longer within reach of Mubarak's taxes.

As a result, Mubarak was forced to relent. He could ill afford to lose both the capital and the labor that the pearling merchants controlled. In exchange for the merchants' return, the emir reduced or eliminated many of the taxes he had imposed. As the British Political Agent observed: "the Shaikh is to have become very tame and courteous after the trouble of the Towashis and pearlers and is now ever ready to listen to reason and to help" (quoted in Crystal 1990: 25).

That the merchants could credibly threaten to flee and inflict damage on the emir's revenue base if their demands were not met, demonstrated that they constituted a powerful interest group that Mubarak could not ignore. Perhaps more alarmingly for Mubarak, the merchants' opposition also took on a distinctly political and nationalist tone. The merchants did agree to return in exchange for Mubarak's redress of their grievances, but their protest was concerned with more than just the immediate economic issue. They were dissatisfied with the arbitrariness with which decisions were made and unmade even if at the moment they did not demand the right to participate in making those decisions. Those demands would come later.

The nationalist overtones of the merchants' protest constituted a reaction to the alliance between Mubarak and the British. As helpful as British protection was in securing Kuwait's territorial integrity and in building the state apparatus, it was also an obstacle in establishing Mubarak's own legitimacy. In addition, the theme of nationalism became an issue around which the merchants could construct a collective identity. So not only did they share economic interests, but the merchants shared a common sense of belonging to the territory. During the crisis, several traders had told the British Political Agent that "they had no desire to leave, emphasizing that they were all Kuwaitis by birth and family tradition" (Crystal 1990: 25).

After their return, Mubarak maintained a truce with the merchants until his death in 1915. His son, Jabir, became emir only to be replaced two years later by his brother, Salim. In the meantime, the merchants sustained heavy economic losses during the interwar period. The pearling industry crashed during the Great Depression, and renewed conflict with the al-Sauds led to a slowdown in trade.

Upon Salim's sudden death in 1921, then, the merchants made a more direct attempt to seek redress for their grievances. Twelve heads of the leading merchant families formed *al-Majlis al-Istishari* (consultative council) to assert merchant participation in administration of the country, particularly regarding the decision over succession. The council proposed three candidates, all of whom were members of the al-Sabah clan. One of the candidates, Ahmed al-Jabir, became emir and pledged to work with the council on future policies. Undoubtedly, the memory of the merchants' exodus and withdrawal of revenues from earlier in the century pushed Ahmed to negotiate. After two months, however, the council collapsed due to internal strife, and Ahmed was spared from having to make concessions to outsiders.

The merchants were able to politically reorganize on a smaller scale in the 1930s. The first institution they developed was the Education Council in 1936. As early as 1912, the merchants had founded some schools to offer Kuwaitis a non-Christian alternative to the missionary schools that had emerged a few years earlier. But merchant-founded schools had closed due to the economic downturn of the interwar years. The Education Council, then, was an attempt to reopen these schools, hire expatriate teachers, and standardize the curriculum.

More comprehensive, however, was the formation of the Kuwait City Municipality. After a visit to Bahrain, where he observed the Manama municipality, a leading merchant, Yusif Isa al-Qinai, spearheaded the movement for a similar organization in Kuwait's capital. The emir agreed, and initially the Municipality's main responsibility consisted of supervising and cleaning the market. It was not long before the Municipality also began supervising traffic, zoning, housing, infrastructure, schools, public health, and city planning while its jurisdiction expanded to outlying villages. The Municipality was important not just for the services it provided but also because its activities were funded by local taxes on imports and businesses, making it financially independent from the emir. In addition, the Municipality was created and run by the merchants who ran elections every two years to fill leadership positions. Only notables were allowed to vote in these elections; in 1932, for example, this electorate consisted of only 250 individuals. Still, the elections were heatedly contested, and the institution provided a model for how decision-making could be decentralized in contrast to absolutist Sabah rule.

The first hint of a greater challenge from the merchants came in 1937. Several leaders of the Municipality along with those of the Education Council demanded greater administrative reforms. The emir's response was to shut down the Education Council. But his reaction only incensed leading merchants who, in turn, began meeting secretly to compose a list of reforms that they disseminated through leaflets and antigovernment wall writings. Some of the underground writings even called for Ahmed to step down.

2.2.3 The *Majlis* Movement and the Regime's Response

In June 1938, the merchants drew up an electorate of the heads of 150 notable families who then proceeded to elect a *Majlis*, or Legislative Assembly, of fourteen members. All of the legislators were well-established Sunni merchants. The merchants asked Abdallah Salim, the emir's cousin, to lead the Assembly. After the election, the politically active merchants organized the National Bloc, Kuwait's first political party. The party was designed to support the Assembly and spread information about proposed reforms.

The emir's initial reaction to the political activity was repression. Before the election of the Assembly, several merchants were detained, accused of "propaganda and intrigue" (Crystal 1990: 47). But the pressure did little to stop the merchants' mobilization, and so a month after the Assembly elections, the emir consented to the legislative body. When the emir persisted in dragging his feet, arguing that the prerogatives of the new institution should be developed gradually, Assembly members issued a strong statement in which they concluded: "We either [march forward] to prosperity, with you leading your people surrounded by glory, appreciation and love from every side, or the opposite" (quoted in Ismael 1993: 74). The legislators were reminding the emir that Kuwait would be significantly harder to govern without their cooperation, which was contingent on the development of parliamentary power.

In asserting its right to participate in decision-making for the country, *Majlis* members prepared a basic law, claiming control over the budget, judicial affairs, and public security. To make good on their powers, the Assembly formed a new police force, introduced several judicial reforms, and created a new finance department. In addition, the Assembly directly challenged some of the ruling family's privileges. New laws were passed forbidding the royal family from taking tribute from butchers and fishermen, owning monopolies in the production of certain commodities, and employing forced labor. Finally, the Assembly demanded a degree of fiscal control that would inevitably make the ruler beholden to it. With new legislation, the *Majlis* cancelled the pearl tax to the emir, seized the collection and allocation of customs revenues from the royal domain, and became responsible for distributing allowances to members of the royal family.

The Assembly also enacted a number of measures to win popular support. It cancelled a variety of taxes that had been levied by the emir: export taxes, import duties on fruits and vegetables, and taxes on goods moving from urban to rural areas. The Assembly passed laws to protect consumers against low quality or adulterated foods. It also expanded educational opportunities, including the opening of a school for girls.

The legislature's powers, however, were to be short lived. The events that led to the end of the Assembly are as follows. On December 17, a dispute between the emir and the legislature led Assembly members to barricade themselves in a palace that stored arms. The standoff ended peacefully after legislators laid down their arms in exchange for amnesty. The emir even held new elections to reconstitute the Assembly. But soon afterwards, some Kuwaiti dissidents, just returned from Iraq, gave nationalist, antiroyalist speeches that led to accusations of treason and provided the perfect excuse for the emir to end this experiment in reform.

The deeper reasons for the Assembly's demise are found in the reasons for which the emir made concessions in the first place: the ruling family's dependence on the merchants for revenue and the involvement of the emir's cousin, Abdullah, in the reform movement. Ahmed recognized the economic importance of the merchants and sought to prevent any repetition of what had occurred in 1910 when Mubarak had tried to impose his will on them. The support of Abdullah for the merchants' demands probably convinced the emir that he had to respond carefully to the merchants' demands. Because a member of the ruling family was part of the movement, the emir could not crush the movement outright.

But these conditions rapidly changed. The presence of oil in Kuwait had been suspected for some time. The Kuwaiti Oil Company (KOC), an American–British consortium, drilled its first well in 1936. In negotiating with the KOC, the emir treated the fields as his own private property, exchanging concessions to extract the resource for a share of the revenues made from sale. But until the oil was actually found, the emir saw little revenue from this deal. Once oil was discovered in 1938 at the Burgan field (which was to become one of the largest oil deposits in the world), Ahmed was sure that he could break free of any dependence on the merchants for revenues, which also meant that he could dispense with their demands for representation. Oil also helped the emir consolidate his ruling family, which partly explains why Abdullah abandoned the *Majlis* movement. His alliance with the merchants likely had been self-serving: he saw it as a way to challenge his cousin and gain a following for his own attempt to take the throne. But once the Assembly ceased to be an effective tool and oil became an inducement to close ranks with the family, Abdullah deserted the movement.

Revenues from oil also enabled the ruling family to eventually buy the political acquiescence of the merchants and of the population as a whole so that Sabah family rule would not be challenged in this matter again (Crystal 1990). The ruling family established direct state control over activities related to oil, but, in exchange, promised to stay out of other commercial activities dominated by the merchants. In addition, state subsidies and land grants to the merchants allowed for them to prosper while remaining shut out of the most lucrative industry of all. For the general population, in turn, the state began to provide a wide array of social services, ranging from education to health care, without cost. In addition, public employment expanded significantly so that the increasing ranks of educated Kuwaitis could be accommodated even if their compensation exceeded their effort. With the strategic use of such resources, the ruling family was able to maintain power without making substantial political concessions.

2.3 MOROCCO: SURVIVAL WITH INSTITUTIONS

2.3.1 The Rise of Monarchical and Nationalist Forces

Alawite rule over Moroccan territory dates back to the 1600s when the first leaders succeeded in driving out Spanish and British settlers and uniting the territory with the capital in Meknes. The succeeding years were a period of consolidation of the Alawis' political power in the area.

European influences, however, began threatening in the mid-1800s. Having engaged in an expensive process of internal reform, the government became dependent on foreign funds from European governments that were eager to penetrate Morocco's domestic market. A 1856 treaty granted Great Britain preferential commercial status to be followed by similar agreements with other imperial powers. Europe's interests in Morocco were more than commercial, however. The British wanted to prevent any other power from gaining control of the Gibraltar Straits. As a result, Britain sought to preserve the integrity of the Moroccan government and territory. French interest in Morocco emerged with the annexation of its eastern neighbor, Algeria, in 1834. Morocco's sultan had aided the Algerian revolt against the French to demonstrate religious solidarity and preserve his reputation as defender of Islam. A potentially hostile neighbor to the west of its most prized colonial possession unsettled French officials. Yet they were not able to address the Moroccan problem until six decades later: after completion of the Tunisian campaign freed up resources and government officials had assembled enough support for colonial expansion within the French metropole (Gershovich 2000: chapter 2).

In 1906 at the Algericas Conference, France gained the assent of other European powers to its plan to share police control with Spain over Moroccan ports to collect customs revenues.[3] The Sultan was

---

[3] In exchange for this acquiescence from Great Britain, Italy, and Spain, France had waived its claims in Egypt and Libya. Germany and Austria-Hungary, however,

forced to sign the agreement as well, and so Morocco was independent in name only. The conspicuous, armed European presence in coastal cities combined with Moroccan anger over the violation of their sovereignty made for a volatile situation. It was perhaps inevitable, then, that street protests and riots broke out, leading to more targeted forms of protest, such as political assassinations. These events provided French authorities with an excuse to intervene beyond their coastal mandates. By the end of 1908 the French had set up two separate, but permanent, occupied areas in eastern and western Morocco.

In the meantime, civil war was raging between supporters of two different claimants to the throne. Morocco's greatest leader, Mawlay Hassan, who had done much to preserve Moroccan independence, had died in 1894. For the following six years, a regent had governed on behalf of Mawlay Hassan's minor sons. In 1900, Mawlay Hassan's son and designated heir 'Abd al-'Aziz was crowned sultan. He was supported by the French, who perceived him as a weak and pliant leader. Domestic groups, in turn, criticized him for his passivity in the face of increasing foreign involvement in Morocco. Under this banner, the sultan's brother 'Abd al-Hafiz (also known as Mawlay Hafid) advanced his claim to the throne with violent tactics. With the country embroiled in civil conflict and no other foreign powers willing to challenge French control in the area, Morocco finally became an official French protectorate in 1912.[4] Among the countries in the Maghreb, it had held out against foreign control the longest.

'Abd al-Hafiz had succeeded in dethroning his brother, but his rule did not endure. Soon after establishment of the protectorate, the French forced him to abdicate in favor of one of his brothers, Mawlay Yussef. Opposition to colonial control continued, the most significant manifestation being the Rif War in the early 1920s, when the French and Spanish were forced to combine forces to defeat a tribal rebellion. But Yussef was not a central figure in the opposition to French control. So when he died in 1927, the French engineered the succession of his youngest son, Sidi Mohammad (who became Mohammad V), believing that he would be as passive as his father.

---

refused to recognize the agreement and continued to support Moroccan claims of independence. Germany later accepted a French free hand in Morocco after it received two French territories in the Congo in 1911.

[4] The Spanish did obtain zones of influence around Tangiers and in southern Morocco.

In contrast to the passivity of Morocco's kings, a nationalist movement developed among the population in the early 1920s. The earliest manifestations of the movement were in education. Denied the chance to attend select schools that were intended for the sons of the French elite, modern Moroccans established their own educational system consisting of "Free Schools" that provided a modern Islamic education in Arabic. Graduates of these primary and secondary schools went on to study in the Arab East or in France itself, where they became acquainted with other Arab nationalists and French leftists. Shortly after Mohammad V ascended to power, these young men began to return home and establish cultural groups and discussion societies (Pennell 2003: chapter 8).

The movement took on a political form with the French establishment of differential policies toward Moroccan Arabs and Berbers. The Berber *Dahir* (Decree) of 1930 instituted customary law, rather than the *shari'a*, as the code that would govern Berber-speaking areas. In reaction, the nationalist movement began to organize campaigns in mosques to protest French intentions toward Islam. The protests were originally peaceful but grew more vociferous as French reactions became increasingly punitive. Mohammad V became an important part of this movement, serving as its public face. By the mid-1930s, working together, the sultan and the nationalists were able to mobilize demonstrations against French rule in almost every urban area. It seems that French authorities had underestimated Mohammad V's intentions and popularity.

The nationalists with the support of the sultan eventually formed the *Parti de l'Istiqlal* (Independence Party) in 1944. The party's manifesto demanded that Morocco become a signatory to the Atlantic Charter, that negotiations for independence include the sultan himself, and that independence be granted. In the meantime, Mohammad V continued to speak out against French policies, rallying more support to the independence movement. In a speech in November 1952, Mohammad V compared the protectorate to "a suit of clothing for a child that he is expected to go on wearing when he is a man" (quoted in Hassan II 1978: 45). In a clumsy attempt to silence him, the French deposed him on August 20, 1953, sending him and his sons into exile. Yet his treatment at the hands of the French only increased Mohammad V's legitimacy and provided another catalyst for more violence. The

French occupiers soon found themselves facing a nationalist insurgency not unlike what was transpiring in neighboring Algeria. In addition, an Army of Liberation, free of *Istiqlal* control, emerged in the countryside.

The French could not countenance such wars in both urban and rural areas across North Africa. Realizing that the status quo was too costly, by August 1955, the French opened talks with Moroccan nationalists in Aix-les-Bains. But the *Istiqlal* refused to participate without involvement of the king. So two months later, the king and his family were brought to France for negotiations, and by November of that same year, Mohammad V was again on the Moroccan throne. Official independence came to Morocco in 1956.

2.3.2 Managing State-Building and Opposition

The French left behind infrastructure (15,000 kilometers of roads, 1,600 kilometers of railways), productive agricultural land (35,000 irrigated hectares), and a valuable phosphates industry (Pennell 2003: 163). Yet the colonial legacy was a bitter one as well. The distribution of land was extremely unequal: most Moroccans had no more than four hectares of unirrigated land, whereas wealthy Europeans had controlled most of the best acreage. Agricultural production was so stagnant that Morocco for the first time became a net importer of cereals – a staple of the Moroccan's diet – by 1960 (Swearingen 1987). In search of opportunities, many rural Moroccans left the countryside only to become frustrated, unemployed inhabitants of *bidonvilles* around Casablanca, Rabat, and other cities. Just a decade before independence, of two million school-age Moroccans, only thirty-six thousand were in school (Waterbury 1970: 42). As a result, 89 percent of the population was illiterate, but very few schools and teachers existed to rectify the problem. Per capita income was just over fourteen hundred dollars, less than a quarter of average income in France. Immediately after independence, income continued to decline.

To confront such challenges, Mohammad V proposed land reform, educational measures, and plans for industrialization. But these reforms would be difficult, and he tried to prepare his people for the long process of nation-building that lay ahead. In a speech shortly after independence, the king proclaimed that "we have finished minor jihad and are ready to start the major one" (quoted in Bourqia 1999: 249).

Yet Mohammad V did not have basic instruments of governance at his disposal to address these problems. For one, the Moroccan state did not even possess a monopoly of violence. After independence, the king and his advisors had to work quickly to create a standing army (Zartman 1964b: chapter 3). In addition, they had to disarm the Army of Liberation, which had formed in 1955 from disparate militia fighting the French. The Army had fought in the name of the king but even after independence refused to lay down their arms until French forces were expelled from Algeria. But because Morocco could ill-afford to be dragged into its neighbor's conflict, Mohammad V had to build a strong enough *Forces Armées Royales* to neutralize the rural militia.

The second obstacle was that the king and his nationalist allies were not in agreement about the form of government that should be adopted. In principle, both Mohammad V and the *Istiqlal* subscribed to the November 1955 joint French-Moroccan Declaration of La Celle-Saint-Cloud in which Morocco was proclaimed a constitutional monarchy. But, in practice, the question was over to what extent the government would be responsible to either the monarch or the parliament. The king wanted to preserve royal prerogatives in part to safeguard his own interests but also because he doubted the ability of other groups to govern. As he declared in 1958:

If we are to give the nation sound and healthy institutions, we must avoid any precipitate action or improvisation. The real danger lies not in the absence of representative institutions; it consists in the establishment of a parliamentary system which is a pure formality, and which might be an agent for disorder and destruction. A true democracy must be an agent for construction and stability (quoted in Hassan II 1978: 65).

Mohammad V had joined forces with the nationalists to expel the French. But he perceived that after the fight for independence was over, nationalism would no longer be enough to hold together the coalition of civilian forces. As a result, Mohammad V would position himself as the arbiter among those interests, maintaining dynastic rule (Waterbury 1970: chapter 7).

For the *Istiqlal*, the king had served as a useful public face for the independence movement, but its earlier support was not an indication of unquestioned fealty. As one nationalist observed about Mohammad

V: "We do not admire him as king, however, but as a man who has acted and succeeded" (quoted in Zartman 1964a: 30). With the form of government at stake, the *Istiqlal* advanced its own republican agenda, which was further encouraged by events in neighboring Tunisia.[5]

As opposition to the king, the *Istiqlal* posed a formidable threat. It was the oldest political party on the scene with immense legitimacy given its role in the struggle for independence. In addition, the *Istiqlal* was capable of coherent action due to its well-defined organization. By 1958 the party was composed of over 1,200 party secretaries, each organized within a centralized hierarchy that was monitored by regional party inspectors and was controlled by active party headquarters in Rabat (Ashford 1964: 5). The party also had active ties to other organizations, such as the *Union Marocaine du Travail* (UMT), the largest trade union. Under the leadership of Mehdi Ben Barka, beginning in 1958, the party went on a campaign to unify its ranks and become the main political organization in opposition to the king. Moreover, Ben Barka was not afraid to challenge the king. After the first two *Istiqlal*-dominated governments appointed by the king had fallen, Ben Barka complained in a veiled reference to the king's interference: " . . . le government actuel – composé presque entièrement de nos camarades du parti – ne possède pas les moyens suffisants pour faire à ses responsibilities entières, et exercer toute son autorité à travers le pays" (Ben Barka 1999: 86–87).[6]

In its battle with Mohammad V, the *Istiqlal* was not a virtuous champion of democracy for all. The *Istiqlal* sought to become the dominant party, co-opting other groups and marginalizing those that it could not incorporate. It was even suspected of a campaign of political assassinations of leaders of the Army of Liberation and other parties. And although the *Istiqlal* demanded a strong legislature in the interests of dominating it, its less-than-democratic motives do not negate the fact that the party was the leader in the conflict with the king to establish a monarchy that was constitutional rather than absolutist.

---

[5] After achieving independence from France in March 1956, Tunisia's citizens quickly elected a Constituent Assembly. The following year, the bey was deposed, and Tunisia was declared a republic.

[6] . . . the current government – composed almost entirely of our colleagues from the party – do not possess sufficient means to carry out their responsibilities and to exert full authority throughout the country.

2.3.3   The Battle over Institutions

Mohammad V made the first move in the battle over the legislature. By decree, the king created the National Consultative Assembly (NCA) to which he appointed seventy-six members. The members included representatives of various professions along with some from political groupings. Included were ten members of the *Istiqlal*. The Assembly operated under considerable constraints given its relationship to the king. Mohammad V reserved the right to invoke and close all sessions, to replace any member, and to renew members' appointments every two years. The king had meant for the Assembly to serve in an advisory capacity rather than as an institution with equal power. It perhaps was fitting, then, that the Assembly convened in Rabat in the former Conservatory of Music and Declamation.

The one useful power the Assembly did have, however, was its right to question ministers from the king's government. Similar to procedures within parliamentary democracies, ministers were required to attend sessions of the Assembly when their relevant issue areas were on the agenda. Assembly members could pose oral or written questions. In the case of the latter, ministers were required to provide written responses within one week. The former resulted in policy debates, and as Zartman (1964a: 46) explains: "Without being able to enforce demands upon the government, the Assembly could prod it into action or at least increase the emotional and political content of the issue." Indeed, the Assembly was sometimes able to go beyond its "fire alarm" function and inject itself into the policy-making process. Assembly resolutions influenced the course of policy in various areas, such as development of the civil service and organization of a nationalist purge. Finally, the Assembly provided a forum in which the government could "explain and justify its program" (Zartman 1964a: 47).

Yet members of the Assembly called for still greater powers. As early as 1957, the president of the NCA suggested that the government be made responsible to the Assembly. Members of the Assembly, however, perhaps undermined their own chances of gaining more independence as partisanship increased within the body itself. The problem stemmed from the growing concern of some groups over the influence of the *Istiqlal* and its allies. The infighting provided the perfect excuse for the king to not reextend the Assembly's term in 1959. What replaced the NCA was an even more temporary and quasi-legislative institution called the Superior Council of the Plan (SCP). The SCP initially had been established in 1957 to examine the government's economic Two Year Plan. Once the NCA disappeared, however, the Council used its appraisal of Plans as an occasion to review all government programs. And if ever the relationship between these institutions and the king was unclear, any doubt was dispelled when Mohammad V went so far as to dissolve the government and install himself as prime minister in 1960. His son, Hassan II, became the deputy prime minister.

The death of Mohammad V in 1961 and Hassan II's ascension to the throne made calls for reform even louder. The new king promised to adhere to the timetable for reforms that had been laid out by his father. The *Istiqlal* and other parties demanded that a constituent assembly be formed to draft a new constitution, but Hassan II maneuvered himself as the sole drafter of the document.

The 1962 constitution curtailed some of the king's powers but did not do enough to appease the *Istiqlal* and its allies. On the one hand, legislation required passage by the parliament or by voters in a referendum, whereas before it needed simply the king's imprimatur. On the other hand, the government was clearly responsible to the monarch rather than to the assembly because selection and dismissal of the prime minister and his cabinet would rest solely in the king's hands. Hassan II, in fact, viewed the government as an intermediary between himself and the bicameral parliament. A referendum on the constitution later in the year delivered an 80 percent approval.

Under these rules, the first parliamentary elections were held in May 1963. Both the crown and the opposition expected proroyalist forces to win a landslide. Yet the results yielded a parliament that was dominated by neither monarchical forces nor the opposition. The *Istiqlal* won 21 seats, whereas the *Union Nationale des Forces Populaires* (UNFP), a party that resulted from a split within the *Istiqlal*, obtained 28 seats.[7] The largest number of seats (69 of 144) went to the *Front de Défense des Institutions Constitutionnelles* (FDIC), a grouping of proroyalist forces. Six members of parliament remained nonpartisan,

---

[7] By 1959, infighting within the *Istiqlal* reached its climax when a small group led by Mehdi Ben Barka left to form the UNFP, which was more leftist and republican than the remaining core of the *Istiqlal*.

leaving the FDIC just four seats short of a simple majority. Nevertheless, the king asked the FDIC's members to form a government. In response, the opposition set out to derail the government's legislative agenda. Deadlock resulted as neither the opposition nor the government could get their legislative initiatives passed.

In the meantime, the economic situation worsened considerably. Tensions culminated in riots in Casablanca in March 1965. For the political and economic chaos, the king squarely placed the blame on the parliament. In a speech to assembly members soon after the riots, Hassan II scolded:

Enough of your speechifying! You don't even believe your own empty words! Although your business is to legislate, here you are in the third year of this parliament, and you have promulgated only three laws I ask you, elected representatives, to give proof of professional conscience, so that the state and the people may have good laws (Hassan II 1978: 77).

But the king did more than chastise the parliament. As he later recalled with detached rationality: "After having employed what the scientist Claude Bernard called the experimental method, our duty was to guarantee the right of the nation to exist, and to end the era of irresponsibility. This I now did by declaring a state of emergency, which suspended the activity of Parliament" (Hassan II 1978: 78). Yet Hassan II eventually would come to learn that repression and refusal to compromise were not the answer. Dissent continued to emerge; most notable was a general student strike in 1970. The king's response was to draft a new constitution that arrogated even more powers for himself. Yet the opposition refused to acquiesce with the *Istiqlal* and the UNFP urging a boycott of the referendum for ratification.

As demonstrations continued into 1971, Hassan faced a more urgent threat in July when a group of army cadets stormed the king's palace as he was celebrating his birthday with a lavish party. Several people were killed, but the king's forces managed to regain control. Just over a year later, however, another coup attempt almost succeeded when the king's plane was attacked while it was in the air. Very lucky to have survived successive coup attempts along with weathering a succession of domestic protests, Hassan returned to the bargaining table, resulting in a 1972 constitution that did not meet all of the opposition's demands but certainly allowed for more legislative prerogative than had been tolerated in the 1970 version. Hassan continued to govern with a plural party system operating within a legislature although constitutional amendments in 1996 transformed the legislature from a unicameral to a bicameral body.

2.4 ECUADOR: THE PERILS OF NONINSTITUTIONALIZATION

2.4.1 Prelude to Military Rule

After the creation of Ecuador from Gran Colombia in 1830, politics in Ecuador was dominated by agricultural, conservative elites from the interior of the country. With the cultivation of cacao in the late 1800s, however, Ecuador's political configuration began to change. Cacao became a lucrative export, financing the rise of more commercial and cosmopolitan interests along Ecuador's coast that challenged conservative groups from the hinterlands. Yet politics was a distinctly elite affair as power alternated between these two groups. Because neither side was strong enough to dominate, they frequently called on the aid of military strongmen to serve as either allies or arbiters. This succession of *caudillos* did not represent military rule because a nationally based administration in control of the armed forces hardly existed. As a result, these types of military interventions were frequent but quite transitory as the conservatives and liberals continuously attempted to oust each other.

The major break in this pattern occurred with the July 1925 coup that occurred in the aftermath of the collapse of the cacao boom. In this case, the League of Young Officers, whose members largely came from the conservative inner regions, seized power from the Liberal Party government, which steadily had been losing support due to deteriorating economic conditions. The officers justified their intervention on the grounds that a succession of Liberal governments had grown increasingly corrupt and sold out to coastal interests.

As a remedy, the officers installed a new civilian government that embarked on the *Transformacion Juliana* – a broad range of political, economic, and social reforms that were meant to radically change Ecuadorian life. The political centerpiece was the 1929 constitution with provisions for habeas corpus and voting rights for women (the first in Latin America). The state expanded its reach into the economy with the establishment of a central bank, comptroller general, budget offices, customs control, and public works projects.

Yet with the onset of the Great Depression, not even this regime could withstand declining popular support. In 1931, the military-controlled civilian regime was forced to step down, ushering in another round of Liberal governments. The military stayed out of politics, particularly after Ecuador suffered a loss of over one half of its territory to Peru in 1941. The disastrous performance of the armed forces led to a complete withdrawal from politics as military leaders concentrated on rebuilding their tattered institution. The notion that preoccupation with partisan politics had so distracted officers from their original security functions even led to the addition of constitutional law classes to the Military College's curriculum. Future officers were "to understand that they do not defend individual men, but ideals and institutions created to serve the fatherland" (Fitch 1977: 20).

After the Depression, military intervention hardly seemed necessary anyway. For many countries, World War II initiated economic recovery, and Ecuador was no different. Industrialization, although still limited, grew in the production of basic goods, such as textiles. But the peak did not come until 1948, when the state consciously intervened in the economy to promote bananas, cacao's successor as primary agricultural export. The civilian government of Galo Plaza Lasso created the *Comisión de Orientación y Crédito para el Banano*, a lending agency devoted to dispensing credit to domestic banana producers. Plaza Lasso's government embarked on a major road-building project with the help of the U.S. government and international lending agencies to improve infrastructural linkages. In addition, Plaza Lasso invited the United Fruit Company, the multinational corporation that dominated commerce in fruit, to take control of the shipping and sales of Ecuador's product around the world. The boon to Ecuador's economy cannot be overstated. From 1947 to 1953, the number of bunches exported increased from 2.6 million to 16.7 million, increasing the value of exports from 5 to 44 million dollars (Conaghan 1988: 38). By the early 1960s, Ecuador had become the world's largest producer of bananas.

In addition, production of the actual fruit occurred on farms that significantly varied in size. Almost half of all land under cultivation, for example, belonged to farms that were less than 100 hectares (Conaghan 1988: 39). The result was that the earnings of the export boom created forward and backward linkages to other industries. Increased profits went to the middle-class landowners who then expanded agricultural employment, putting more money in the pockets of wage laborers. The expansion of purchasing power by all classes not only encouraged the revitalization of existing plants but also facilitated further industrial diversification.

History seemed destined to repeat itself, however, once the banana boom collapsed in the early 1960s. Amidst a worsening economic situation, the military under General Ramon Castro Jijon seized power with the intent to continue the *Transformacion Juliana*. But Castro Jijon's tenure was short lived as the regime encountered resistance both within society and the armed forces. Consequently, only three years after taking power, military leaders were forced to return to the barracks in 1966.

After two years under an interim leader, Ecuadorian voters selected José Velasco Ibarra as president. Elected president four times in the past, Velasco Ibarra faced a daunting economic situation with declining export revenues, stagnant industrial growth, depleted foreign reserves, and a climbing budget deficit. To address the crisis, Velasco Ibarra presented a stabilization package to Congress. Instead of ratifying the measures, however, the legislature adjourned for the summer in May 1970. Velasco Ibarra, in turn, bypassed Congress and issued the laws as emergency decrees. Eventually, the president carried out a complete *autogolpe*, dissolving the legislature and ruling solely by decree.

In spite of his unconstitutional encroachment on congressional powers, Velasco Ibarra, however, did agree to hold presidential elections scheduled for June 1972. In an atmosphere of economic crisis and political uncertainty, Assad Bucaram, a populist leader, seemed poised to win these elections. Bucaram had been mayor of Guayaquil when the 1963 military junta of Castro Jijon removed him from office. He won reelection in 1967 and later went on to win the prefecture of the coastal province of Guayas. Having won these electoral contests with massive support, Bucaram had set his sights on the presidency (Isaacs 1993: 21).

2.4.2 The Military's Agenda

Bucaram's victory, however, was preempted by a military coup led by General Guillermo Rodriguez Lara in February 1972. Although its agenda was similar to that of the regimes in 1925 and 1963, this military regime was unique in the conditions under which it arose. The exhaustion of the easy phase of import substitution industrialization was evident in Ecuador as it was throughout Latin America. Yet the situation in Ecuador did not appear as bleak as in some neighboring states. In 1967 the Texaco-Gulf Consortium discovered massive petroleum reserves in the eastern jungle region, and the estimated yield was close to 250,000 barrels per day. As one high-ranking Ecuadorian official claimed: "within a year every day will be Christmas and Ecuador will soon become the Kuwait of the Western hemisphere" (Isaacs 1993: 16).

Yet it was for this very reason that military and civilian elites worried about Velasco Ibarra's current administration and Bucaram's populist movement. As a member of the Quito Chamber of Commerce explained:

We accepted the Rodriguez Lara dictatorship because Bucaram would have been a very unreliable leader. The only way to avoid this was with a dictatorship. Oil also gave the government a chance to be rich and paternalistic. We thought it had the potential to be a great government. Yes, without a doubt, given the slight administrative capacity of either Velasco or Bucaram and the untested capacity of the military, we preferred the military (Isaacs 1993: 70).

The discovery of oil unleashed momentous hopes that Ecuador would be able to alter its historical trajectory. Oil would replace cacao and bananas. But unlike these agricultural exports, its demand would never be satiated and Ecuador's position as a supplier would not be undermined easily because other countries could not simply decide one day to start producing oil and glut the market. With stable and generous export earnings, Ecuador would be able to use the funds to industrialize and to initiate a host of economic and social reforms designed to spread the wealth.

It was in this spirit that the military junta announced its intention to establish "'a revolutionary government' in which civilians and the military would unite 'to serve the interests of the people and implant a regime of social justice'" (Isaacs 1993: 37). Indeed, in private,

Rodriguez Lara explained that leaders of the regime "didn't want this to be just another coup" (Isaacs 1993: 37).

Agrarian reform was to be the foundation of the government's plans to transform Ecuador's economy. The armed forces and technocrats from *Junta Nacional de Planificación* (JUNAPLA) believed that the unequal distribution of land was the main cause of stagnant agricultural production that hindered the expansion of industrial production because it impeded most of the rural population from becoming consumers of manufactured goods.[8] Initial proposals of reform required expropriation of all land that was deemed to be inefficiently cultivated.

Contingent on the success of the agrarian reform, industrial production was expected to increase. According to the *Plan Integral*, import substitution industrialization would be broadened and deepened with the expanded production of more consumer goods and new intermediate and capital goods. To facilitate development, the government started with the basics, making investments in physical and human capital. In addition, the state would both aid private agents in boosting manufactures and become more involved in the production process itself. The military, for example, planned to fund over 200 major industrial projects in conjunction with domestic entrepreneurs (Neuhouser 1996: 649). The military also nationalized key industries, such as the national airline, and created almost fifteen new public enterprises (Schodt 1987: 117). Increased profits to private and public firms would lead to trickle-down benefits to the working class in the form of increased employment and wages. The minimum wage, which had been increased only once since the previous military regime of 1963, was raised for three consecutive years (Neuhouser 1996: 649). Workers, in turn, would fuel further expansion of the domestic market.

Mindful that reform had been promised many times before, military leaders believed they would succeed where others had failed because, this time, oil would make much more possible. Yet the presence of resources alone was not enough. The new government needed the help of outsiders to develop those resources and implement its plans.

---

[8] JUNAPLA was created in 1954 to formulate and implement plans for more state intervention in the Ecuadorian economy. It was formed with the direct participation of the United Nations Economic Commission for Latin America (ECLA) which was heavily influenced by Raul Prebisch's campaign to end the asymmetries caused by "dependent development" (Hidrobo 1992).

2.4.3   The Rise of Opposition

The first set of actors with whom the government negotiated consisted of the oil companies. In June 1972, the junta issued Decree 430, which required companies that wished to maintain their operations in Ecuador to renegotiate the terms of their concessions. No longer could any concession exceed 160,000 hectares: all foreign companies were now required to engage in exploration, an additional 15 percent tax on petroleum exports was levied, and the government's production royalties increased from 11 to 16 percent (Isaacs 1993: 42). In addition, Ecuador joined the Organization of Petroleum Exporting Countries (OPEC). The net effect of the renegotiations was to increase resource rents to the government but also to make it more dependent on the largest company, the Texaco-Gulf Consortium, as many smaller companies exited with the increasing costs and risks of doing business in Ecuador.

Texaco-Gulf's dominant position was not without consequence. In 1974, the Consortium requested expansion of production to take advantage of soaring prices. The government demanded that in exchange, the company engage in more exploration, especially because fewer companies now remained to do so. After the 1972 renegotiations, Texaco-Gulf claimed that such demands were unreasonable, and in response, halted exports of Ecuadorian oil. It also threatened to end its operations in the country, cancelling purchase orders and agreements with subcontractors to increase the credibility of the threat (Isaacs 1993: 44–45). The results were a dramatic decrease in export earnings and economic growth that forced the government to increase its foreign borrowing. And although production resumed a few months later, the point was well made to the Rodriguez Lara government: resources would not enable unilateral actions by the state because development of that resource would require the cooperation of others.

The government encountered a similar lesson with other elements of its agenda for reform. The actual Agrarian Reform Law that was issued in October 1973, for example, was significantly less radical. The law established no limits on the size of private holdings and guaranteed ownership rights to those private agents who efficiently cultivated at least 80 percent of their land (Isaacs 1993: 47). In addition, the law's vague language and a two-year moratorium on enforcement neutralized the threat of expropriation for all intents and purposes (Schodt 1987: 122). The government's retreat on agricultural reform was due to pressure from landowners who refused to cede their land without a fight.

For workers, the results produced by the regime did not match its promises. Between 1968 and 1975, the share of national income to the poorest quintile of the population actually dropped from 4 to 2.5 percent (Neuhouser 1996: 651). As a result, labor unions began to mobilize to protect the interests of their members. By 1974, Ecuador's three major labor unions joined forces for the first time in the formation of the *Frente Unitario de Trabajadores* (FUT) to redirect their efforts from fighting among themselves to protesting against the regime.[9] They successfully held a one-day strike on November 13, 1975, which crippled the country.

In a parallel development, the *Cámaras de la Produccion* became centers of opposition as disillusionment set in among industrialists. The state had created the *cámaras de industrias* in 1936 with the stated purpose "to impel the progress of industry in cooperation with the state" (Hidrobo 1992: 158). In essence, the *cámaras* served as the institutional link between the state and domestic entrepreneurs. Because membership in one of the *cámaras* was mandatory, the *cámaras* could monitor the activities of business groups fairly easily. In addition, the *cámaras* were helpful in the explanation and implementation of government decisions affecting local businesses. Eventually, the *cámaras* also provided feedback to the government about the reaction, suggestions, and complaints of domestic capitalists. But during the Rodriguez Lara regime, the *cámaras* ceased to be the cooperative partner of the state and instead became extremely critical publicly.

The opposition of the landowners to the Rodriguez Lara government was not surprising because their interests were clearly hurt by the proposed reforms. But the rising discontent among industrial and labor groups was a puzzle (Neuhouser 1996). A more diversified industrial base would create greater profits for domestic entrepreneurs and greater purchasing power for workers. If they were the ostensible

---

[9] These unions were the *Confederación de Trabajadores Ecuatorianos* (CTE), the *Central Ecuatoriana de Organizaciones Clasistas* (CEDOC), and the *Confederación Ecuatoriana de Organizaciones Libres* (CEOSEL), which together represented almost one-half of all organized workers (Schodt 1987: 126–127).

beneficiaries of the military regime's policies, what grievances motivated their actions?

Repression could have been one obvious culprit. At this time, military governments governed every country on the continent except for Guyana, Suriname, and Venezuela. In many of them, the degree of repression was evident from stadiums used as holding grounds, police stations transformed into torture centers, and disappearances that ended with the dropping of bodies into the sea from airplanes. Yet the Rodriguez Lara regime did not follow the Argentine and Chilean examples. Certainly violations of individual rights and media censorship did occur, but as a trade unionist in Ecuador explained: "Here we do not have dictatorships with fascist tendencies like those of the Southern Cone or Central America... there is a certain amount of respect for human rights. It is the kind of dictatorship that we call *dictablanda*" (Isaacs 1993: 91). The cries of opposition that domestic groups voiced, in fact, were possible only because the regime did not stifle them.

2.4.4   Underinstitutionalization and Its Consequences

The protest by labor and industrial groups appears to have been motivated by their exclusion from the regime's policy-making process. Upon seizing power, Rodriguez Lara had closed the legislature and banned political parties, closing off the institutional routes available to industrialists and workers for expressing their demands. The junta debated the idea of establishing a regime party similar to that of the hegemonic organization, *Sistema Nacional de Apoyo a la Movilización Social* (SINAMOS), in neighboring Peru (also under leftist military rule at this time), but in the end, decided not to do so. As Rodriguez Lara explained: "We did think about forming a party, but then we reconsidered because we felt it might divide the spontaneous support. So we did not pursue it. I guess that we just did not think it was that important; we preferred to retain spontaneous support" (Isaacs 1993: 93). A civilian minister echoed this idea: "Rodriguez thought that the building of infrastructure to benefit the people replaced politics and that as long as the government built roads and schools no one had to discuss politics" (Isaacs 1993: 93).

There were potentially other institutions through which outside groups could have influenced the regime. The industrialists, in the past, had used the *cámaras* to advance their interests. Rodriguez Lara's government continued to maintain direct relations with the *cámaras*, soliciting their members' opinions on government policy and allowing for their participation in the *Junta Monetaria*. In this regard, a government minister defended the regime's record: "The government kept its doors open. Rodriguez Lara himself received businessmen. Ministers had permanent contact so it was not difficult to arrange a meeting and come in and talk. Look the *Junta Monetaria* is an excellent forum that permits a fluid relationship to develop between the business sector and the government..." (Isaacs 1993: 71).

But the "open door" policy had distinct limits. The input of domestic entrepreneurs was welcomed but in no way binding on the government. As Rodriguez Lara himself emphasized: "I met with them [the private sector] and listed to them. They were heard and listened to but not consulted. I was not going to be governed by what they had to say. Until then the *cámaras* had controlled the economy and the political process. I was not prepared to accept this" (Isaacs 1993: 72).

For a group that was accustomed to being heard, the government's attitude was infuriating. León Febres-Cordero, director of the *Cámaras de Guayaquil*, one of the largest producer associations, tied the erosion of support for reforms with the government's exclusionary stance: "Is it possible by chance that one could demand a genuine participation by private enterprise for the accomplishment of development goals while pretending that we should not have a role in the organs of planning, credit, or monetary policy?... We cannot accept the assignment of great responsibilities without participation" (Conaghan 1988: 104–105).

The lack of institutionalized access appears to have galled the industrialists for two very specific reasons. For one, a number of entrepreneurs were of the opinion that the government's reform plans were misguided. Following the announcement of land reform, agricultural production fell as current landowners lost the incentive to produce given the likelihood of losing some of their property. The industrial *cámaras* pointed to this fact to argue that because land redistribution was leading to a slowdown in agricultural production that impeded industrial expansion, the government's land reform was the primary culprit in slowing industrial growth.

Certainly, ideological bias and prejudice motivated some of the industrialists' claims. Many of them had reflex-like opposition to increased state intervention in the market and carried deeply ingrained prejudices against the rural poor, who, according to the government's plan, were supposed to become new landowners and to drive greater agricultural production. As one entrepreneur claimed: "The Ecuadorian experience has demonstrated that land distribution caused a decrease in agrarian production due to the fact that peasants do not have education and technological capabilities" (Hidrobo 1992: 116). Aside from their views about the proper division between the state and the market and the capacity of the rural poor, many industrialists also had technical beliefs about the reform plans that fundamentally clashed with those of government planners.

The second reason why domestic entrepreneurs opposed the exclusive policy-making process is that they feared for their own interests. Rodriguez Lara's government patronized domestic capital, but at the same time also stoked the demands of workers. Greater industrialization was supposed to benefit both entrepreneurs and workers who would form a coalition in support of the regime. Yet the military's populist rhetoric only fueled the suspicions of domestic industrialists who were fearful that what the military had attempted to do to the landowners could one day be foisted on them. And because they had no institutional mechanism by which they could guarantee some access, the industrialists refused to cooperate with a regime that ostensibly was attempting to implement policies that would be in their benefit.

Workers harbored similar suspicions. The result was increasing protest by all sectors of society that exacerbated tensions within the military itself. Factionalization within the armed forces reared its ugly head on August 30, 1975, when disenchanted Ecuadorian officers, led by General Raul Gonzalez Alvear, attempted to oust Rodriguez Lara. The coup attempt failed but set in motion Rodriguez Lara's eventual replacement one year later by a military triumvirate that abandoned any notion of radical transformation and prepared for the return of civilian rule. Ecuador's return to democracy came with the election of Jaime Roldós Aguillera in April 1979.[10]

---

[10] As a side note, Bucaram again ran for the presidency in these elections, but the military managed to disqualify him by claiming that because Bucaram's immigrant parents were not Ecuadorian by the time of his birth, he was not Ecuadorian born and could not become president according to the constitution.

2.5 CONCLUSION

The cases in this chapter illustrate that dictators confront two basic problems of governance: they must solicit the cooperation of some part of their citizenry even to achieve the most modest of aims in addition to counteracting any active opposition to their rule. Nondemocratic incumbents face these problems in varying degrees. Some rulers, such as the Kuwaiti emirs after the discovery of oil, are more financially independent from their citizens than other leaders. In fact, the revenues from oil helped Kuwaiti leaders buy the acquiescence of the merchants who previously had constituted the loudest voice of opposition. Other powerholders, however, such as the dynastic family in Morocco or the military regime in Ecuador, faced greater challenges of state-building with fewer resources. After Morocco's independence, Mohammad V and, later, his son Hassan had to exert newfound authority and pull their country into the modern era. And in Ecuador, after continuous cycles of economic booms and busts, military leaders faced the challenge of constructing a more stable and equitable economy. In tackling these daunting tasks without the resources available to states such as Kuwait, authoritarian incumbents in Morocco and Ecuador had to enlist the help of significant segments of their populations.

In exchange for assistance, dictatorial rulers undoubtedly offered material benefits. Yet rents alone are not all the potential opposition seeks. Groups within society also demand participation, even if limited, in the determination of policy. In Kuwait, the merchants resisted the government's attempts to interfere in their commercial activities and sought to play a role in determining the fiscal priorities of the state. In Morocco, after independence, the *Istiqlal* and its supporters pushed for a form of constitutional monarchy, indicating the desire to be wholly included in the setting of all possible policies. Finally, in Ecuador, both entrepreneurs and workers did not trust the military regime's ideological commitment to act in their interests. To avoid potential arbitrariness, these groups sought to have a permanent place in the decision-making process. As these examples illustrate, informal arrangements and formal interest group associations were not enough. Although business groups in Ecuador had some access to the government of Rodriguez Lara through the *cámaras*, they demanded a restoration of the assembly and political parties as a way of organizing themselves and gaining concessions from the regime. Similarly, the *Istiqlal* in Morocco was adamant that the king cooperate in establishing a parliament with both *de jure* and *de facto* power. To guarantee real policy concessions, then, outside groups demand the presence of nominally democratic institutions in dictatorships.

In summary, then, the Kuwaiti case shows that when the emirs no longer needed the cooperation of the merchants after the discovery of oil, they disbanded the movement for parliamentarism because they no longer needed to make concessions to this group. In contrast, in Morocco, after independence, the king and his son had to establish their legitimacy and reconstruct their country. Facing such Herculean tasks with few resources and an opposition that had grown strong in the nationalist struggle, the ruling family had to make some concessions. After some turmoil, both sides settled on a full panoply of legislative parties that survive to this day under monarchical rule. Finally, in Ecuador, the challenges of establishing a sound footing for the economy were no less pressing. But after misguidedly dismantling the legislature and parties, the military junta could not obtain the cooperation of even those who were the ostensible beneficiaries of its program. The result was the quick demise of the regime at the hands of a well-mobilized opposition. Although these cases are quite heterogeneous, taken together, they provide some intuitions for why dictators govern with nominally democratic institutions. A formalization of these ideas to generate additional systematic hypotheses follows in the next chapter.

3

Use of Institutions to Co-opt

3.1 INTRODUCTION

As seen in the previous chapters, dictatorships vary in their institutional arrangements. In 12 percent of all dictatorial country-year observations, neither a legislature nor a political party existed. Monarchs are most likely to govern without institutions; one-third of them dispense with nominally democratic institutions. In contrast, civilian dictators rely heavily on them: there are almost two times as many civilian dictatorships with a single party rather than multiple parties, but almost all of them govern with legislatures. The organization of military regimes is much more varied.

The illustrative cases also display the variation in institutions under dictatorship. In Kuwait, the ruling family at first conceded institutions to the merchant opposition, only to rescind them after the discovery of oil. After independence, the kings of Morocco attempted to renege on institutional concessions as well, only to find that they could not engage in state-building and neutralize the opposition without the aid of nominally democratic legislatures and parties. Because they did not have the resources of the Kuwaiti emirs, Morocco's rulers wisely established these institutions to co-opt the opposition. In contrast, Rodriguez Lara failed to incorporate crucial elements of Ecuadorian society. By not providing a forum in which outside groups could issue demands, negotiate with the regime, and influence policy, the military

government alienated even those segments of society that were designated beneficiaries of its programs.

This chapter systematically addresses the questions that emerge
from both the aggregate patterns and the aforementioned cases: what
accounts for the institutional variation in nondemocratic regimes? Why
do some rulers create broadened dictatorships with a panoply of legislative parties, whereas others govern more narrow regimes with either
a single party or no institutions at all? To answer these questions, the
chapter begins with a description of the conditions under which dictators may choose to govern with nominally democratic institutions,
followed by a discussion of how these institutions facilitate the exchange of policy concessions for political support. The second part of
the chapter formalizes these arguments to produce predictions about
when we should expect to observe these institutions that are tested empirically for all dictatorships from 1946 to 2002. A brief conclusion
ends the chapter with a summary of the findings and a discussion of
why institutions are expected to affect policies and outcomes.

3.2   DICTATORIAL CONCESSIONS

All dictatorships face two problems of governance: first, how to thwart
rebellion and second, how to obtain cooperation. Leaders want to
survive in office either to reap the benefits of being in power or to
implement policies. For democratic leaders, surviving in office requires
negotiating with constituencies and parties and winning elections. But
for authoritarian rulers who do not face electoral constraints, the task
of maintaining power is considerably more difficult.

Foremost are the threats posed by the ruling elite. As Geddes (1999:
121) observes, politics in authoritarian regimes "involves factional-
ism, competition, and struggle. The competition among rival factions, however, takes different forms in different kinds of authoritarian regimes. . . . " Accordingly, to co-opt the ruling elite, dictators
frequently set up inner sanctums where real decisions are made and
potential rivals are kept under close scrutiny. As discussed earlier, the
heads of dynastic monarchies rely on consultative councils and extensive kin networks to staff important government positions. To prevent
internecine fighting and to rationalize decision-making, military officers form juntas and other power-sharing arrangements within the

armed forces. Finally, civilian dictators who often govern with a regime party create a smaller political bureau within the party. These smaller bodies and inner sanctums are the first institutional trench by which dictators protect themselves.

Yet discontent with dictatorship also may come from larger segments of society. The previous chapter highlighted domestic entrepreneurs as the source of opposition under both the monarchy in Kuwait and the military regime in Ecuador. Other examples emphasize the importance of popular mobilization in challenging authoritarian regimes. In Algeria, for example, Islamic organizations spearheaded the opposition before the military government banned the most popular Islamic party and closed the legislature. Workers who organized under the banner of Solidarity, in contrast, constituted the strongest challenge to Poland's communist regime.

Observers of democratic transitions are divided as to the relative importance of elite ruptures and mass mobilization in ending non-democratic regimes. In several Latin American cases, popular protest seems not to have been the initial spark for democratization but rather emerged as democratization already was underway (Collier 1999). These cases seem to confirm O'Donnell and Schmitter's (1986: 19) observation that "there is no transition whose beginning is not the consequence – direct or indirect – of important divisions within the authoritarian regime itself" (see also Haggard and Kaufman 1995, Przeworski 1991). Indeed, Svolik (2007) finds that the vast majority of authoritarian rulers lose power through coups staged by insiders although their deposals do not necessarily usher in democratic rule. Yet in their study of 42 sub-Saharan African countries, Bratton and van de Walle (1997: 83) observe that "[democratic] transitions in Africa seem to be occurring more commonly from below . . . " because rulers "resist political openings for as long as possible." In addition, regime transitions that have occurred in the wake of the Soviet collapse seem to have been driven by forces from below.

The problems of elite defections and mass protest most likely intersect and jointly threaten authoritarian regimes. Neutralizing threats to their rule that emerge from within society is important for dictatorial rulers not only for easing the problem of governance but also for demonstrating to colleagues within the ruling elite that they have control over the situation. Yet to insure political acquiescence among citizens, dictators may have to offer groups within society some concessions.

Certainly dictators can rely on repressive tools to neutralize threats to their rule. The secret police is a specialized institution of dictatorial rule.[1] Yet the use of force is costly, requiring resources "devoted to producing repressive legislation, to publicizing these laws, to policing their obedience, and to punishing offenders" (Wintrobe 1998: 46). Furthermore, repressive methods may not always be effective. Writing of military dictatorship in Latin America, Cardoso (1979: 48) observes that the "State is sufficiently strong to concentrate its attention and repressive apparatus against so-called subversive groups, but it is not as efficient when it comes to controlling the universities, for example, or even the bureaucracy itself." As a result, the dictator may find it useful to rely on other strategies to neutralize threats to his rule. He may offer a mix of carrots and sticks: repressing some and co-opting others. Alternatively, periods of repression may be punctuated by moments of openness. Mao, for example, orchestrated both the Cultural Revolution and the One Hundred Flowers Movement.

But repression is not the only instrument by which dictators maintain power because dictators must do more than just avert rebellion. They rule over states, and the task of governance is difficult. Even if dictators act merely in their own interest, if they are "predatory," up to a point they benefit more when the country is militarily secure and the economy functions well (Levi 1988, McGuire and Olson 1996). Yet a state with full monopoly over the means of coercion requires citizens who are willing to serve as loyal soldiers and police. Similarly, a functioning economy requires the regime to provide incentives for people to reveal their private information, to work, and to save. As

---

[1] The degree and the method by which the secret police infiltrate society differs: only certain groups may be targeted, such as unions, media, leftist organizations, and ethnic or religious minorities, or the system may be more extensive, designed to monitor the whole society. In this case, monitoring and punishment may be through cells in the workplace or in schools or through a system of personal denunciations among neighbors and friends. As important as monitoring citizens is, so is watching the military. In military regimes, it is not uncommon for each branch to set up its own intelligence service to monitor not only citizens, but also its own and other branches' members. Finally, dictators sometimes rely on paramilitary groups to terrorize both the civilian and military populations. Systematic work on coercive institutions, however, is lacking.

the merchants of Kuwait and entrepreneurs of Ecuador demonstrated, the owners of productive assets have little incentive to cooperate with regimes if they do not receive concessions in return. In speaking about labor under dictatorship, Valenzuela (1992: 89) summarizes the incentives for incumbents to do more than just repress: "Most authoritarian regimes would simply prefer to eliminate worker organizations altogether, but twentieth-century technology, management, and marketing provide workers with many opportunities to disrupt production, for which a totally repressive stance towards labour is counterproductive." Hence, dictators must make concessions to induce the cooperation of outsiders.

What are these concessions that dictators must offer to induce cooperation from outsiders and neutralize threats of rebellion? Concessions frequently take the form of perks, privileges, and spoils. Yet dictators may be required to offer more than just rents. Sometimes, the opposition demands policy compromises to satisfy its own constituents and to justify its engagement with the regime.

Not all dictators will make concessions. The disbursement of rents and the degree of policy compromise depends on the size of the threat authoritarian rulers face and the degree to which they need cooperation from the rest of society. But if the threat is large and they need cooperation, they will make concessions to maintain power.

3.3 DICTATORIAL INSTITUTIONS

As concessions, rents may be distributed through a variety of means. Rents may include bribes to individuals or distribution to a wider swath of society through state employment and public works programs. The distribution of spoils may be organized through the bureaucracy or distributed within institutions, as much of the literature on dictatorship recognizes (Binder 1964, Collier 1982, Wintrobe 1998, Zolberg 1969). In reference to regime parties, Friedrich and Brzezinski (1965: 29) observe, "it is the role of the party to provide a following for the dictator." A party offers individuals willing to collaborate with the regime a vehicle for advancing their careers within a stable system of patronage. In exchange for perks, privileges, and prospects of career advancement, members of a single party mobilize popular support and supervise behaviors of people unwilling to identify themselves with the dictator. In contrast to repression, rents are an alternative means by which dictators can bind parts of the population to them.

Policy concessions are another concession, but they differ from rents in that that they are best made through some institutional forum that lowers the transaction costs of exchanging them for political support. In this regard, legislatures and political parties are ideal.

For the dictator, legislatures are ideal because they allow for an environment of controlled bargaining. The dictator can select the groups to be granted access. Polish communists, for example, repeatedly sought participation of some Catholic groups: in a 1990 interview (translated from Rolicki 1990), the former first secretary of the Polish United Workers' (Communist) Party, Edward Gierek, revealed that he "intended to introduce to the *Sejm* [Parliament] a significant group of 25 percent of Catholic deputies." "It would have permitted us...," Gierek continued, "to broaden the political base of the authorities." Encapsulating these groups within a legislature allows the dictator to negotiate over various policy realms without having to reconstitute his bargaining partner each time.

An assembly also serves as a forum for negotiations in which preferences and information can be revealed. As President Jomo Kenyatta said in 1964 in a speech to the Kenyan House of Representatives: "What this House must contribute to the Republic is something far more than just machinery which can give the plans and requirements of the Government their lawful status. This must be our forum, for discussion and proposal, for question, objection, or advice.... serving as the place where the elders and the spokesmen of the people are expected and enabled to confer" (quoted in Stultz 1970: 325–326).

The flow of information about negotiations can be controlled. The subcommissions of the Supreme Soviet, for example, "[could] collate suggestions from experts and the public on the circulated draft, then deliberate upon the incorporation of these suggestions without revealing the dirty linen" (Vanneman 1977: 162).

A regime party can serve the same functions. Yet a single party may not suffice to co-opt a sufficient range of the opposition. As a consequence, although some dictators allow participation within legislatures only as nonpartisans or as members of a single party, other rulers must allow for multiple parties within legislative assemblies.

Multiple parties still can be an effective instrument of dictatorial rule if they can be tightly controlled by the dictatorship: these are "fronts." Consider communist Poland. Even though in 1948 communists forced their major rival, the Polish Socialist Party, into a "merger," thus creating the Polish United Workers Party (PUWP), they tolerated a prewar left-wing United Peasant Party (ZSL), a small private business party (SD), and a Catholic group with direct ties to Moscow. After 1956, two other Catholic groups were allowed to organize. Even though these parties functioned under separate labels in the legislature, they were presented to voters as a single list, with all candidates approved by the communists. Hence, elections only ratified the distribution of parliamentary seats and the specific appointees of the Communist Party. One way to think of this "multipartism" is that it represented a menu of contracts, allowing people characterized by different political attitudes (and differing degrees of opportunism) to sort themselves out. Membership in each party entailed a different degree of identification with the regime: highest for members of the PUWP, lower for those joining the Peasant Party, the lowest for the Catholic groups. In exchange, these memberships offered varying amounts of perks and privileges, in the same order. Someone not willing to join the Communist Party, with the social opprobrium this membership evoked among Catholic peasants, may have joined the Peasant Party. This choice entailed a less direct commitment and fewer perks, but it did signify identification with the regime. This separating equilibrium maximized support for the regime and visibly isolated those who were not willing to make any gesture of support.

For the dictator, legislatures and parties are institutions that ease the task of governing. Opposition demands can be made and contained within these institutions. As Brownlee (2007: 203) observes: "Parties do not merely transmit societal concerns: They create an arena in which those perspectives are renegotiated and reconciled." What is true for parties, however, is also true for legislatures in that assemblies provide the arena in which parties can interact. In addition, concessions made in response to opposition demands can be revealed within a closed forum rather than on the street. Within the halls of an assembly, demands do not appear to be acts of resistance and concessions do not seem like capitulations. Compromises can be hammered out without undue public scrutiny, and the resulting agreements can be dressed in a legalistic form and publicized as such. In Jordan, for example, once King Hussein offered the Muslim Brotherhood some influence over educational and religious policies, the group shifted from denouncing the regime on the streets to articulating its demands within the legislature (Schwedler 2006).

For domestic groups, participation in institutions yields several benefits. For leaders of these groups, legislative seats may result in lucrative appointments and other perks. Yet these leaders also must provide for their constituents if they are to remain leaders for long. For groups within society, having an institutional forum in which they can learn the regime's intentions and voice their own demands without precipitating punishment is also beneficial. Outside groups obtain more than just information and expressive benefits, however. In discussing the cooptation of labor, Valenzuela (1992: 87) observes that "placing the labour movement as one of the main constituencies of the party also enhances the ability of the labor leadership to pressure the authorities in favour of their programmes and interests. Co-optation is a two-way street."

Finally, dictatorial institutions reduce the political transaction costs that the potential opposition and the regime may incur in negotiating over rents and policies. Neo-institutionalism emphasizes the gains in efficiency that institutions can provide for transactions in both the economic (Greif et al. 1994, Milgrom et al. 1990, North and Weingast 1989) and political spheres (Aldrich 1995, Cox 1987). What is true for the marketplace and for democratic institutions also is true for legislative and partisan arrangements under dictatorship. For the potential opposition, an inclusive authoritarian regime reduces uncertainty over whether the incorporated groups will be included in future bargaining with the regime. Lust-Okar (2005: 37), for example, broadly argues that the mere permission to "make their demands legally" – whether through the formation of parties and associations or the publication of material – provides important access to the political arena. In a similar vein, I argue that legislatures that allow for multiple political parties are an important form of access to the political arena, which reduces some uncertainty for outside groups. As for the dictator, institutions make the granting of concessions easier for the reasons discussed above: the identification of reliable bargaining partners, the revelation of information, and the avoidance of popular mobilization.

That these institutions promote more efficient bargaining between the potential opposition and the authoritarian regime does not deny their significant distributional impact (Knight 1992). Large and stable coalitions within a parliament may have a better chance of challenging the dictator and extracting more concessions. In Brazil, for example, the *Movimento Democratico Brasileiro* (MDB), constituted as the voice of the opposition in parliament, successfully rejected a government-sponsored tax bill, an international trade bill, and an effort to lift the immunity of a parliamentarian whom the military wished to prosecute for insulting the armed forces during a speech. Yet it is likely that the dictator still maintains the upper hand because he retains the power to close these institutions. As a result, institutions under authoritarianism do not completely resolve problems of time inconsistency and uncertainty for participating groups as much as they do for the dictator himself. Yet even in the shadow of this potential arbitrary power, institutions still reduce some of the insecurity and costs of bargaining for incorporated groups (even if these costs are not zero) because dictators cannot close institutions without some costs. When the Algerian military, for example, closed the legislature after FIS was poised to win a majority of seats in 1991 elections, even members of the regime party, the *Front de Libration Nationale* (FLN), protested and the country was plunged into civil war. Because closing institutions entails some costs, dictators cannot so easily renege on bargains.

The result, then, is that when dictators face threats and need cooperation, they must make concessions. If these concessions are in the form of policies, they need institutions to deliver them. In the next section, I develop these intuitions more formally in a model in which dictators may need cooperation to generate rents and may face a threat of rebellion. The rents available for distribution – monetary rewards, perks, and privileges – increase when more people cooperate with the dictatorship. Yet dictatorships differ in their need for cooperation: those that can extract rents from mineral resources need little of it, whereas those that must rely on bankers to loan them money, peasants to produce food, and scientists to do research need extensive cooperation. In turn, dictators are dictators because they cannot win competitive elections, because their preferences diverge from those of the majority of the population. Hence, dictators may face a threat of rebellion, and the magnitude of this threat is again not the same for different dictators because potential opposition within society varies. The simple model, then, demonstrates under what conditions the dictator will make concessions, the opposition will accept them, and peace or turmoil will reign.

3.4 ACTORS AND PREFERENCES

That dictators are concerned with remaining in power goes without saying. Yet maintaining power is a means to an end. While in power, dictators may have substantive goals they seek to fulfill. Many Latin American militaries seized power to extinguish leftist threats. Other dictators in the developing world wanted to lead the modernization of their newly independent states. In addition, dictators frequently have more personal, less salutary aims. They seek enrichment through the accumulation of perks and privileges both for while they are in power and for when they might be forced to live as ordinary citizens or exiles. The popular portrayal of dictators makes it appear as if these goals are mutually exclusive. Some dictators, like General Park in South Korea, are widely credited with improving material conditions and security for their citizens while engaging in little personal graft. Other dictators, like Mobutu Sese Seko in Zaire, are notorious for the amounts and the ways in which they pilfered their nations. Yet examples such as General Pinochet in Chile and General Suharto in Indonesia should be enough to caution against thinking of dictators dichotomously on the basis of these two goals. Pinochet, perhaps denounced for his brutality but lauded for his personal integrity, was discovered in the end to have stashed away eight million dollars in a secret Riggs Bank account. Suharto, credited with presiding over Indonesia's economic miracle, also managed to take forty billion dollars.[2] Dictatorial leaders care about both policies and rents even if they vary in the weights they attach to each goal.

Let policy, then, be a number $x \in [0, 1]$. The policy dimension may refer to any type of issue whether it is government provision of secular education, censorship of the press, nationalization of industries,

---

[2] Estimates of the Suharto family's fortune vary with 40 billion dollars being the highest estimate (cited in *The Economist*, September 24, 1998).

or international alliances. Nevertheless, the policy space is unidimensional.

Let x^i stand for the peak of quasi-concave preference of individual i. Peak preferences are distributed according to $f(x^i)$ over the population of a unit mass. The ideal point of the dictator, x^D, is larger than the median ideal point, x^M. That the dictator has preferences that differ from those that would prevail in free and competitive elections is generically true of dictatorships: a chief executive whose preferences converged with those of the median voter would be able to win competitive elections and hence, would be democratically elected. The assumption that $x^D > x^M$ is made just for convenience and without loss of generality.

In turn, even if antidictatorial coalitions sometimes fall apart as soon as they are victorious, whether the dictatorship is succeeded by democracy (e.g., Solidarity in Poland) or another dictatorship (e.g., Iran after the fall of the Shah), to fight against the current dictator, any opposition must present itself as "the people united." Hence, whoever resists the dictator must appeal to the individual with the median preference so the potential opposition's preferred policy is characterized by $x^O = x^M \equiv F^{-1}(1/2)$.

The set of people who might oppose the dictator is thus $\Omega = \{x^i | x^i \leq x^O + \frac{1}{2}(x^D - x^O)\}$. Letting the distance $\theta \equiv x^D - x^O$ stand for the degree of policy polarization, the measure of this set is $F(x^D - \frac{1}{2}\theta) > 1/2$. Policy concessions are defined as

$$\gamma \equiv \frac{x^D - x^*}{x^D - x^O} = (x^D - x^*)/\theta, \tag{3.1}$$

where x^* is the actual policy chosen by the dictator. When the dictator makes policy concession $\gamma > 0$, the opposition becomes reduced to $F[x^D - \frac{1}{2}\theta(1 + \gamma)]$. Hence, a proportion $F(\gamma\theta/2)$ is induced to cooperate with the dictator.

Rents consist of a variety of monetary payoffs, perks, and privileges. Bribes are the most obvious example. Leaders such as Mobutu Sese Seko, Ferdinand Marcos of the Philippines, and the Duvaliers of Haiti accepted millions of dollars in kickbacks that were recycled into conspicuous consumption of real estate and other personal vanities (shoes, most famously, in Marcos's case). Rents may also accrue to dictators who personally (or through their families) own substantial portions of the national economy. The family of Rafael Trujillo, for example, owned a significant share of firms in the Dominican Republic. Yet the perks of office need not be extravagant to be considered rents. Communist rulers squirrelled away little in terms of hard currency but had access to dachas, private services, and special stores with imported goods, whereas the rest of the population had to queue for poorly made domestic goods.

Whether these rents are bribes, outright theft of the public treasury, or income produced by firms owned by dictators, they are produced in cooperation between the dictator and some part of the potential opposition – when the country is peaceful internally and economic activity is productive. Because cooperation from the potential opposition occurs when the dictator makes policy concessions, total rents, R, are an increasing function of policy concessions, $dR/d\gamma > 0$.

Dictatorships differ, however, with regard to the need for cooperation, α. Dictators who can rely on mineral resources need little cooperation to secure rents, $\alpha \approx 0$. With an "enclave economy," the dictator does not need the cooperation of broad sectors of society to maximize state revenue.[3] Other dictators need varying degrees of cooperation. Hence, rents are produced according to

$$R(\gamma) = \gamma^{\alpha}, 0 \leq \alpha \leq 1. \tag{3.2}$$

Both the dictator, D, and the opposition, O, have a linearly separable utility function

$$U^{j}(R^{j}, x) = v(R^{j}) + u^{j}(x), j \in \{D, O\}, \tag{3.3}$$

where R^{j} stands for the total amount of rents accruing to j.

The function $u(x)$ is given by[4]

$$u^{j} \equiv u(x^{j}, x) = -(x^{j} - x)^{2}. \tag{3.4}$$

---

[3] "Enclave" economies require little labor inputs, as distinct from "plantation" economies, which also export primary commodities but are labor intensive (Cardoso and Faletto 1978).

[4] The assumption that the loss from policy distance is quadratic, even if standard, is not innocent. One way to justify the concavity of this function is that although political leaders care about spoils from office, their followers care about policy, and the followers' preferences constrain the leaders on both sides.

Rents are divided with the opposition receiving share s of the total and the dictator keeping share $(1 - s)$. The function $v(.)$ is simply $v(R) = R$.

Using Eqs. (3.1) through (3.4), the dictator's utility function can be rewritten as

$$U^D = (1 - s)\gamma^\alpha - (x^D - x^*)^2 = (1 - s)\gamma^\alpha - (\gamma\theta)^2. \tag{3.5}$$

The derivative of the dictator's utility with regard to the policy concession is then

$$\frac{\partial U^D}{\partial \gamma} = (1 - s)\alpha\gamma^{\alpha-1} - 2\theta^2\gamma, \tag{3.6}$$

which is positive when γ is low and negative when it is high. Hence, a dictator may have an incentive to make some policy concessions, if only to induce cooperation.

Similarly, the utility function of the opposition is rewritten as

$$U^O = s\gamma^\alpha - (x - x^O)^2 = s\gamma^\alpha - \theta^2(1 - \gamma)^2, \tag{3.7}$$

which increases in the policy concessions:

$$\frac{\partial U^O}{\partial \gamma} = s\alpha\gamma^{\alpha-1} + 2\theta^2(1 - \gamma) > 0. \tag{3.8}$$

The opposition always wants concessions.

Yet the opposition differs in its strength. Let the probability that the opposition overturns a dictator if it acts against him be $q < 1.$[5] If the opposition wins, it gets all the rents and its ideal policy. If the opposition is defeated, the dictator imposes the policy that maximizes his utility and punishes the opposition. The net severity of punishment is $L \le 0.$[6] Putting these assumptions together, the expected value of acting against the dictator is

$$q[V(R^O = 1) + u^O(\gamma = 1)] + (1 - q)L = q + (1 - q)L \equiv z, \tag{3.9}$$

---

[5] I assume that $q < 1$, because if the opposition were certain to be able to overthrow the dictator, the dictator would not be around. This assumption excludes some corner solutions; see below.

[6] This is net punishment because when the dictator maximizes his utility he makes policy concessions that maximize his gains from cooperation. But he also takes reprisals against the opposition, so that in the end the severity of loss is L, which is taken as exogenous.

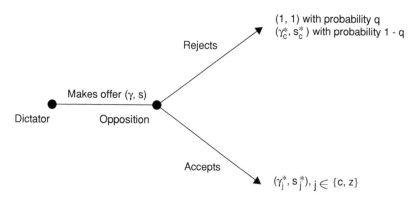

FIGURE 3.1. Logic of dictatorial concessions.

where $z(q, L)$ summarizes the strength of the opposition. The opposition is strong when it has a good chance to overturn the dictator (i.e., q is high) and when the loss it would suffer from defeat in a struggle against the dictator is small (i.e., L is low). In the model, both q and L are exogenous. Their values, or the strength of the opposition, may depend on a variety of factors: the degree to which the opposition is organized, the stability of the regime, and even the international environment that may prove encouraging or discouraging of challenges to the regime. In addition, the strength of the opposition may depend on the repressiveness of the regime. Although this model is about the co-optative strategies employed by dictators, it does not exclude the possibility that dictators may use both coercion and cooptation to achieve their aims. In other words, co-optative and repressive strategies are not substitutes.

3.5   TIMING

The timing is as follows. The need for cooperation, α, the degree of polarization, θ, and the strength of the opposition, z, are given and observed by everyone. The dictator offers policy concessions and a share of rents, $\{\gamma, s\}$. Then the opposition decides whether to rebel. If the opposition does not rebel, policy and rents are allocated according to this offer. If the opposition decides to fight, nature moves and resolves the conflict. Figure 3.1 shows the sequence of moves.

3.6 RESULTS: THREE EQUILIBRIA

The model is a constrained maximization problem for the dictator in which he decides what amount of policy concessions and rents to provide to deter the opposition from rebelling. Solution of the model results in equilibria characterized by the dictator's offer of policy compromises and a share of rents, $\{\gamma, s\}$, and the opposition's decision to accept or reject the concessions. The model generates three equilibria: one in which the dictator makes few concessions which the opposition accepts (i.e., cooperation equilibrium), another in which the dictators makes more concessions and the opposition accepts (i.e., cooptation equilibrium), and a final possibility in which the dictator makes few concessions, but the opposition rejects them (i.e., turmoil equilibrium). From here, I discuss each of the three equilibria and the conditions under which these scenarios are likely. Details of the model's solution and comparative statics are in the Appendix to the chapter.

3.6.1 Cooperation Equilibrium

In this case, the potential opposition to the dictator is relatively weak. Yet even if the threat posed by the opposition is low, the dictator may still find it in his interest to make some concessions as long as he needs some, even if minimal, cooperation from segments within society. These policy concessions increase as the need for cooperation grows. But as policy polarization increases, the dictator finds additional policy concessions to be more costly.

Figure 3.2 makes this point visually by showing policy concessions as a function of the dictator's need for cooperation for differing degrees of policy polarization between him and the potential opposition. The thick line indicates policy concessions when $\theta^2 = 1/2$, the thin line when $\theta^2 = 1$. That for all values of the need for cooperation (on the x-axis), the thick line is higher than than the thin one illustrates that whether the ruler needs little or much cooperation from groups outside the ruling elite, he offers more policy concessions when his preferred policy is closer to that of the potential opposition.

In this equilibrium, when the strength of the opposition is relatively low, the dictator will offer some policy concessions but no rents. The exact size of this cooperation offer will depend on the degree to which

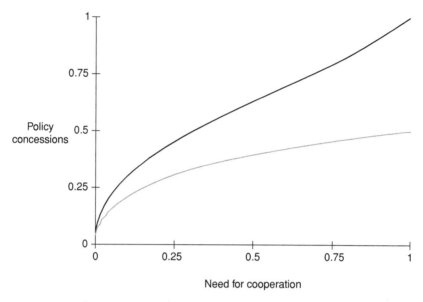

FIGURE 3.2. "Cooperation" policy concessions. Policy concessions, γ_c, under different degrees of policy polarization, θ^2 (thick line indicates γ_c when $\theta^2 = {}^1/_2$; thin line indicates γ_c when $\theta^2 = 1$).

the dictator needs cooperation. And because the opposition is relatively weak, it will accept such an offer.

3.6.2 Co-optation Equilibrium

If the potential opposition within society is stronger, the dictator must offer more in the way of concessions to co-opt it. As a result, the dictator's concession will entail more policy compromises (i.e., offer policies further away from his ideal point and closer to the opposition's) and spoils than under the cooperation equilibrium.

Similar to the cooperation equilibrium, under co-optation equilibria, an increase in the need for cooperation raises the policy concession. Hence, under the threat of rebellion as well, an increase in the need for cooperation results in greater policy concessions. Increasing polarization makes policy concessions relatively more expensive for the dictator, resulting in smaller concessions. Figure 3.3 shows co-optation policy concessions as a function of the need for cooperation, for different degrees of policy polarization. Again, the thick and thin lines

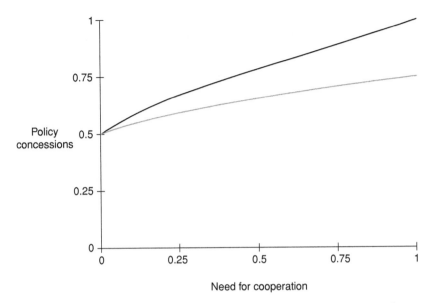

FIGURE 3.3. "Co-optation" policy concessions. Policy concessions, γ_z, under different degrees of policy polarization, θ^2 (thick line indicates γ_z when $\theta^2 = \frac{1}{2}$; thin line indicates γ_z when $\theta^2 = 1$).

track policy concessions when $\theta^2 = 1/2$ and 1, respectively. As in the previous picture, Figure 3.3 illustrates that holding constant the need for cooperation, dictators make fewer policy concessions when their preferred policies exhibit greater divergence from those of the potential opposition. In both types of equilibria, policy concessions are an increasing function of the need for cooperation but a decreasing function of policy polarization.

Comparing Figures 3.2 and 3.3 also shows that in this model "rentier states," which need little or no cooperation to generate rents, make substantial policy concessions whenever the power of the dictator is threatened. This conclusion goes against the vast rentier state literature, which typically claims that dictators in resource-rich countries counter political threats only by distributing rents (Crystal 1990, Karl 1997, Luciani 1987, Ross 2001). There is no reason to believe that dictators have a lexicographic preference for policy over rents, that is, that they would give away all the rents before making any policy concessions. Smith (2004: 242), finding no evidence that regime survival is contingent on oil booms and busts within the oil-rich states, also concludes that "there is more to the durability of regimes in oil-rich state than patronage and coercion." He speculates that the types of coalitions supporting resource-rich regimes may better explain their durability.

Although the model predicts that even resource-rich dictators make policy concessions, these results are in agreement with the rentier state literature's finding that these rulers will rely more on sharing rents than those who need more extensive cooperation because rents and policy concessions are substitutes. In turn, dictatorships that need less cooperation, give away a larger share of spoils when they are threatened.

The amount of spoils given away under the co-optation offer is determined by q and L. The higher the likelihood the opposition would rebel successfully and the lower the losses the dictatorship can inflict on the opposition should rebellion fail, the greater the offer of spoils must be. Finally, as under the cooperation equilibrium, the opposition will accept the co-optation offer.

3.6.3 Turmoil Equilibrium

In this case, the dictator makes a cooperation offer because such an offer maximizes his utility. But the opposition refuses and rebels, resulting in low-level conflict and possibly overthrow of the dictator. This outcome is possible when the opposition has a low probability of overthrowing the dictator, but the dictator is unable to punish the opposition for trying. This model, even though it is based on complete information, does admit an outcome in which a dictatorial ruler may be overthrown – in contrast to most models in which incumbents are never overthrown (Bertocchi and Spagat 2001, Bueno de Mesquita et al. 2003) or, if revolutions do occur, they happen because information is incomplete (Ginkel and Smith 1999).

Note that although q and L determine the size of the rents offered under the co-optation equilibrium, they do not affect the content of the cooperation offer. These parameters, however, determine, whether a cooperation or co-optation offer is made. It is useful, then, to see the equilibria graphically in $(q, -L)$ space, as shown in Figure 3.4.

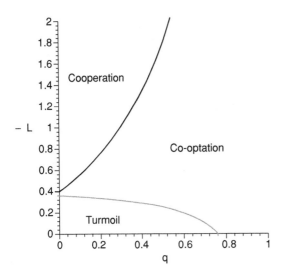

FIGURE 3.4. Three equilibria in $(q, -L)$ space. Ranges of q and $-L$ for which "cooperation," "co-optation," or "turmoil" occur.

In Figure 3.4, the thick line increasing in q separates cooperation from co-optation equilibria; and the thin line decreasing in q separates co-optation from turmoil. When the losses, L, the dictator can inflict on the opposition should its rebellion fail are high but the likelihood, q, that such a rebellion would succeed in the first place is low, the opposition accepts the cooperation offer even though it does not include a share of rents. As q, or the chances of successful rebellion, increases, however, the dictator must offer more. Hence, the range of co-optation offers to the right of the cooperation equilibria entail greater policy concessions and a share of the spoils. When the chances of successful rebellion are low, but the dictator cannot credibly threaten significant punishment, turmoil results.

We thus learn that when the opposition is weak, so that the probability that it could overthrow the dictator is low and the loss it would suffer in the eventuality that it would fail is high, the dictator will set the policy so as to maximize his rents from cooperation and not share them, whereas the opposition will not rebel. When the loss the dictator could inflict on the opposition, were a rebellion to fail, is smaller, or the probability the opposition would prevail is higher, the dictator will make additional policy compromises and share the rents from cooperation, whereas the opposition will again not rebel. When, however, the opposition has a low chance to overthrow the dictator but the dictator can do little to hurt the opposition, the dictator is not willing to move beyond a pure cooperation offer and the opposition does rebel. The dictator is not afraid of the opposition when the prospects that it would overthrow him are low and the opposition does not fear to rebel when the dictator cannot punish it. Because additional policy compromises as well as the sharing of rents are costly to the dictator, he is not willing to make a co-optation offer. And because the opposition has little to lose by rebelling, a turmoil ensues.

3.7   PREDICTING DICTATORIAL INSTITUTIONS

The model's predictions relate dictators' need for cooperation and the strength of the opposition they face to the degree of policy concessions they make. Because policy compromises are best made within an institutional framework (an assumption discussed in Section 3.3), the degree of institutionalization is expected to increase in γ. Hence, although γ cannot be observed, it is possible to use the comparative statics of γ with regard to the particular parameters, provide an empirical interpretation of these parameters, and by implication, formulate hypotheses relating the degree of institutionalization to the observed conditions. Hence, policy concessions are expected to be greater, and therefore the degree of institutionalization to be greater, when the dictator needs more cooperation, when polarization between the dictator and the opposition is lower, when the opposition is more likely to succeed in overturning the dictator, and when the loss the opposition would suffer were it to fail is small. These are the conclusions to be tested statistically with a sample of all dictatorships from 1946 to 2002 for which the requisite data are available.

3.7.1   Data

As seen from Chapter 1, dictators may organize their legislatures and party systems in a myriad of ways. Legislatures serve a common purpose, but the variation in party systems reflects substantive differences in the degree to which dictators co-opt groups within society. Hence, the dependent variable is *Institutions*, coded 2 if the dictatorship has a legislature with multiple political parties (i.e., broadened dictatorship), 1 if the regime party occupies all seats within the assembly (i.e., narrow dictatorship), and 0 otherwise (e.g., noninstitutionalized dictatorship).[7]

Testing the predictions derived from the model requires indicators of the need for cooperation and of the threat originating from the opposition. Within the limits of the available data, these indicators are considered in turn (for definitions and sources of all variables, see the *Codebook of Variables*).

Proxies for Need for Cooperation. The need for cooperation depends on the existence of ready-made institutions capable of organizing rule. As discussed earlier, monarchs and military rulers have ready-made institutions with which to organize their rule: the dynastic family and the armed forces, respectively. Civilian dictators, in turn, must rely on regime parties. Table 3.1 shows the variation in nominally democratic institutions, indicating *de jure* political parties and legislatures across types of dictators.

Table 3.1 shows that some correlation exists between the types of dictators and organization of their regimes. Monarchs are more likely to govern without institutions. Military rulers vary considerably in their institutional arrangements. Two dichotomous variables (*Military dictator, Civilian dictator*), which indicate the military and civilian identity of the dictator, are included, leaving monarchs as the omitted category. Because they cannot rely on kin networks and the armed forces as easily, civilian dictators are expected to face a higher need for cooperation than monarchs and military dictators and, consequently, govern with more institutions.

The need for cooperation is lower in economies that can rely on mineral exports. In such economies, the dictator does not need the cooperation of broad sectors of society to maximize state revenue. Moreover, resource wealth makes it easier for dictators to maintain their rule by sharing rents in exchange for political acquiescence (Crystal

---

[7] Coded as 0 are those cases in which there is no legislature and those in which a legislature exists, but members are not allowed to have partisan affiliations. These two types of cases are treated similarly on the grounds that without the support of party organizations, the potential opposition is in as weak a position as if it had no access to a legislative arena. Of the 1,593 country-year observations in which *Institutions* is coded as zero, the absence of a legislature constitutes over 70 percent of the cases.

TABLE 3.1. *Institutions by Type of Dictator*

Type of Dictator	Political Parties	Legislature		Total
		None	Extant	
Monarch	None	241	193	434
	Single	7	32	39
	Multiple	61	137	198
	Total	309	362	671
Military	None	269	46	315
	Single	122	243	365
	Multiple	229	648	877
	Total	620	937	1557
Civilian	None	36	82	118
	Single	43	551	594
	Multiple	117	1480	1597
	Total	196	2113	2309

1990, Ross 2001, Wantchekon 2002). A dichotomous variable measuring resource wealth, *Resources*, is coded 1 if the average ratio of mineral exports to total exports exceeds 50 percent, 0 otherwise.[8] The coefficient of the variable is expected to be negative.

Proxies for Policy Polarization. Measuring policy polarization between the dictator and the opposition is difficult in part because policies are many and preferences are unobservable. One might expect that societies that are fragmented along ethnic lines may closely approximate polarized relations between the dictator (and his small band of supporters) and the rest of society. Hence, greater polarization among ethnic groups proxies policy polarization, resulting in fewer concessions.[9] *Ethnic polarization* then should have a negative impact on institutions.

---

[8] I also experimented with several alternative measures that distinguish between fuels and mineral ores: two dummy variables, each coded 1 if the average ratio of oil and mineral ores, respectively, exceeds 50 percent (International Monetary Fund 1999); ores and metal exports as a percentage of merchandise exports (World Bank 2000); fuel exports as a percentage of merchandise exports (World Bank 2000); and crude oil and natural gas production in thousand barrels per day (EIA). They all have the same sign and are all significant. Given that the qualitative results do not depend on the particular operationalization of the need for cooperation, I use the cruder measure to minimize the loss of observations.

[9] Again, several alternative indicators were tried, including religious polarization and religious and ethnic fractionalization measures. The results do not qualitatively differ by other proxies.

Alternatively, a measure of income inequality may serve as a crude proxy for policy polarization because many dictatorships arose with the support of monied interests to resolve political and economic crises and restore order.[10] Therefore, higher income inequality may signify greater class conflict and, hence, more polarization between the dictator and most of society. As measured by the Gini coefficient of gross income (posttransfers, pretax), *Income inequality* should be negatively correlated with institutions.

Proxies for Strength of Potential Opposition. The threat presented by the opposition depends on its chances to overthrow the dictator and the stakes entailed in being violently defeated. I assume that the success of a rebellion will depend both on the organization of the opposition and on the ability of the dictator to repress dissent. I use various proxies to characterize the strength of the opposition vis-à-vis the dictator, as discussed below.

Opposition to the dictatorship may be widespread, but it does not pose a threat to the regime unless it is organized. The role of organizations outside the state (e.g., religious organizations, student groups, labor unions, and professional associations) in mobilizing popular protest is crucial in organizing political opposition. Yet the absence of a cross-national measure of the organization of civil society under these regimes leads to the question of whether there are other vehicles through which opposition can mobilize.

In dictatorships that have inherited political parties, some segments of society are already organized and capable of using preexisting structures. Those dictators who seize power and must contend with existing parties face the difficulty of dealing with organizations that have provided leaders and members with the infrastructure and experience of political participation. In contrast, authoritarian rulers who inherit no political parties from their immediate predecessors are more likely to face weaker challenges from the potential opposition. An indicator for the *de facto* number of parties inherited by the particular dictator either from the previous democratic regime or his immediate predecessor, *Inherited parties*, is included. It is a trichotomous

---

[10] This story has a long intellectual history, spanning Marx (1994 [1869]), Cardoso and Faletto (1979), and O'Donnell (1979).

variable with the same categories as those of *Institutions*, but it is not the lagged dependent variable. It is the number of extant parties a particular dictator finds when assuming power. A new dictatorship, for example, may have replaced a nondemocratic regime in which political parties were allowed, but the regime party controlled all of the seats within the assembly. In this case, the ascendant regime faces *Institutions* = 1 but *Inherited parties* = 2.[11] The opposition is expected to be stronger when it can rely on more networks from inherited parties, resulting in more institutional concessions from the current dictator. Consequently, the coefficient on *Inherited parties* should have a positive sign.

Past turnover among rulers in dictatorships indicates whether the regime is relatively stable. Under stable regimes, much of society may already have been co-opted, and if not, the ruling elite is united in repelling any challenges. It is expected that the fewer the past accumulated number of leaders, the more stable is the dictatorship.[12] In this case, opposition strength is likely to be low, resulting in fewer institutional concessions. The correlation between *Leadership changes* and *Institutions* should be positive.

Repression affects the strength of the opposition by determining how well it can mount a challenge and the loss it would suffer were rebellion to fail. A direct indicator of dictators' propensity and ability to repress is the number of purges they carry out. Higher numbers of purges, as indicated by the variable *Purges*, signifies higher capacity and propensity to repress, diminishing the strength of the opposition and resulting in fewer concessions from the dictator. *Purges*, then, should have a negative effect on institutions.

The external pressure for countries to liberalize may help the opposition mount a challenge and create obstacles for regimes trying to answer with repression. This pressure increases when more countries are democratic, so that the remaining ones are isolated. The number

---

[11] As the example illustrates, the number of inherited parties is not endogenous to the number of parties allowed within the legislature. Although the degree to which society is organized in parties affects to what extent dictators decide to co-opt them within the legislature, the degree of partisan participation within the assembly likely does not affect whether parties simply are allowed to exist.

[12] Dictators who died of natural causes while still in office neither stepped down nor were removed by others; so their exit from power says little about the stability of the regime. If they are excluded from the analysis, the results do not change.

TABLE 3.2. *Descriptive Statistics of Variables in Institutions Analysis*

Variable	Mean	Standard Deviation	Minimum	Maximum	Cases
Institutions$_t$	0.972	0.818	0	2	4559
Military dictator$_t$	0.344	0.475	0	1	4588
Civilian dictator$_t$	0.509	0.500	0	1	4588
Resources	0.213	0.410	0	1	4588
Ethnic polarization	0.587	0.232	0.005	0.986	4169
Income inequality$_t$	42.717	11.583	17.830	64.000	532
Inherited parties$_t$	1.122	0.957	0	2	3179
Leadership changes$_t$	2.226	2.593	0	19	4588
Purges$_t$	0.253	0.943	0	34	3874
Other democracies$_t$	0.394	0.106	0.266	0.605	4588

of other democracies in the world (*Other democracies*) serves as a proxy for external conditions that may strengthen the threat posed by the opposition.[13] More democracies throughout the world should increase opposition strength and dampen the dictator's enthusiasm to repress, leading to more institutional concessions. The coefficient on *Other democracies* should be positive.

To summarize, the dictator's need for cooperation, α, is indicated by (1) the type of dictator and (2) the availability of mineral exports. Policy polarization, θ, is indicated by ethnic polarization and income inequality. Finally, the strength of the opposition, z, is measured by the number of parties he inherited, the amount of executive turnover, the number of purges, and the percentage of other countries that are democratic.

Table 3.2 provides the descriptive statistics for all the variables used in the analysis. The contemporaneous value of all variables is used because several variables are time invariant for an entire leader spell (e.g., *Military dictator, Civilian dictator, Inherited parties,* and *Leadership changes*) or country spell (e.g., *Resources* and *Ethnic polarization*), but the results of the analysis are substantively similar when the lagged values of all independent variables are used instead. The effects of these factors on the number of legislative parties under dictatorship is

---

[13] Because the number of independent states increases over time, I use the percentage, rather than the absolute number, of other democracies.

TABLE 3.3. *Explaining Dictatorial Institutions*

Variables	Model 1	Model 2	Model 3
	Need for cooperation		
Constant	−3.139***	−1.290***	−0.910***
	(0.611)	(0.169)	(0.131)
Military dictator	0.114	0.611***	0.622***
	(0.304)	(0.104)	(0.080)
Civilian dictator	0.909**	1.452***	1.486***
	(0.307)	(0.105)	(0.077)
Resources	−1.828***	−0.443***	−0.467***
	(0.325)	(0.061)	(0.051)
	Policy polarization		
Ethnic	−1.343***	−0.662***	−0.290***
polarization	(0.296)	(0.115)	(0.088)
Income inequality	0.030***		
	(0.007)		
	Opposition strength		
Inherited parties	0.200*	0.191***	
	(0.084)	(0.026)	
Leadership	0.074***	0.077***	0.042***
changes	(0.022)	(0.009)	(0.007)
Purges	−0.007	−0.070*	−0.054**
	(0.060)	(0.030)	(0.023)
Other	6.952***	1.950***	1.643***
democracies	(1.276)	(0.285)	(0.235)
μ	0.506***	0.915***	1.152***
	(0.059)	(0.030)	(0.027)
N	428	2468	3510
% correctly predicted	0.657	0.551	0.534
Log-likelihood	−336.876	−2304.891	−3352.981

Standard errors in parentheses.
*** $p < 0.01$; ** $p < 0.05$; * $p < 0.10$.

determined using an ordered probit model due to the ordinal nature of the dependent variable. The results are presented in Table 3.3.

Table 3.3 shows that the predicted degree of institutionalization tracks observations very closely. In Model 1 (column 1), almost all coefficients are statistically significant and have the predicted signs. Availability of mineral resources reduces the need for institutions. Civilian dictators are most likely to govern with institutions because they cannot rely on either the armed forces or extensive kin networks for support. When leaders are bequeathed a history of leadership instability and the potential for popular mobilization through parties, they are more likely to neutralize such potential opposition through institutions. Finally, the mere presence of an increasing number of democracies may increase the strength of the opposition, leading to greater institutional concessions.

Repression, as it turns out, appears not to have an effect on institutions, whereas the results on policy polarization are mixed. Ethnic divisions, as a proxy for policy polarization, does have the expected negative effect on institutions. Its magnitude of impact is among the largest of all the variables. Yet income inequality as a measure of policy polarization also has a statistically significant impact on institutions but in an unexpected positive direction. The unexpected sign on *Income inequality* may be due to its poor capacity as a proxy of policy polarization or to the selected sample of countries for which income inequality data are available. Over one-third of the observations are from Latin America, whereas the sample contains no observations from the resource-rich states of the Middle East. Only 7 percent of the sample is from sub-Saharan Africa. Due to the paucity and unrepresentativeness of the sample, results must be interpreted with caution.

Column 2 shows results when the inequality indicator is omitted. The sample size expands by five, and the substantive effects of all the other variables remain. In addition, the differences in institutionalization among types of dictators are more pronounced. Now monarchs (the omitted category) are less likely to have institutions than the military, who, in turn, have fewer than civilians. Because most monarchies govern resource-rich states, the increased importance of the dictatorial type variables diminishes the magnitude of the effect of resources. The positive and strongly significant impact of inherited parties, leadership instability, and global prevalence of democracy remain. As a countervailing influence, *Purges* now exhibits a small, negative impact on institutions.

Finally, Column 3 shows the results after the variable with the second least observations, *Inherited parties*, is dropped along with *Income inequality*. With over an additional 1,000 country-year observations, the analysis yields similar substantive findings as in Column 2.

The signs and significance of the indicators of need for cooperation and strength of the opposition are robust in a sample that is more likely representative of the population.

It is far from clear that the empirical implementation accurately captures the theoretically relevant variables: the constraint of data availability is very tight. But there is no doubt that dictators establish and maintain political institutions for systematic reasons and these institutions can be predicted quite well.

3.8 CONCLUSION

To mobilize cooperation and to deter larger segments of society from forming active opposition, dictators try to protect themselves with institutions. A system of institutions – a legislature and a political party or parties – provides a means by which autocrats can encapsulate the potential opposition. Nominally democratic institutions serve as the channel through which rents can be distributed, and more importantly, as the forum in which policy compromises can be organized. By offering to particular groups of potential opposition a place in the legislature, dictators induce these groups to vest their interests in the status quo. By creating a single party, dictators offer a vehicle for career advancement within a stable system of patronage. By allowing autonomous parties, dictators coax some political forces into channeling their activities within their institutional creations. For both the dictator and the potential opposition, nominally democratic legislatures and parties reduce political transaction costs although not without distributive consequences because incumbents retain the power to alter or close such institutions.

Yet not all nondemocratic rulers govern with these institutions. The institutional structures of dictatorships differ for systematic reasons: the degree of cooperation dictators must mobilize and the strength of the threat they face. The illustrative cases from the previous chapter provided some intuition about how to proxy these conditions, whereas the quantitative analysis in this chapter more systematically shows the correlation between these conditions and the institutionalization of authoritarian regimes. The degree of cooperation that rulers must solicit is related to the structure of the economy and to the type of dictatorship. Mineral-rich dictatorships, particularly those headed by monarchs but also by professional military, need little cooperation from their populations. When, in addition, dictators inherit a politically unorganized population and face few international pressures, they can rule as pure autocrats without institutions, extracting all the rents without making any policy concessions. In contrast, those dictators who cannot generate rents without mobilizing cooperation and who are forced to co-opt some of the potential opposition to survive in power, build, and maintain a full panoply of institutions.

Given that dictators use assemblies and parties strategically – to organize policy concessions without appearing weak – an implication is that policies should differ across institutionalized and noninstitutionalized regimes. Policies in authoritarian regimes with legislatures and parties should reflect more of a compromise between the autocrat and the potential opposition than the policies adopted in noninstitutionalized regimes where rulers need not make concessions. Furthermore, if institutions have policy consequences, they also may affect outcomes or the performance of dictatorial regimes either directly or indirectly through their effects on policies. Finally, if dictators maintain legislatures and parties and make policy concessions to broaden their bases of support, institutions should have effects on their political survival. These are the consequences of dictatorial institutions that the remaining chapters will explore.

3.9   APPENDIX

3.9.1   Solutions

The problem of the dictator is to

$$\max_{\gamma,s} U^D(R^D, x), \tag{3.10}$$

s.t.

$$U^O \geq z$$

$$0 \leq s \leq 1$$

$$0 \leq \gamma \leq 1$$

with the Lagrangian

$$\pounds = (1-s)\gamma^{\alpha} - \gamma^2\theta^2 + \lambda\left[s\gamma^{\alpha} - \theta^2(1-\gamma)^2 - z\right] + \mu_0 s$$
$$+ \mu_1(1-s) + \eta_0\gamma + \eta_1(1-\gamma), \tag{3.11}$$

where λ is the multiplier on the opposition's incentive constraint and the $\mu's$ and the $\eta's$ are, respectively, multipliers for the constraints on s and γ.

To avoid the proliferation of cases, I focus on the complementary slackness condition

$$\lambda\left[s\gamma^{\alpha} - \theta^2(1-\gamma)^2 - z\right] = 0 \tag{3.12}$$

and consider corner solutions only as they arise.

Consider first the case $\lambda = 0$, $s\gamma^{\alpha} - \theta^2(1-\gamma)^2 - z > 0$. The dictator does not need to fear the opposition and all he does is maximize his utility from cooperation. First-order conditions are then

$$\frac{\partial\pounds}{\partial s}|_{\lambda=0} = -\gamma^{\alpha} + \mu_0 \le 0 \tag{3.13}$$

and

$$\frac{\partial\pounds}{\partial\gamma}|_{\lambda=0} = \alpha\gamma^{\alpha-1} - 2\gamma\theta^2 = 0, \tag{3.14}$$

implying that the dictator offers $s_c = 0$ and

$$\gamma_c = \left(\frac{\alpha}{2\theta^2}\right)^{\frac{1}{2-\alpha}}, \tag{3.15}$$

where the subscript c stands for "cooperation" offer.[14]

This offer is accepted by the opposition if

$$z < -\theta^2(1-\gamma_c)^2, \tag{3.16}$$

which defines the conditions for the "cooperation" equilibrium, in which the dictator offers $\{\gamma_c, 0\}$ and the opposition does not rebel.

---

[14] This solution is logically consistent when $\gamma_c = 1$ or $\alpha \ge 2\theta^2$. Note that if $\gamma = 1$, $x = x^M$, so that the dictator sets policy according to the median preference but he takes all the spoils.

Now consider the case $\lambda > 0, 0 < s < 1, 0 < \gamma < 1$. First-order conditions are now

$$\frac{\partial \mathcal{L}}{\partial s}\Big|_{\lambda > 0} = -\gamma^\alpha + \lambda \gamma^\alpha = 0 \Rightarrow \lambda = 1 \tag{3.17}$$

and

$$\frac{\partial \mathcal{L}}{\partial \gamma}\Big|_{\lambda > 0} = \alpha \gamma^{\alpha-1} - 4\gamma\theta^2 + 2\theta^2 = 0, \tag{3.18}$$

with the implicit solution γ_z, where the subscript z stands for "co-optation." Observe that when the dictator fears rebellion, he makes a policy concession at least as large as that needed to maximize his rents from cooperation, $\gamma_z \geq \gamma_c$. This can be seen by rewriting Eq. (3.18) as $\alpha \gamma_z^{\alpha-1} - 2\gamma_z\theta^2 = 2\theta^2(\gamma_z - 1) \leq 0$. Comparing this expression with Eq. (3.14) shows that it cannot be satisfied by the same value of γ.[15] In turn, because the left-hand side declines in γ, it must be true that $\gamma_z \geq \gamma_c$.

Finally, because $\lambda > 0$, it must be true that $s\gamma^\alpha - \theta^2(1-\gamma)^2 - z = 0$, so that s_z is given by

$$s_z = \frac{z + \theta^2(1-\gamma_z)^2}{\gamma_z^\alpha}. \tag{3.19}$$

I refer to $\{\gamma_z, s_z\}$ as the "co-optation" offer.

Note that because $\gamma_c \leq \gamma_z$, the dictator's utility under cooperation, U_c^D, is strictly larger than his utility under co-optation, U_z^D. But if the opposition is sufficiently strong to reject the cooperation offer, will dictators always make the offers necessary to deter the opposition from acting against them? The expected value for the dictator of facing a revolt is

$$q[V(R^D = 0) + u^D(\gamma = 1)] + (1 - q)U_c^D$$
$$= -q\theta^2 + (1 - q)[\gamma_c^\alpha - \theta^2\gamma_c^2], \tag{3.20}$$

and the dictator makes the co-optation offer as long as his utility from co-optation is at least as high as the expected value of rebellion:

$$U_z^D \geq -q\theta^2 + (1 - q)U_c^D. \tag{3.21}$$

---

[15] Equality will hold only if $\alpha \geq 2\theta^2$ and $\gamma_c = 1$.

Substituting s_z into U_z^D, writing out z from Eq. (3.9), and rearranging terms, the above condition can be rewritten as

$$q(U_c^D + \theta^2 - 1 + L) \geq U_c^D + \theta^2 - [\gamma_z^\alpha + 2\theta^2 \gamma_z(1 - \gamma_z)] + L. \quad (3.22)$$

Let $C = U_c^D + \theta^2 - [\gamma_z^\alpha + 2\theta^2 \gamma_z(1 - \gamma_z)]$ and $D = U_c^D + \theta^2 - 1$. Then this condition becomes $(D + L)q \geq C + L$. Now, for all feasible values of parameters it is true that $C \leq D$, which leaves three cases: (1) If $C \leq D < -L$, this condition is satisfied for all $q < 1$; (2) If $C < -L < D$, the condition is satisfied for all $q \geq 0$; (3) If $-L < C \leq D$, the condition is satisfied only for $q \geq (C + L)/(D + L)$.

Hence, the game has three equilibria. They are best characterized in the $\{q, -L\}$ space.

PROPOSITION 1   *(1) If* $-L \geq \theta^2(1 - \gamma_c)^2 + q/1 - q$, *a cooperation equilibrium ensues: the dictator makes a cooperation offer and the opposition does not rebel. (2) If* $U_c^D + \theta^2 - [\gamma_z^\alpha + 2\theta^2 \gamma_z(1 - \gamma_z) -q]/1 - q \leq -L < \theta^2(1 - \gamma_c)^2 + q/1 - q$, *a co-optation equilibrium occurs: the dictator makes a co-optation offer and the opposition does not rebel. (3) If* $-L < U_c^D + \theta^2 - [\gamma_z^\alpha + 2\theta^2 \gamma_z(1 - \gamma_z) - q]/1 - q$, *a turmoil equilibrium transpires: the dictator makes a cooperation offer and the opposition rebels.*

Proof. Part (1) results from solving (3.16) for L in terms of q. In turn, when $-L < \theta^2(1 - \gamma_c)^2 + q/1 - q$, the dictator does not make a cooptation offer only if $q < (C + L)/(D + L)$. Substituting for C and D and solving for L yields the condition in Part (3). Finally, it can be shown that for all values of parameters $U_c^D + \theta^2 - [\gamma_z^\alpha + 2\theta^2 \gamma_z(1 - \gamma_z) -q]/1 - q < \theta^2(1 - \gamma_c)^2 + q/1 - q$.[16]   **Q.E.D.**

To complete the analysis, corner solutions must be considered. Note first that $\gamma = 1, s = 1$ is not feasible, because it would occur only if $z = 1$ or $q = 1$, and no dictator would be in power if the opposition

---

[16] It is necessary to check that $U_c^D + \theta^2 - \frac{\gamma_z^\alpha + 2\theta^2 \gamma_z(1-\gamma_z)-q}{1-q} < \frac{\theta^2(1-\gamma_c)^2 + q}{1-q}$ or
$(1 - q)(\gamma_c^\alpha - \theta^2 \gamma_c^2 + \theta^2) - \gamma_z^\alpha - 2\theta^2 \gamma_z(1 - \gamma_z) + q < \theta^2(1 - \gamma_c)^2 + q$.
This must be true for $q = 0$, so that
$\gamma_c^\alpha - \theta^2 \gamma_c^2 + \theta^2 - \theta^2(1 - \gamma_c)^2 < \gamma_z^\alpha + 2\theta^2 \gamma_z(1 - \gamma_z)$, or after rearranging
$2\theta^2[(\gamma_c - \gamma_z)(1 - \gamma_z + \gamma_c)] < \gamma_z^\alpha - \gamma_c^\alpha$.
But $(\gamma_c - \gamma_z) \leq 0, 1 - \gamma_z + \gamma_c \geq 0$. Hence LHS ≤ 0 and RHS ≥ 0.

were certain to overthrow him. Hence, when $s_z = 1$, it must be true that $\gamma_z < 1$. This case, however, is also unfeasible. At $s = 1$,

$$\frac{\partial \pounds}{\partial s}|_{s=1} = -\gamma^\alpha + \lambda\gamma^\alpha - \mu_1 \geq 0 \Rightarrow \lambda - 1 \geq \mu_1\gamma^{-\alpha} > 0$$

$$\frac{\partial \pounds}{\partial \gamma}|_{s=1} = -2\gamma\theta^2 + \lambda[\alpha\gamma^{\alpha-1} + 2(1-\gamma)\theta^2] = 0,$$

which implies

$$\lambda = \frac{2\gamma\theta^2}{\alpha\gamma^{\alpha-1} + 2(1-\gamma)\theta^2}.$$

But

$$\lambda - 1 = \frac{2\gamma\theta^2 - \alpha\gamma^{\alpha-1} - 2(1-\gamma)\theta^2}{\alpha\gamma^{\alpha-1} + 2(1-\gamma)\theta^2} = 0,$$

by Eq. (3.18). Hence, μ_1 cannot be positive, implying that $s < 1$.

In turn, when $\alpha \geq 2\theta^2$, $\gamma_z = \gamma_c = 1$, and [from Eq. (3.19)] $s_z = z$.

$$\frac{\partial \pounds}{\partial s}|_{\gamma=1} = -\gamma^\alpha + \lambda\gamma^\alpha = 0 \Rightarrow \lambda = 1$$

$$\frac{\partial \pounds}{\partial \gamma}|_{\gamma=1} = \alpha\gamma^{\alpha-1} - 2\gamma\theta^2 + 2(1-\gamma)\theta^2 - \eta_1 \geq 0,$$

which is feasible. Hence, when their policy position does not diverge much from the median, dictators may be willing to abdicate control over the policy in their quest for cooperation. But they never give away all the rents.

3.9.2 Comparative Statics

Consider first the cooperation offer. Policy concessions increase as the need for cooperation grows:

$$\frac{\partial \gamma_c}{\partial \alpha} = \left(\frac{\alpha}{2\theta^2}\right)^{\frac{1}{2-\alpha}} \frac{1}{2-\alpha}\left[\frac{1}{2-\alpha}\ln\frac{\alpha}{2\theta^2} + \frac{1}{\alpha}\right] > 0, \qquad (3.23)$$

if $2 - \alpha[1 - \ln(\alpha/2\theta^2)] > 0$, or $\ln(2\theta^2) \leq 1$, or $\theta \leq 1.16$, which is true by construction (because $x \in [0, 1]$, so is θ).

In turn,

$$\frac{\partial \gamma_c}{\partial \theta} = \left(\frac{\alpha}{2}\right)^{\frac{1}{2-\alpha}} \left(\frac{2}{\alpha - 2}\right) \theta^{\frac{2}{\alpha-2}-1} < 0, \tag{3.24}$$

which shows that as policy polarization increases, the dictator finds additional policy concessions to be more costly.

To derive comparative statics under co-optation equilibria, recall from Eq. (3.18) that the policy concession is characterized by $F(\alpha, \theta, \gamma_z) = \alpha\gamma^{\alpha-1} - 4\gamma\theta^2 + 2\theta^2 = 0$, with second-order condition $\partial F/\partial \gamma = \alpha(\alpha - 1)\gamma^{\alpha-2} - 4\theta^2 < 0$. By the implicit function theorem, an increase in the need for cooperation raises the policy concession if

$$\frac{\partial \gamma_z}{\partial \alpha} = -\frac{\partial F/\partial \alpha}{\partial F/\partial \gamma} = -\frac{\gamma^{\alpha-1}(1 + \alpha \ln \gamma)}{\alpha(\alpha - 1)\gamma^{\alpha-2} - 4\theta^2} > 0, \tag{3.25}$$

or if $1 + \alpha \ln \gamma > 0$. This is obviously true for $\alpha = 0$, $\gamma_z(\alpha = 0) = 1/2$ and for $\alpha = 1$, $\gamma_z(\alpha = 1) = 1/2 + 1/4\theta^2$. I cannot show analytically that it is also true for $0 < \alpha < 1$, but the implicit plot in Figure 3.3 shows that this derivative is positive in the entire range. Hence, under the threat of rebellion as well, an increase in the need for cooperation results in greater policy concessions.

The impact of a change in polarization on policy concession is $\partial \gamma_z/\partial \theta = -(\partial F/\partial \theta/\partial F/\partial \gamma.)$ It is known from above that $\partial F/\partial \gamma < 0$, whereas $\partial F/\partial \theta = -8\gamma\theta + 4\theta < 0$ for $\gamma \geq 1/2$, which is guaranteed by $\gamma_z(\alpha = 0) = 1/2$ and $\partial \gamma_z/\partial \alpha > 0$. Increasing polarization makes policy concessions relatively more expensive for the dictator, resulting in smaller concessions, or

$$\frac{\partial \gamma_z}{\partial \theta} < 0. \tag{3.26}$$

Rents and policy concessions are substitutes[17]:

$$\frac{ds_z}{d\gamma_z} = -\frac{1}{\gamma^\alpha}\left\{2\theta^2(1 - \gamma) + \frac{\alpha}{\gamma}[\theta^2(1 - \gamma)^2 + z]\right\} < 0. \tag{3.27}$$

In turn, because $ds/d\alpha = (ds/d\gamma)(d\gamma/d\alpha) < 0$, dictatorships that need less cooperation give away a larger share of spoils when they are threatened.

---

[17] That the expression in square bracket is positive is guaranteed by the condition (3.16) and $\gamma_z \geq \gamma_c$.

4

Institutions and Policies under Dictatorship

4.1 INTRODUCTION

Jordan, a dynastic monarchy since independent statehood in 1946, was dominated by King Hussein. During his 47 years in power, he made a number of institutional changes. After a failed coup attempt and wrangling with a socialist-led parliament, Hussein dissolved the assembly and banned political parties in 1957. Elections to a new legislature were held in 1962 and again in 1967, but candidates had to run as independents. By 1978, Hussein had marginalized the parliament in favor of a National Consultative Council, a sixty-person council charged with giving advice to the king. Hussein reconstituted the legislature, however, in 1984 with the first competitive general elections held five years later. The elections were a huge success for Islamist groups, who were expected to win seven to fifteen seats, but instead garnered thirty-four. A further ten deputies were elected from opposition parties (six nationalists and four leftists).

In the face of opposition victory, the king made a conciliatory choice of prime minister in Mudar Badran, who had already served in the post in the early 1980s. Nevertheless, assembly members were in no mood to compromise. In Badran's initial appearance before the parliament, he was "subject to a bruising three-day debate" in which parliamentarians criticized the government's past record in managing the economy. Robins (2004: 172) reports that "in order to succeed with the confidence vote, Badran was therefore obliged by this grilling to go much further than he originally seemed intent upon doing, and adopted much of the platform of the vocal opposition... Badran agreed to amend or revoke a number of draconian laws, to make the security apparatus more transparent and to ensure that an investigation into corruption was less restricted than initially envisaged."

Laws regarding rights and freedoms have constituted an important issue dimension on which opposition parties in parliament consistently have agitated. In 1991, for example, the government, led by a new prime minister, Tahir al-Masri, submitted two draft laws to the parliament: one on the legalization of political parties and the other on restrictions on the press. Both bills were debated in parliament with the Political Parties Law going into effect in 1992. Yet the Press and Publications Law was not agreed on until another year later. The delay was due to extensive deliberation about the law within the Law Committee of the House of Deputies, which suggested numerous revisions of clauses concerning the definition of a journalist, confidentiality of sources, direct restrictions on the press, and penalties for violators. The Committee did not always succeed in persuading the full parliament to demand maximum concessions. As a result, as Lucas (2005: 61) observes, "The final text of the law reflected a great deal of the government's original language. However, the Parliament made some significant changes during its deliberation."

With looser restrictions on the press, Jordanians found a means by which to criticize the regime, and they had much to criticize. The election law of 1993, which was a manipulation of the electoral rules to disadvantage the opposition, the peace treaty with Israel in 1994, and the cutting of consumer subsidies in 1996 in fulfillment of IMF requirements, all induced massive critical opinion within the media. Not surprisingly, then, in 1997, the government sought to limit the "excesses" of the press with an amendment to the 1993 Press and Publications Law. To enact the changes, however, the king did not endorse the amendments until May, two months after the parliament had ended its regular session. In this situation, according to Article 94 of the constitution, the cabinet could use its power to decree temporary legislation if urgency was deemed necessary. This end-run around the legislature, however, was blocked when the High Court of Justice struck down the law as unconstitutional.

In 1998, the regime tried yet again to pass amendments to the press law. This time it was successful since the 1997 legislative elections had delivered a more pliant assembly (due to the manipulation of the electoral rules in 1993). The government, under Prime Minister Abd as-Salam al-Majali, curtailed press freedoms, but the victory was short lived. Majali's government soon fell in part due to popular dissatisfaction with the law. He was replaced by Fayiz al-Tarawnah, who "promised that, despite the law's harsh conditions, his government would offer a 'soft implementation'" of the law (Lucas 2005: 121). To further show its willingness to compromise with the parliament and opposition parties, Tarawnah's government ordered that journalists who violated the new amendments would not be prosecuted in court. Instead, the state-sponsored Jordanian Press Association should discipline its own members. Even though in this case, the institutionalized opposition did not succeed in defeating the restrictions, it induced the regime to compromise on enforcement.

What the episodes in Jordan demonstrate is that legislatures and parties can have an impact on policies in nondemocratic states. By using their rights to question ministers, to debate government proposals, and to oversee implementation of policies, opposition parties within parliament can influence the substance and enforcement of laws under dictatorship.

Indeed, we have seen the systematic reasons that explain why dictators govern with legislatures and political parties. Given that these institutions are used as instruments of co-optation, they should influence policies and outcomes. Dictators need to make concessions when they need cooperation and when the potential opposition is strong. When these concessions must take the form of policy compromises, nominally democratic institutions provide a useful forum in which demands can be controlled, information can be shared, and negotiations can proceed. As the theory predicts and the example from Jordan suggests, we should expect to see systematic differences in policies across differently institutionalized dictatorships.

This chapter develops the theoretical underpinnings and determine the extent of empirical support for this argument. It is the first of three chapters devoted to assessing the various effects of dictatorial legislatures and parties. (Chapters 5 and 6 go on to examine the impact of institutions on economic outcomes and the survival of dictators,

respectively.) Although the model of concessions and institutionalization from the previous chapter does not always provide direct implications for the effects examined in the remainder of the book, theoretical
implications for these effects can be derived indirectly. Where additional assumptions are included, they are made clear.

4.2   WHICH POLICIES?

Governments make a wide array of decisions, the set of which has been
ever expanding as the size of government has grown. In evaluating the
effect of dictatorial institutions on policies, however, the range of policies that can be sensibly analyzed is restricted. The issue is that the
theoretical framework from the previous chapter entails assumptions
that must be met for the implications about policy variation across differently institutionalized regimes to follow through. First, the potential
opposition is a unified actor with a unified preferred policy. Second,
the preferred policy of the dictator differs from that of the potential
opposition. Only policies that satisfy these two assumptions are worth
examining; otherwise, the logic of institutional effects on policy under
dictatorship does not hold.

   The problem, of course, is that policy preferences are not observable.
Consequently, which policies are suitable for analysis is not readily apparent. A typical approach in this context is to assume that dictators
prefer private goods – both for themselves and for the ruling elite.
As discussed in Chapter 3, the spoils that dictators take for themselves
range from shoes to real estate, purchased with monies from the public
treasury. But they also may funnel these goods to those within the elite
who can threaten their power. Hence, positions within juntas, dynastic networks, and political bureaus of regime parties provide not just
participation within decision-making but also perks and privileges. As
a result, regimes with small winning coalitions (Bueno de Mesquita et
al. 2003), less "encompassing interest " (Olson 1993), and more monopolistic power (Lake and Baum 2001) provide more private goods
at the expense of public goods that would benefit the larger citizenry.
Policies that can be characterized as decisions over the provision of
private and public goods, then, can be analyzed here if the standard
assumption that the dictator prefers private goods whereas the potential opposition is united in preferring public goods appears reasonable.

If this assumption is satisfied, then the expectation would be that institutionalized dictatorships would yield more public goods because, within legislatures and parties, nondemocratic rulers must engage in policy compromises with the potential opposition. In contrast, in non-institutionalized regimes, autocrats unilaterally can determine policy and implement their preference for more private goods.

Information on private goods or rents that are consumed only by the dictator or the elite is difficult to obtain. A crude proxy may be found in military spending. Consider that authoritarian rulers must constantly worry about their security in office, and as a result, are more likely to channel money to the armed forces because they often constitute the greatest threat to power. Belkin and Schofer (2003: 596) report that from 1945 to 2000, there were 432 coup attempts, of which over one-half were successful. A variety of factors, ranging from wealth to past military interventions, affect the likelihood of coups (Belkin and Schofer 2003, Brooker 2000, Londregan and Poole 1990). But one coup-proofing strategy for leaders is to allocate enough resources to appease military officers and the rank and file. In this case, the resources directed to the armed forces benefit a small group in addition to the dictator who has guaranteed his security by appeasing the men with guns. Because the dictator and only a small segment of the population benefit from military expenditures, one might think of them as private goods.[1]

Spending on the military, however, inevitably leads to fewer resources for other publicly provided services, such as social programs in education, health, social security, and welfare. Yet there are some reasons why dictators may care about spending on social programs. They may be committed to providing material benefits to certain segments of society for ideological reasons. Draped in nationalism along with various ideological cloaks, many founding fathers of newly independent states and successive military leaders in the developing world were committed to the modernization of their societies and devoted monies to building physical and human capital to achieve this goal. Dictators also may invest in education and social security out of concern for their own survival in power. Along with buying domestic

---

[1] Note that typically national defense is considered to be a public good, whereas many social programs and education, for example, are club goods.

support, these programs may be attractive to leaders of states suffering from "systemic vulnerability" (Doner et al. 2005).

Spending on social programs constitutes a long-term investment. Raising the literacy rates of the population, for example, requires the building of schools, the training of teachers, the purchase of textbooks, and the attendance of children for several years until the fruits of such programs are apparent. Money spent on prenatal care and vaccinations does not serve dictators' immediate needs of fending of challenges to their rule. Although providing these goods may help dictators build support among the population, fend off external threats, and satisfy ideological ends, the payoffs in terms of outputs and legitimacy are long term.

Yet authoritarian rulers have incentives to focus on short-term goals, such as insuring the loyalty of the armed forces or establishing a praetorian guard. Social spending may yield important benefits, but these investments will not be made at the expense of protecting their power – even by the most benevolent of dictators. On balance, then, we can expect that in the trade-off between spending on military resources and personnel versus other social programs that benefit the civilian population, authoritarian leaders will choose to allocate more resources to the armed forces.

More ambiguous are the preferences of the potential opposition participating within dictatorial legislatures and parties. Considered as a bundle, these types of programs provide benefits to a broad range of citizens. Participation within the PRI's governing coalition in Mexico, for example, gave labor organizations significant material benefits for their members, including government-financed housing, health care, low-cost consumer goods, and a legally mandated share of enterprise profits (Middlebrook 1995). Leaders of unions, religious groups, and professional organizations who participate within dictatorial institutions are likely to demand funding for these types of programs because they allow for credit-claiming among members and cement their own bases of support within their organizations. As Valenzuela (1991: 37) notes about labor leaders within authoritarian regimes: they "must try to avoid the buildup of worker discontent that could contribute to the development of alternative opposition leadership groups among the rank and file, which means that they cannot simply accept – or be perceived as accepting – state policies that may

TABLE 4.1. *Transition Probabilities of Institutional Arrangements*

Institutional Arrangement in Year t	Institutional Arrangement in Year $t+1$			
	No Institutions	Single Institution	Multiple Institutions	N
No institutions	0.852 (0.357)	0.058 (0.235)	0.084 (0.278)	155
Single institution	0.283 (0.453)	0.628 (0.485)	0.088 (0.285)	113
Multiple institutions	0.415 (0.494)	0.011 (0.104)	0.574 (0.496)	183

Standard deviation in parentheses.

have a visibly negative impact on the rank and file's working or living conditions."

Yet because leaders of social groups that participate within these institutions are collaborating with the regime, they, too, may be invested in its survival. As a consequence, the groups within these institutions may also support spending on the military at the expense of other priorities in which case, the preferences of the dictator and the opposition would converge, and we would not expect to see differences in spending policies across differently institutionalized regimes.

Although these institutions are not wholly independent of the dictator, they frequently survive changes in dictatorial rulers. Table 4.1 shows the probability of institutions changing during a given year when one dictator is replaced by another.

When dictators rule without institutions, the likelihood that their successors will continue to rule without legislatures and parties is high (over 85 percent). The likelihood of retaining the same institutional arrangement decreases as dictatorships are more institutionalized. When rulers govern with multiple parties within a legislature, their replacements govern with the same arrangements in only 57 percent of cases. Yet all of the probabilities in the diagonal cells are higher than the ones in the other cells of the same row, indicating that even if the dictator changes, the likelihood that the institutional arrangement remains the same is high.[2] Because legislatures and parties frequently

[2] From these figures, we cannot be certain that the same legislature or parties are retained from one dictator to the next. A dictator may close his predecessor's single party and

survive beyond the ruler who maintained them, the extent to which their members are willing to aggrandize the military at the expense of social programs should be less. As a result, it may be reasonable to assume that groups within these institutions have preferences different from those of authoritarian rulers: they favor allocating more resources to broadly beneficial social programs than to the armed forces.

In addition to decisions regarding the allocation of resources, governments make policies determining the boundaries of political and civic participation. On "rights" issues such as freedom of speech, association, and movement, it is likely that most people would prefer to have these freedoms. Hence, the assumption that the potential opposition has a unified policy preference may be more easily satisfied.

In addition, it is likely that dictators would not want to allow such freedoms. Why? It is no coincidence that when coming to power, many dictators try to consolidate their power by banning parties, unions, and other types of organizations. They may go on to establish institutions of their own in the form of regime parties, state-controlled unions, youth groups, and the like. Yet both deinstitutionalization and the creation of institutions when necessary are to prevent the emergence of autonomous groupings that may advance alternative ways of conducting political life. As Przeworski (1991: 54–55) observes: "What is threatening to authoritarian regimes is not the breakdown of legitimacy but the organization of counterhegemony: collective projects for an alternative future." Echoing Havel (1985), he continues: "Only when collective alternatives are available does political choice become available to isolated individuals... This is why they are so afraid of words, even if these words convey what everyone knows anyway, for it is the fact of uttering them, not their content, that has the mobilizing potential." The emergence of an alternative is more likely to appear when people have the freedom to talk about it, to organize it, to mobilize support for it – when citizens have liberties and freedoms. Hence, it seems reasonable to assume that policy polarization over the issue of rights would exist between the dictator and the potential opposition.

open one of his own. In Table 4.1, this situation is counted as retention of the same institutional arrangement even though the body's membership may have changed. Nevertheless, the new institution may look similar to the old one because leaders of these groups have a comparative advantage in negotiating policy compromises between the government and their members.

To summarize, regarding rights policies, dictators prefer to grant fewer freedoms because the use of these rights may lead to the emergence of challenges to their rule. Groups within society, in contrast, prefer more liberalization and openness. In allocating resources, dictators prioritize spending on the armed forces, whereas the potential opposition champions social spending that may benefit the wider citizenry. Although exceptions certainly exist, these stylized characterizations of the preferences of regimes and opposition groups under authoritarianism are reasonable enough to provide a starting point for analyzing the impact of dictatorial institutions on various policies.

The theoretical framework from the previous chapter combined with the assumptions laid out here provide some testable hypotheses about policies under differently organized nondemocratic regimes. When dictators do not need cooperation and face weak opposition, they do not need to co-opt groups within society. Hence, they do not govern with institutions and, unconstrained, can enact policies close to their own preferences. In contrast, when dictators need cooperation and face strong potential opposition that must be co-opted, they govern with institutions in which they can make policy concessions to broaden their bases of support. Concessions, however, require compromise so that authoritarian leaders cannot unilaterally make decisions that satisfy only their preferences. As a result, in an institutionalized dictatorship, policy will be further away from the dictator's ideal point and closer to the opposition's than had the dictator governed without institutions. More concretely, here, institutionalized dictatorships should have more liberties and freedoms, lower military spending, and higher social spending.

The remainder of the chapter is devoted to testing these propositions. In the following section, I examine an array of civil liberties to determine whether institutions are associated with greater freedom of speech, press, and association. The second half of the chapter is devoted to assessing institutional effects on government expenditures on the armed forces and social programs. The cross-national evidence confirms the effect of dictatorial institutions on civil liberties and on military expenditures. Yet these institutions do not exhibit the expected effects on social spending. A summary and discussion of these results concludes the chapter.

4.3 CIVIL LIBERTIES

Governments make numerous policies that affect the rights of individuals and organizations. Cross-national studies of political and civil liberties, however, are conflated frequently with the study of political repression in general (Davenport 1996, 1998). Yet following Poe and Tate (1994), it is worthwhile to separate acts that violate the "integrity of the person" (e.g., murder, torture, and forced disappearances) from political and civil rights more broadly construed. Due to their extralegal nature, human rights abuses and state terrorism cannot be the object of negotiations between the government and opposition. For one, governments rarely admit to these actions. Second, because these actions are not governed by laws, legislatures would have little to say regarding them. In contrast, restrictions on speech, the press, and worker's rights constitute legal pronouncements that are publicly known and applicable to all. As such, we can think of these restrictions, as opposed to the use of political terror, as policies over which the regime and opposition can bargain and, consequently, that are suitable for analysis here.

The distinction between the protection of liberties and freedom from state terror is important for empirical reasons as well. Early studies examined formal institutional measures, such as the proportion of years in which constitutions were declared not in full force or leftist parties were banned (McKinlay and Cohan 1975, 1976). More recent studies have used either an events data approach or a standard-based approach. Events data measures, such as Taylor and Jodice (1983), are created through counts of state coercive behaviors (e.g., political execution and imposition of media ban) found in newspaper accounts of human rights-related issues or events.[3] These measures would not serve as an appropriate dependent variable in this analysis because they conflate violations of civil liberties with state terror in addition to the more general problems associated with these indicators (for a discussion, see Stohl et al. 1986).

The alternative, then, is a standards-based approach that involves the creation of indices that incorporate political background

---

[3] Several studies have used these data, including Davenport (1996, 1998), Davis and Ward (1990), and Hibbs (1973).

knowledge through expert surveys and/or content analysis of governmental and nongovernmental reports on human rights issues. Freedom House, for example, provides widely used ratings of political and civil liberties based on a checklist of questions. The organization's research team along with academic advisors use a broad array of written sources and make visits to countries to assign raw points for each of the questions. Because the index does not conflate political and civil liberties with state terror, it would have served as an ideal dependent variable. The problem is that the survey on which the ratings are based asks questions about individuals' rights to form and join political associations, such as parties. Because legislative parties under dictatorship is the institutional variable of interest on the right-hand side of any model, any correlation between this factor and the Freedom House rating may occur simply by construction.

4.3.1 Data

The key, then, is to find measures of specific civil liberties that do not include evaluations of political liberties and of state terror. Three dependent variables fulfill this criteria and are used in the analysis.

The first is a measure of freedom of speech developed by Cingranelli and Richards (2004). The indicator, *Speech freedom*, is an ordinal variable indicating the extent to which freedoms of speech (including art and music) and press are affected by government censorship, including ownership of media organizations. The lowest value, 0, indicates complete censorship, whereas the highest value, 2, signifies few or no restrictions. As expected, the vast majority (94 percent) of dictatorships practice either complete or limited censorship. The few nondemocratic regimes that do not have significant restrictions are found in places such as Botswana, Fiji, Gambia, Mexico, and Paraguay. Data are available for 125 countries between the years 1981 and 2002.

The second indicator examines a subset of the rights in the Cingranelli–Richards measure of speech. Van Belle (1997) measures freedom of the press on a 4-point scale with a value of 1 indicating that the press is clearly free and "capable of functioning as an arena of political competition" up to 4 signifying that the press is under direct government control or subject to severe restrictions (Van Belle 1997: 408). About 10 percent of the cases score as either 1 or 2, indicating a fairly free press. These cases include ones similar to those found in the Cingranelli-Richards measure although the correlation between the two measures is only 44 percent. Nevertheless, the variable *Press freedom* allows for isolation of the effect of dictatorial institutions on freedom of the media more particularly rather than on general freedom of speech. Van Belle's measure covers the period 1948 to 1995 for 133 countries.

Finally, the last indicator is a composite measure of workers' rights created by Cingranelli and Richards (2004).[4] The variable indicates the extent to which workers are free from compulsory or child labor and enjoy freedom of association within the workplace, the right to bargain collectively with their employers, and acceptable work conditions that include minimum wage, hours of work, and occupational safety and health. The ordinal scale of *Workers' rights* begins with 0, which indicates severe restrictions on labor rights and ends with 2 signifying that their rights are largely protected. Again, in the vast majority of cases (87 percent), workers' rights are limited or nonexistent. Fuller protection of workers' rights has occurred in countries such as Lesotho, Senegal, Sierra Leone, and Taiwan. Data coverage extends from 1981 to 2002 for 125 countries.

Because all three dependent variables are ordinal, the effects of institutions and other control variables are estimated using an ordered probit model. The variables on the right-hand side of these models are discussed in turn.

Institutions remains the independent variable of interest. When institutions exist, authoritarian rulers must reach policy compromises with those groups that have agreed to be incorporated within legislatures and parties. Consequently, nondemocratic regimes with greater institutionalization are expected to show more respect for freedom of speech and the press along with workers' rights.

All three dependent variables are modeled as a function of a set of independent variables that has been identified as important within the literature on state coercion. Among the control variables that are included is *Per capita income*, indicating a country's level of

---

[4] Cingranelli and Richards (2004) has variables coding freedom of movement, association, and religion as well. I do not use these measures because they are dichotomous and, consequently, exhibit very little variance within this sample.

development. Poor countries are more likely to be politically unstable because most citizens are materially deprived, leading to a greater propensity for the elite to enact restrictions and use repression to control the situation (Henderson 1991, Mitchell and McCormick 1988, Poe and Tate 1994). In addition, in poor countries, most citizens may be depoliticized, too engaged in material survival rather than agitating for political and civil rights. Hence, as income increases, respect for civil liberties is also expected to increase.

Pressure for civil liberties also may come from the international community. Since the end of World War II, awareness and consensus about the importance of protecting individual rights and liberties has grown, as evinced by the emergence of international conventions and the increasing number of states that sign on to them. The mechanism for this diffusion effect is unclear. It may due to the increased role of nongovernmental organizations (NGOs), intergovernmental organizations, and democratic states in making restrictions and repression more transparent. Organizations and agencies ranging from Amnesty International to the United States Department of State issue country reports on human rights practices. It may be due to domestic opposition groups, encouraged by NGOs and democratic states, agitating for more liberties (Vreeland 2003). The "orange revolution" in Ukraine, for example, occurred in part due to the support of transnational NGOs and democratic governments that encouraged, taught, and supplied groups challenging Leonid Kuchma. It may be due to the benefits and sanctions that democratic governments provide to other governments on the basis of their rights records (Risse et al. 1999). In 2002, the Organization of African Unity (OAU), for example, considered joining the European Union in sanctioning the Mugabe regime in Zimbabwe. That the OAU even considered the matter is likely due to the increasing number of democracies within the region. Whatever the mechanism, it appears that as more and more states become democratic, the remaining authoritarian regimes face growing pressure to respect civil liberties. So it is expected that as the number of democracies (*Other democracies*), as a share of the total number of independent states in the world, increases, respect for civil liberties increases as well.

Yet aside from domestic and international pressures, states may still restrict liberties under certain circumstances. War, either interstate or civil, is often a context in which governments restrict liberties.

Governments often restrict liberties as part of their strategy to combat subversives. Citizens are more likely to accept that such restrictions are necessary when the sovereignty of the state is threatened. Rasler (1986) found evidence that the United States government increased the level of repression during wartime in the twentieth century. In cross-national analysis, Davenport (1996) and Poe and Tate (1994) find that both external and internal conflict lead to more restrictions on liberties. To control for the effect of conflict on civil liberties, a dichotomous variable, *War*, indicating interstate or intrastate conflict, is included.

Politically destabilizing events short of war, however, may also induce authoritarian leaders to curtail civil liberties. Riots and demonstrations may influence the government's stance on civil liberties although whether internal disorder leads to a more accommodative or repressive posture is unclear (Gurr 1970, Lichbach 1987, Moore 1998). In Indonesia in the late 1950s, for example, antigovernment rioting led to Sukarno's declaration of martial law. Yet events in Congo in the early 1990s serve as just one of many counterexamples: after civil unrest paralyzed Brazzaville's commercial sector and opposition legislators led open confrontation with state security forces, the regime under Pascal Lissouba liberalized. A result consistent with the theoretical framework offered here, however, is that rioting should have either a negative effect or no effect at all. Because nondemocratic rulers have legislatures and parties in part to induce groups to make their demands within a controlled institutionalized setting rather than on the street, they presumably would avoid making compromises in response to protests. Such a response would seem to undermine one of the main reasons for having nominally democratic institutions in the first place.

The type of dictatorship may also influence the degree to which liberties are curbed. As usual, military regimes are singled out as being distinct. In their analysis of political repression, Poe and Tate (1994: 858) observe that "Military juntas are based on force, and force is the key to coercion." Yet they later note that "in many of the nations in which soldiers forcibly take power, they do so alleging that the leader they are replacing were themselves violating the constitution" – the implication being that the military will try to gain legitimacy by respecting civil liberties. Another reason for the ambiguity of the effect of the type of regime may simply be due to the fact that most heads of nondemocratic states – military or otherwise – come to power through force because typically there is no regularized mechanism for choosing leaders. As a result, the use of force or the restriction of liberties should not be unique to military regimes. The dichotomous variables, *Military dictator* and *Civilian dictator*, are included to determine whether the type of dictator has an impact on respect for liberties.

For many authoritarian states within the developing world, the historical legacy of colonialism has many consequences, one of which may be the degree to which civil liberties are respected. Mitchell and McCormick (1988: 480) state directly: "British colonial rule ... is commonly thought to be strongly associated with the post-colonial development of democracy. The British legacy may be a relatively greater respect for human rights. By contrast, other colonial experiences (Spanish, for instance) are generally assumed to have introduced a greater degree of hierarchy and authoritarianism. The legacy here may well involve higher levels of human rights violations." British colonialism may have had a positive influence on civil liberties through a number of channels. It may be the result of the tutelary form of parliamentarism the British cultivated within their colonial holdings. The British also may have successfully instilled a greater appreciation for individual rights and liberal democracy. In addition, arguing that inherent in British common-law tradition is a greater respect for the rule of law, La Porta et al. (1998) show that these countries offer better protection to investors and have overall better quality of government. Analogously, they also may lead to greater respect for civil liberties when such legislation is in place. For all of these reasons, former British colonies, as indicated by the dichotomous variable *British colony*, are expected to allow for greater individual freedoms.

Finally, also included is the lagged dependent variable for both conceptual and practical reasons. Policies are sticky such that the current year's rights legislation and enforcement may be shaped by what already exists. In addition, the previous year's values serve to address the serial correlation within the data on civil liberties.[5]

---

[5] Inclusion of the observed, rather than the latent, lagged dependent variable, means that a restricted, rather than a full, transition model is being estimated (Beck et al. 2001). But following Londregan and Poole (1990), this technique seems appropriate given the theoretical reasons for expecting that current outcomes are contingent on past ones.

TABLE 4.2. *Descriptive Statistics of Variables in Civil Liberties Analysis*

Variable	Mean	Standard Deviation	Minimum	Maximum	Cases
Speech freedom$_t$	0.600	0.604	0	2	1681
Speech freedom$_{t-1}$	0.590	0.605	0	2	1572
Press freedom$_t$	2.518	0.752	0	3	3713
Press freedom$_{t-1}$	2.516	0.755	0	3	3678
Workers' rights$_t$	0.614	0.702	0	2	1679
Workers' rights$_{t-1}$	0.604	0.699	0	2	1570
Institutions$_{t-1}$	0.979	0.817	0	2	4443
Per capita income$_{t-1}$/1000	4.362	7.129	0.171	84.408	3383
Other democracies$_{t-1}$	0.390	0.103	0.266	0.605	4471
Riots$_{t-1}$	0.389	1.436	0	32	3835
War$_{t-1}$	0.108	0.310	0	1	4471
Military dictator$_{t-1}$	0.336	0.472	0	1	4471
British colony	0.272	0.445	0	1	4588

Descriptive statistics of all the variables are provided in Table 4.2. The dependent variables (*Speech freedom, Press freedom, Workers' rights*) are subscripted t. Not surprisingly, the means of *Speech freedom* and *Workers' rights* are closer to the low end, whereas the average value of *Press freedom* is on the high end, indicating relatively tight restrictions for the sample of nondemocratic states. The remaining variables enter on the right-hand side and are lagged by one year with the exception of *British colony* which is time invariant.

4.3.2 Effect of Institutions

The results of the ordered probit model for all three dependent variables are shown in Table 4.3. Column 1 of Table 4.3 shows that a number of factors contribute to freedom of speech within nondemocratic regimes. The extent to which the regime respected freedom of speech in the previous year has a large and positive impact on speech freedoms in the current year. Having been a British colony also makes permissive speech laws more likely while, not surprisingly, involvement in conflict leads to a more restrictive atmosphere. Finally, the variable of main interest, *Institutions*, has a positive and highly significant impact on speech freedoms. Regimes that are more

TABLE 4.3. *Effect of Institutions on Civil Liberties*

	Speech Freedom	Press Freedom	Workers' Rights
Dependent variable$_{t-1}$	1.145***	2.906***	1.161***
	(0.073)	(0.064)	(0.061)
Institutions$_{t-1}$	0.197***	−0.038	0.188***
	(0.052)	(0.045)	(0.052)
Per capita income$_{t-1}$	0.002	0.006	−0.004
	(0.007)	(0.006)	(0.007)
Other democracies$_{t-1}$	0.586***	−1.391***	−0.491
	(0.449)	(0.428)	(0.452)
Riots$_{t-1}$	0.028	−0.014	0.017
	(0.028)	(0.020)	(0.026)
War$_{t-1}$	−0.243**	0.035	−0.016
	(0.122)	(0.112)	(0.120)
Military dictator$_{t-1}$	0.001	−0.137*	0.102
	(0.088)	(0.077)	(0.089)
British colony	0.194**	−0.166**	0.138
	(0.087)	(0.081)	(0.087)
μ_1	1.009***	0.700***	0.724***
	(0.211)	(0.214)	(0.212)
μ_2	3.139***	3.473***	2.259***
	(0.231)	(0.210)	(0.221)
μ_3		6.429***	
		(0.227)	
log-likelihood	−747.416	−721.780	−794.499
Observations	1043	2627	1039

Standard errors in parentheses.
*** $p < 0.01$; ** $p < 0.05$; * $p < 0.10$.

institutionalized allow for greater freedom of the press because groups within nondemocratic legislatures and parties demand concessions on civil liberties.

As an illustration of the effects of institutions along with the other variables, Table 4.4 provides predicted probabilities for the outcomes of the dependent variable – *Speech freedom* – for some paradigmatic types of dictators. The examples do not reflect the impact of institutions alone because the values of other variables also vary. Yet they allow for interpretation of the ordered probit coefficients whose signs cannot be unambiguously interpreted for the middle category [i.e., Prob($y = 1$)].

TABLE 4.4. *Predicted Probabilities for Speech Rights*

Type	Examples	Pr ($y = 0 \mid x$), Severe Restrictions	Pr ($y = 1 \mid x$), Moderate Restrictions	Pr ($y = 2 \mid x$), No/Few Restrictions
Extremely poor (per capita income ~$800) military regime at war with no institutions	Burundi under Buyoya, Nigeria under Gowon	0.615 (0.514, 0.715)	0.378 (0.374, 0.381)	0.008 (0.001, 0.014)
Poor (~$3,000) civilian regime at peace with a single party	Djibouti under Gouled, Uzbekistan under Karimov	0.440 (0.383, 0.496)	0.537 (0.527, 0.546)	0.024 (0.013, 0.035)
Middle-income (~$6,500) military regime at peace with multiple legislative parties	South Korea under Chun, Tunisia under Ben Ali	0.360 (0.291, 0.430)	0.602 (0.588, 0.616)	0.038 (0.020, 0.056)

For calculating predicted probabilities for all types: *British colony* is set to zero, whereas other variables (lagged dependent variable, *Other democracies*, and *Riots*) are set to to their means. 95-percent confidence interval indicated in parentheses.

The table shows three types. The first is of a military regime in a country that was never occupied by the British but is currently very poor (i.e., per capita income of around 800 dollars), engaged in war, and without institutions. In these cases, the likelihood of strong speech restrictions is 0.615, of moderate restrictions 0.378, and of no prohibitions 0.008. In contrast, a country with almost three-and-one-half times per capita income (i.e., 3,000 dollars) at peace under a single-party regime headed by a civilian dictator, such as Hassan Gouled Aptidon in Djibouti or Islam Karimov in Uzbekistan, is most likely to have moderate prohibitions on speech. Finally, fully institutionalized military regimes at peace found in middle-income countries that never experienced a British colonial past also are most likely to place some restrictions on speech. Yet the probabilities that speech would be free or moderately free are the highest in comparison to the previous types.

Returning to Table 4.3, Column 2 shows the results for press freedoms, a subset of the liberties coded by the speech variable. The analysis here benefits from a substantially larger set of observations, and a number of control variables affect the degree of press freedom.

TABLE 4.5. *Predicted Probabilities of Workers' Rights Conditional on Institutions*

	Pr ($y = 0 \mid x$), No Rights	Pr ($y = 1 \mid x$), Moderate Rights	Pr ($y = 2 \mid x$), Full Rights
No institutions	0.591 (0.515, 0.666)	0.371 (0.359, 0.382)	0.039 (0.020, 0.057)
Single institution	0.516 (0.459, 0.573)	0.426 (0.410, 0.442)	0.058 (0.038, 0.077)
Multiple institutions	0.441 (0.380, 0.503)	0.476 (0.455, 0.497)	0.083 (0.056, 0.110)

For calculating predicted probabilities for all types: *British colony*, *War*, and *Military* are set to zero whereas other variables are set to to their means. 95-percent confidence interval indicated in parentheses.

Beyond the effect of the previous year's press restrictions, the share of democracies in the world exhibits the strongest effect in terms of magnitude and statistical significance. The greater the share of democracies in the world, the less restrictive are a country's press laws. Consistent with the results on speech freedoms, a British colonial past again is correlated with fewer restrictions. Unexpectedly, press restrictions are less severe under military governments. *Institutions*, however, does not have an effect significantly different from zero.

The last column of Table 4.3 provides results on workers' rights. As with the other civil liberties, the degree of rights provided depends very much on past history; the lagged dependent variable is large, positive, and statistically significant. The only other factor affecting workers' rights is *Institutions*. Institutionalization under nondemocratic regimes is correlated with a more protective environment for the labor force.

To better understand the effects of institutions on workers' rights, Table 4.5 shows the predicted probabilities of particular environments for workers (i.e., no, moderate, and high protection of rights) under different institutional frameworks. When the legislature is closed or parties are not allowed within the assembly, workers are most likely to receive no concessions, as the top left cell in Table 4.5 indicates. The predicted likelihood of workers having no rights is 0.591. Single-party states also are fairly restrictive. Dictatorial regimes do not concede even a moderate amount of labor protection unless there are partisan legislatures. Only under a broadened dictatorship is the predicted probability of moderate rights (e.g., 0.476) higher than the likelihood of other possible rights environments.

Governments under dictatorship are most likely to trample on workers' rights when they do not have to contend with legislative parties. These results regarding labor legislation comport with the findings of Gandhi and Kim (2005) who show that dictatorial institutions lead to higher wage benefits for workers in manufacturing and fewer strikes. Taken together, these findings provide confirmation for the theoretical account of nominally democratic institutions advanced here. As a forum in which outside groups, such as workers, can announce their demands, legislatures and parties should result in fewer expressions of these demands on the street in the form of strikes. Yet because these institutions are to aid in the forging of policy compromises, they should result in policies that advance workers' interests.

4.4   MILITARY EXPENDITURES

Governments enact a range of policies that affect the lives of citizens. The previous section examined the effect of institutions on the rights of citizens to speak freely, to have access to independent media, and to organize collectively as employees. This section and the following one examine government expenditures. As discussed in Section 4.2, it is assumed that to remain in power, dictators must not only build coalitions within society but also insure monopolistic control over the means of coercion. A well-funded military is crucial for deterring and eliminating opposition within society. In addition, an authoritarian incumbent seeks to appease the men with guns lest one of them decide to overthrow him. Consequently, nondemocratic leaders are expected to prioritize spending on the military above all else. In the presence of nominally democratic institutions, however, dictators may not be able to provide such generous allocations to the military. Because assemblies and parties allow groups within society to wrangle policy concessions from the dictator, they may divert resources to other priorities. As a result, spending on the armed forces is expected to decline with greater institutionalization.

4.4.1 Data

The dependent variable, *Military spending*, is measured as a percentage of gross national product. The figures are provided by the Stockholm International Peace Research Institute (SIPRI) and are based (wherever possible) on the North Atlantic Treaty Organization's definition that includes all current capital expenditures on the armed forces, including peacekeeping forces, the defense ministry, other government agencies engaged in defense projects, and paramilitary forces. The definition is broad, encompassing activities, such as military space programs, that may not bear on the immediate survival of rulers. But the figures also capture the amount of spending on military operations and maintenance along with the pensions of retired military and civilian members of these organizations. Allocating enough resources to these items is of importance to any leader interested in appeasing the armed forces.

Data coverage is extensive, including 418 dictators in 130 countries, beginning in some cases as early as 1952 and extending to 2002.[6] Military expenditures as a percentage of total income range from 0.2 percent in Fiji, Guinea-Bissau, Togo, and Uganda, to 48.5 percent in Kuwait during the Iraqi invasion. Over 90 percent of country-year observations are of expenditures of less than 10 percent. For the entire sample of nondemocratic states, average military spending is just over 4 percent of GDP.

The independent variable of primary interest is *Institutions*, coded 2 if multiple legislative parties are allowed, 1 if only the regime party controls seats within the legislature, and 0 otherwise. As the degree of institutionalization increases, the portion of total income devoted to the armed forces is expected to decline.

To estimate the impact of institutions on military spending, a number of control variables are included. Engagement in conflict is an obvious determinant (Gupta et al. 2001). Governments defending their territories against aggressors or attacking as belligerents need sufficient arms and personnel. Hence, included as a control is a dichotomous variable, *War*, coded 1 if the state is engaged in an armed conflict

---

[6] There are fewer observations in the statistical analysis due to missing data for other variables.

TABLE 4.6. *Descriptive Statistics of Variables in Military Spending Analysis*

Variable	Mean	Standard Deviation	Minimum	Maximum	Cases
Military spending$_t$	4.149	4.352	0.200	48.500	3092
Military spending$_{t-1}$	4.159	4.373	0.200	48.500	3011
Institutions$_{t-1}$	0.979	0.817	0	2	4443
War$_{t-1}$	0.108	0.310	0	1	4471
Military dictator$_{t-1}$	0.336	0.472	0	1	4471

(either civil or interstate wars) on its territory or abroad and 0 otherwise. *War* should be correlated positively with military expenditures.

Corporatist interest is one reason why militaries are thought to stage coups. Yet even if material deprivation is not the reason for seizing power, once in office military rulers are thought to favor the interests of their own men and the organization of which they are members, possibly resulting in greater spending on the armed forces (Nordlinger 1977, Perlmutter 1977). The evidence here is mixed as well, however. Zuk and Thompson (1982) show that the military's impact on spending depends on the type of dependent variable used. They find a statistically significant difference between military and civilian regimes when spending as a share of total income, but not post-coup growth of spending, is examined. In addition, military rulers can use their status as heads of the chain of command to demand obedience; civilian dictators cannot. As a result, nonmilitary dictators may throw resources at the armed forces in an attempt at appeasement in which case regime type may matter but in a different way. To determine whether military dictators display corporatist interests, a dummy variable, *Military dictator*, distinguishes military from nonmilitary regimes. The variable's expected sign is positive. Table 4.6 shows descriptive statistics of the variables used in the analysis.

Government finances exhibit a great deal of inertia in that the current value is highly correlated with past values. This attribute of government budgets and fiscal data have consequences for the appropriate method of estimating the impact of political factors on fiscal outcomes. First, from a theoretical perspective, it seems likely that any factors influencing fiscal outcomes do so through short-term and long-term processes. Institutions during a particular year, for example, may have a direct contemporaneous effect on spending in that year but also an indirect equilibrium effect on future spending. The two impacts should be separated. Second, from the empirical side, augmented Dickey–Fuller tests indicate that government expenditures may have unit roots. Because some right-hand-side factors also may have unit roots, making co-integration likely, simple regressions (either with or without a lagged dependent variable) may provide spurious results.

Beck (1992) and Franzese (2002) suggest a method of estimation, similar to an error correction model (ECM), that addresses both concerns. The method (hereafter referred to as pseudo-ECM) involves regressing the change in the dependent variable on its lagged level, its lagged differences as necessary, and the lagged levels and differences of whatever other variables theory or empirics suggest. This approach addresses the possibility of unit roots and produces estimates that asymptotically have properties equivalent to those of the error correction model as long as the coefficient on the lagged dependent variable is "comfortably negative" (Franzese 2002: 82). Its virtue over the error correction model is that the model does not require *ex ante* decisions about either the choice of variables to co-integrate with the dependent variable or the order of co-integration.

In addition, the model allows for intuitive interpretation of the long- and short-term impacts of independent variables. The coefficients of differenced independent variables refer to their short-run, transitory effects on the dependent variable. If x increases once to a new level, for example, the transitory impact on y lasts only that one period as well and then diminishes as determined by the dynamics in y and Δy. In contrast, when the independent variables are levels, their estimates reflect long-run equilibrium effects. These coefficients indicate that increases in x may result in permanent increases in y.

Because there are no strong theoretical grounds to believe that some right-hand-side variables are likely to have exclusively short-run or long-run effects, both the difference and the lagged value of each independent variable are included.

Table 4.7 provides the results of the analysis. For comparison, the first and second columns show results from a random effects and a fixed effects model, respectively, in which only one-period lags of the independent variables are included. The third and fourth columns

TABLE 4.7. *Effect of Institutions on Military Expenditures*

	OLS		Pseudo-ECM	
	Random Effects	Fixed Effects	Random Effects	Fixed Effects
Military spending$_{t-1}$	0.919***	0.798***	−0.066***	−0.203***
	(0.023)	(0.043)	(0.020)	(0.043)
Institutions $_\Delta$			−0.043	−0.012
			(0.066)	(0.068)
Institutions$_{t-1}$	−0.091**	0.009	−0.098**	−0.003
	(0.046)	(0.047)	(0.044)	(0.047)
War$_\Delta$			1.026**	1.171***
			(0.406)	(0.439)
War$_{t-1}$	0.294**	0.548***	0.537***	1.012***
	(0.128)	(0.156)	(0.140)	(0.219)
Military dictator$_\Delta$			0.121	0.206
			(0.132)	(0.139)
Military dictator$_{t-1}$	−0.153**	−0.065	−0.155**	−0.045
	(0.066)	(0.075)	(0.066)	(0.084)
Constant	0.477***	0.816***	0.402***	0.781***
	(0.110)	(0.171)	(0.100)	(0.169)
N	2901	2901	2900	2900

Standard errors in parentheses.
*** $p < 0.01$; ** $p < 0.05$; * $p < 0.10$.

provide results from the pseudo-error correction model with random and fixed effects, respectively. To remind, the models in columns 1 and 2 and the models in columns 3 and 4 differ in two important ways. The dependent variable in the former is military spending in a given year t, whereas in the latter, it is the change in military spending. In addition, the column 1 and 2 models contain only lagged values of the independent variables, whereas the pseudo-ECM models have both differences and lagged values in an attempt to model both short- and long-run impacts.

Results from the models in columns 1 and 2 show that much of the variance in the current year's budget is accounted for by spending in the previous year. Even after inclusion of country effects, the coefficient on the lagged dependent variable is still positive and highly significant.

Also not surprisingly, involvement in either interstate or civil war increases military expenditures. Results from both the random and fixed effects models in columns 1 and 2 show that participation as a combatant significantly increases military spending. According to the results from the fixed effects model in column 2, involvement in either civil conflict or interstate war increases military spending by one-half of one percentage point.

The results from both models regarding military dictatorships is surprising. Although the fixed effects model shows no statistically significant difference in spending between military and nonmilitary dictators, the random effects model indicates that military dictators actually devote fewer resources to the armed forces in comparison to their civilian counterparts.

Finally, consistent with expectations, the main variable of interest, *Institutions*, has a negative and significant impact on military spending according to the results from the random effects model. A one-unit increase in the degree of institutionalization reduces military spending by 0.091 percent. The fixed effects model, however, shows that the difference in military spending across institutional arrangements is not significantly different from zero.

The pseudo-ECM models allow for more precise distinction between transitory and equilibrium effects of both institutions and various other factors. Note first the negative and statistically significant coefficients on military expenditures lagged one year. The estimate from the pseudo-ECM model with random effects in column 3, for example, shows that military spending adjusts very slowly: just about 93 percent $(1 - 0.066)$ of a shock in one year persists into the next, and then 93 percent of that into the following year, and so on. Thus, the long-run effect of any permanent shock is 15 times $(1/0.066)$ its immediate impact.

Again, war is the second most important determinant of resource allocation to the armed forces, exhibiting both short- and long-run effects. In the pseudo-ECM models, the positive and significant coefficients on the lagged value and difference dwarf the impact of other variables. In the random effects model, the coefficient on War_Δ indicates that involvement in war leads to an immediate 1.026 percent increase in spending. If war is long-term, the effect of conflict results in an even greater $(1.026 + 0.537)$ long-run increase in military expenditures.

The pseudo-ECM results differ in estimating the impact of both military leaders and institutions. Results from the random effects model in column 3 indicate that military dictatorship has a long-term decreasing effect on military expenditures. The model estimates of the effect of institutions is similar: the reduction in spending happens only over the long-run, suggesting that although a particular legislative session or extent parties may not have an immediate impact, their presence eventually leads to policy compromises. Yet the results on neither military dictators nor institutions are robust to the inclusion of fixed effects.

In summary, results from all models indicate that budgets exhibit inertia, and so current spending is largely a function of allocations of the previous year. In addition, conflict, whether external or internal, is the next strongest determinant of military expenditures. As expected, the effects are immediate as states fight to maintain their sovereignty. But the impact of conflict persists over time as well. The effects of military dictatorship and institutions, however, are less clear because results depend on model specification. In only random effects models do military dictatorships and, more importantly, institutions have a long-run negative impact on military spending. These institutions result in reductions in military spending primarily in the long-run as dictators seek to compromise with those groups that they have incorporated within these structures.

4.5   SOCIAL SPENDING

If institutions succeed in reducing allocations to the armed forces, do they also result in greater social spending? The assumption is that budgets entail distributional trade-offs and that groups within society that are incorporated within legislative and partisan institutions will prefer to steer resources to satisfy their interests. Social programs in education, health, welfare, and social security are considered as a bundle to minimize the importance of determining the precise coalition of groups participating within dictatorial institutions. Indeed, on matters of education, for example, a number of historical examples demonstrate how broad-based coalitions have supported its public extension (Galor and Moav 2006, Lindert 2004). For these reasons, it does not seem wholly unreasonable to believe that a substantially large portion of the population will support a wide variety of social programs in these areas.

4.5.1 Data

The *Government Finance Statistics* of the International Monetary Fund provides separate indicators of central government expenditures on education, health, social security, and welfare, as shares of gross domestic product. The expenditures in these three areas have been added to create the dependent variable, *Social spending*. Data on these types of expenditures are much less available than figures on military spending analyzed in the previous section. Coverage begins in 1972 for 124 dictators in sixty-four nondemocratic states. Average social spending within the sample is 7.77 percent. The low of 0.11 percent was in Guinea, whereas Kuwait spent a high of 30.26 percent to recover just after the invasion by Iraq.

Institutions is again the primary independent variable of interest. As authoritarian regimes are more institutionalized, it is expected that social spending will increase, reflecting policy compromises with social groups incorporated within legislatures and political parties. Therefore, the coefficient on *Institutions* should have a positive sign.

Provision of social programs also depends on the demand from citizens and the ability of governments to meet these needs. The demographic profile of the population can serve as a proxy for potential demand within society for these services. Education is consumed by the young, particularly in the developing world where the focus is on the provision of primary education. Brown and Hunter (2004) and Stasavage (2005) both find statistically significant effects of a young population on educational spending. Health services are most often demanded by both the young and the old because mortality rates are highest within these two groups. Finally, because pensions constitute a large share of social security and welfare spending, a large retired elderly population requires greater resources in this area. Rudra (2002) and Avelino et al. (2005) find that the size of the elderly population is a strong predictor of social security spending. As a result, a bundle of education, health, and social security programs is most in demand when youth and elderly make up a large share of the population.

TABLE 4.8. *Descriptive Statistics of Variables in Social Spending Analysis*

Variable	Mean	Standard Deviation	Minimum	Maximum	Cases
Social spending$_t$	7.772	4.093	0.112	30.256	774
Social spending$_{t-1}$	7.729	4.111	0.112	30.256	760
Institutions$_{t-1}$	0.979	0.817	0	2	4443
Dependent population$_{t-1}$	44.914	5.337	26.813	60.451	3577
Open economy$_{t-1}$	67.969	48.066	0.847	425.340	3428

Dependent population, the proportion of the population that is less than 14 and above 65 years old, should be positively correlated with social expenditures.

Demand for social programs also increases as more citizens are exposed to greater economic risks (Cameron 1978, Garrett 1998, Rodrik 1998). As countries open their borders to freer trade, competition from outside goods and services becomes fiercer. Domestic industries, no longer cushioned by trade protection, may be forced to lay off workers to become more competitive or may have to shut down all together. Greater numbers of unemployed workers will seek welfare and pension benefits. Young workers may demand greater education to develop marketable skills in an increasingly competitive economy. Hence, the demand for social spending is expected to increase as *Trade openness*, the total exports and imports as a share of gross domestic product, increases.

Finally, social spending from the previous year is included to capture the inertia of government finances and to model the serial correlation within the data. Table 4.8 shows descriptive statistics for all the variables used in the analysis. Because a priori there is no reason to think that some variables have exclusively short- or long-run effects, both differences and lags of each are included.

The size of the sample in this analysis is significantly smaller than that used in the previous analysis. For postwar dictatorships, data on social spending are available for only 17 percent of the sample. The smaller sample is due in part because fiscal data for much of the developing world are not available before 1972. In addition, Eastern Europe and Central and East Asia are underrepresented due to the dearth of

TABLE 4.9. *Effect of Institutions on Social Spending*

	OLS		Pseudo-ECM	
	Random Effects	Fixed Effects	Random Effects	Fixed Effects
Social spending$_{t-1}$	0.863***	0.684***	−0.100***	−0.320***
	(0.040)	(0.054)	(0.030)	(0.052)
Institutions $_\Delta$			0.331	0.129
			(0.249)	(0.199)
Institutions$_{t-1}$	−0.198*	−0.326	−0.095	−0.299
	(0.104)	(0.210)	(0.075)	(0.186)
Dependent population$_\Delta$			0.047	0.007
			(0.103)	(0.099)
Dependent population$_{t-1}$	0.001	0.009	−0.009	−0.014
	(0.042)	(0.090)	(0.020)	(0.065)
Open economy$_\Delta$			−0.036**	−0.031**
			(0.016)	(0.013)
Open economy$_{t-1}$	0.006	0.020	0.002	0.009
	(0.004)	(0.013)	(0.002)	(0.006)
Constant	0.845	0.897	1.214	2.781
	(2.291)	(5.256)	(1.072)	(3.550)
N	632	632	632	632

Standard errors in parentheses.
*** $p < 0.01$; ** $p < 0.05$; * $p < 0.10$.

data on communist states. Because many health, welfare, and pension benefits were provided by state-owned enterprises, government expenditures would have been poor measures of public provision of these services in these states.

4.5.2 Effect of Institutions

The impact of institutions along with economic and demographic factors on social spending is determined again in both random and fixed effects models that include one-period lags and differences of the independent variables. Table 4.9 shows the results from the various models. Columns 1 and 2 show results from random and fixed effects models in which only one-period lags of the variables are included. Columns 3 and 4 provide results from the random and fixed effects pseudo-ECM models, respectively, which include both lags and differences to demonstrate long-run and short-run effects.

All of the models in Table 4.9 shows that current social spending greatly reflects the previous year's expenditures. Although the effect of the previous year's spending on current social expenditures is not as great in magnitude as was the case with military expenditures, the impact is still positive and highly statistically significant.

The coefficients on the other control variables, however, either are unstable or have no statistically significant impact. Social expenditures are not a function of demand. All of the models show that the impact of the size of the dependent population is not significantly different from zero. The effect of an open economy on social spending is significant in the short-term, as indicated by the pseudo-ECM models, but is not of the expected direction. Both the random and fixed effects models in columns 3 and 4, respectively, show that an increase in imports and exports as a share of national income leads to a short-term decrease in social spending. Furthermore, the effects of increasing trade in the long-run are zero, providing no evidence for the compensation thesis.

Finally, the results from all of the models do not indicate a significant impact for institutions on social spending in the anticipated direction. The pseudo-ECM models in columns 3 and 4 provide no evidence of either transitory or equilibrium effects of institutions on spending. The one model in which the impact of *Institutions* is just barely statistically significant shows this effect to be negative. A one-step increase in institutionalization, according to the results in column 1, leads to a 0.198-percent decrease in social expenditures. The results run counter to theoretical expectations that predicted that institutions would have a positive effect on social spending as leaders of social groups incorporated within legislatures and parties would press for services that would benefit their constituents.

Several factors may account for the unexpected result. One problem is the poor data coverage. Data on social spending begin late (1972), are largely unavailable for communist states, and are spotty for many developing countries. Another reason is conceptual, drawing on the distributional nature of governments' fiscal decisions. On fiscal issues, it may be too much to assume that opposition groups speak with one voice. After all, the bundle of goods and services under the rubric of "social spending" is still composed of a variety of programs that benefit different constituencies. The standard label of "public goods" for education, health, welfare, and pension benefits is misleading because it hides the fact that these programs emerge from conflicts of interest (e.g., young versus old, sick versus healthy, and employed versus unemployed). As a result, the degree to which social spending is supported by groups incorporated by authoritarian regimes depends on which groups participate within these institutions. Until these details are included, it is difficult to determine which types of social programs might be supported by those participating within institutions under dictatorship.

4.6 CONCLUSION

From Chapters 2 and 3, we learned that under some conditions, non-democratic leaders must make concessions to the potential opposition – in the form of both spoils and policy. The crucial assumption linking concessions to institutions, however, is that policy compromises cannot be made outside the shelter of legislatures and parties. Within these institutions, leaders of religious organizations, business and labor associations, and various other groups can express demands that do not appear as acts of public resistance to the regime. The dictator, in turn, uses legislatures and parties as a way to control dissent and to make concessions while appearing to be magnanimous rather than weak. Because dictators vary in their need to make concessions and, consequently, to have institutions, there should be differences in policies across differently organized authoritarian regimes.

The results in this chapter confirm this is the case in some areas of policy-making in authoritarian regimes. Consistent with expectations, more institutionalized dictatorships spend less on the armed forces than their noninstitutionalized counterparts. Yet they do not compensate with more resources for education, health, and welfare. In the context of a "guns versus butter" trade-off, this finding is surprising and begs the question of where the money goes in institutionalized dictatorships. It could be that institutionalized regimes engage in more corruption. In this case, authoritarian leaders might siphon more funds from public monies to distribute to members of these institutions, leaving less for official government budgetary categories. Alternatively, lower social spending within institutionalized regimes may indicate the difficulty of building coalitions for programs that are not truly public goods. In any case, at this stage, it is difficult to draw any definitive conclusions given the restricted scope of the sample.

Civil liberties, however, should command widespread support among citizens. As a result, members of nominally democratic institutions should be more able to coordinate their efforts to demand these rights in the face of authoritarian power. Institutionalized dictatorships, then, should have more liberalized rights policies. The analysis in this chapter reveals support for this idea. More institutionalized regimes allow for greater freedom of speech along with better protection of workers' rights. So although participation in these nominally democratic institutions under dictatorship may taint some groups as collaborators and cronies, they do result in benefits for the wider population.

5

Institutions and Outcomes under Dictatorship

5.1 INTRODUCTION

Some countries experience phenomenal rates of economic growth while governed under dictatorship. By the end of General Franco's reign in 1975, Spain's per capita income was eight times as large as it had been since the end of World War II. China's average income nearly tripled under Deng Xiaoping. The East Asian "tigers," such as Malaysia, Singapore, Taiwan, and South Korea, all achieved growth rates of over 10 percent under the thumb of dictators. Yet some of the worst economic disasters also occur under dictatorial regimes. Zambia under Kenneth Kaunda witnessed its average income fall: from 996 dollars in 1964 when he took power, to 817 dollars shortly before he left in 1991. The revolution led by Ayatollah Khomeini was costly for average Iranians: their per capita income when he died was almost 1,600 dollars less than when he seized power. It is only now that average income in Iran is returning to its pre-revolution levels.

South Korea and Zaire constitute the paradigmatic comparison. In 1960, per capita incomes in South Korea and Zaire were similar. In fact, as the second largest state in Africa and endowed with copper, cobalt, and diamonds, Zaire faced considerably brighter prospects than small, resource-poor Korea still dealing with postwar devastation. Yet the reversal of fortune could not have been more complete. Under General Park during the 1960s, Korea expanded its total exports by more than forty times, manufacturing's share of total domestic product increased from 17 to 35 percent, and three million jobs were created (Im 1987). In contrast, under Mobutu Sese Seko's long rule over Zaire, fourteen billion dollars of external debt accumulated; total capital flight exceeded twelve billion dollars; and, 70 percent of the population lived in poverty (Ndikumana and Boyce 1998). The end result was that by 1990, average income in Korea was forty-five times greater than in Zaire.

In general, the variance in performance is higher in dictatorships than in democracies (Weede 1996). Among all dictatorial country-years for which data are available, over 20 percent of all observations are of negative growth rates. Only 15 percent of democratic country-years experience declining growth. During the tenure of a single dictator, average annual growth rates range from -11.85 percent to 25.03 percent. These stark differences beg the question: what accounts for the differences in economic growth among dictatorships?

The literature on the effects of democracy and dictatorship on economic growth is immense and has been useful in posing the possible theoretical channels through which political regimes affect economic performance even if empirical results have been inconclusive (for summaries, see Aron 2000, Przeworski and Limongi 1993). Yet much of this work emphasizes the difference in incentives that public officials and private agents have in the presence or absence of elections. The increased accountability, credibility of commitments, and protection of property rights induced by the electoral connection between citizens and public officials appears unable to explain the variance among nondemocratic regimes.

In this chapter, I argue that nominally democratic institutions remain relevant in accounting for differences in economic performance even if the relevant mechanisms differ from those in the literature contrasting democracies and dictatorships. As discussed earlier, dictatorships vary in the degree to which domestic groups within society threaten their rule and the extent to which they need the cooperation of outside groups to govern. To both neutralize threats to their rule and solicit cooperation, some dictators coopt potential domestic opposition by providing rents and policy concessions within nominally democratic institutions, such as legislatures and political parties. These institutions, designed as instruments of co-optation, insure cooperation between the regime and outside groups that is necessary for development.

The mechanisms by which these co-optative institutions lead to higher economic growth are several. First, as a forum in which domestic groups can negotiate with the regime, institutions help dictatorships to avoid the expression of demands on the street and, consequently, to create a more conducive investment climate. Second, due to their role in reducing political transaction costs between the regime and the potential opposition, legislatures, and parties exhibit some institutional stickiness that also signals to firms that they may expect some stability of policy-making on the part of the government. Finally, institutions facilitate the spread of information between government officials and private economic agents, potentially increasing allocative efficiency. Although these mechanisms are theoretically distinct, they point to a similar empirical expectation: greater institutionalization should lead to higher economic growth within nondemocratic regimes.

Of course, there are alternative explanations for accounting for the variance in performance between a Korea and a Zaire. These include purely economic explanations that focus on initial conditions and inputs to growth along with additional political accounts that stress the importance of internal and external security threats and conflicts. In quantitative analysis, controls for these factors can easily be introduced so that we can assess the true effect of institutions on growth.

Yet one of the most prevalent explanations for the differences in economic performance among nondemocratic regimes is based on the notion that the "personal inclinations of autocrats might matter much more than personality differences between democratic rulers" (Weede 1996). So Korea developed because it had the luck of having a "competent, honest, and efficient bureaucracy to administer the interventions, and a clear-sighted political leadership that consistently placed high priority on economic performance" (Rodrik 1995: 91), whereas Zaire had the misfortune of being governed by someone who thought nothing of amassing a personal fortune of over four billion dollars while 70 percent of his citizens lived in poverty (Ndikumana and Boyce 1998).

Qualitative accounts of particular cases can illustrate such differences in motives or ideology, whereas quantitative approaches appear disadvantaged in their inability to capture and code systematically such "unobservables." Yet ignorance of such unobservable factors in quantitative analysis has great costs – particularly if we are interested in determining the effect of institutions on economic growth (as we are in this case). The problem stems from the fact that dictators who prioritize economic development may also have "tutelary" motives in politics, believing that their societies must be prepared before they can govern responsibly under democracy. If "developmental" and "tute- lary" motives go hand in hand, however, dictators who govern with nominally democratic institutions may be "unusual" in comparison to rulers who preside over noninstitutionalized regimes. In this case, the selection of political institutions and the decision to prioritize eco- nomic development are not independent, and empirical approaches that assume so will produce biased estimates. To deal with this poten- tial problem, the effect of institutions on economic growth is estimated using a Heckman selection model after the results of more conventional approaches are shown.

The chapter proceeds as follows. The next section (5.2) incorporates a theoretical discussion of the mechanisms by which legislatures and parties facilitate economic growth within nondemocratic regimes. At the end of this section, the empirical expectations generated by this account of authoritarian politics are contrasted with some hypotheses in the extant literature. Section 5.3 tackles the issue of motives or other unobservables as possible determinants of economic performance. The heterogeneity of dictators and the resulting problem for estimating the effect of institutions on economic growth are discussed. These issues are taken into account in the empirical portion of the chapter, which includes several methods of estimating the effect of institutions on growth. A discussion of the statistical results and speculation about likely causal mechanisms precedes the conclusion of the chapter.

5.2 INSTITUTIONAL MECHANISMS FOR ECONOMIC DEVELOPMENT

Chapter 3 has shown that dictators who face a weak threat of opposi- tion from domestic groups and do not need the support of outsiders, make no concessions to society. As a result, they do not need to govern with the institutional apparatus that is necessary to compromise with outside groups. Potential opposition will be pacified, but the regime is unlikely to have the active cooperation of substantial portions of the population.

In contrast, other dictatorships that face potentially strong threats to their rule and need the support of outsiders have institutions so they can make concessions necessary to neutralize these threats and to solicit cooperation. Institutions, however, do more than just quell the potential opposition. They provide a framework through which the regime and interest groups can cooperate. As a result, dictatorships with institutions produce policies that reflect a compromise between regimes and potential opposition. The previous chapter showed the differences in policies that these institutions can produce. But if institutions influence policies, then they also should affect outcomes.

Consider some additional empirical expectations generated by the theory. The first hypothesis emerges from the idea that when the potential opposition participates within dictatorial institutions, they no longer have incentives to make their demands on the street. Domestic groups risk losing their privileged status and access to decision-making if they express their demands outside of officially designated arenas. In Morocco, Jordan, and Egypt, for example, Lust-Okar (2005) shows that politically privileged parties, even though they possessed the means, did not mobilize the masses in times of economic crisis due to this very fear of losing their standing with the ruling class. Because legislatures and parties serve as a safety valve for the expression of domestic demands, institutionalized dictatorships should experience less open protest. And because private firms seek to minimize the risk of losing returns on their investment, they should be attracted to nondemocratic states that experience less political instability in the form of strikes, demonstrations, and protests. Gandhi and Kim (2005), in fact, show that institutionalized dictatorships experience fewer strikes and grant greater labor compensation than their noninstitutionalized counterparts. The finding suggests that in exchange for material benefits and social protection, workers and their representatives desist from strikes and other forms of open protest that may portray the regime as vulnerable and scare away investors.

In addition to instability generated by conflict between the state and society, entrepreneurs are concerned about the constancy of the state's own actions. The state's failure to respect contracts and to provide a stable set of rules by which economic transactions can be conducted are likely to deter investment as entrepreneurs seek to minimize risk and potential loss of returns. Mobutu, in late 1973, for example, embarked on a nativist "Zairinization" campaign that included the nationalization of all foreign-owned firms. In a deft move to consolidate his political support, he later nationalized all firms exceeding two million dollars in turnover, distributing confiscated properties to party loyalists. But the political strategy had a price: as investment plummeted, Mobutu was forced to reconsider and returned firms to foreign ownership in 1976. Yet having witnessed the capriciousness of the state, entrepreneurs remained wary, and investment never recovered to pre-"Zairinization" levels.

How can dictatorial legislatures and parties induce dictators to behave predictably? Because institutions reduce the political transaction costs of dealing with potential opposition, dictators who face strong opposition have incentives to maintain them. The mere existence of a legislature with semiautonomous parties signals to investors that, at least, the dictator is willing to abide by a process by which he must announce his wishes and follow some internal rules. Otherwise, he would not receive the benefits of these institutions in the first place. As a result, entrepreneurs can count on some degree of stability in policy-making that should include the protection of their property rights.

Institutions also may facilitate growth by transmitting information, providing a forum for negotiations, and allowing the dictatorship to align incentives with effort. Nationalist leaders embarking on development projects have recognized legislatures as invaluable for these reasons. As President Jomo Kenyatta said in 1964 in a speech to the Kenyan House of Representatives: "What this House must contribute to the Republic is something far more than just machinery which can give the plans and requirements of the Government their lawful status. This must be our forum, for discussion and proposal, for question, objection, or advice serving as the place where the elders and the spokesmen of the people are expected and enabled to confer" (quoted in Stultz 1970: 325–326).

In addition to serving as a forum, legislatures may become a critical component of the regime's project to mobilize cooperation among citizens with its policies to promote development. Legislators may be expected to convey the regime's message to the people. As Kenyatta explained: "Members of this Parliament have a most important duty in the rural areas, to urge their people to follow the advice of technicians ... We must all work together to capture their imagination, and to see that they are interested and trained" (quoted in Stultz 1970: 322). One way in which cooperation can be obtained is through the constituency service performed by legislators. Several studies of "peripheral" or "developing" legislatures show that members take their duties of constituency service very seriously (Kim et al. 1983, Mezey 1983, Musolf and Smith 1979). Under the military government in Thailand, for example, legislators regularly intervened with the bureaucracy for their constituents to modify the substance and implementation of local development projects (Morell 1979). Without the legislature as a conduit, the regime would have more difficulty in getting private agents to comply with its goals.

Political parties, in turn, serve many of the same functions as legislatures. Negotiations between the potential opposition and the dictator may occur within parties. In Kenya, for example, backbenchers of the regime party, the Kenyan African National Union (KANU), did not restrict itself to criticism of the small details of legislation; they challenged the government on major issues of policy such as land reform, nationalization of firms, and education (Gertzel 1966: 497). Debate over the content of bills occurred within the party caucus rather than the assembly.

Parties also may serve as a conveyor belt of information between the regime and the people. Of the Tanganyika African National Union (TANU), President Julius Nyerere once said: "It is also necessary to have a strong political organization active in every village, which acts like a two-way all-weather road along which the purposes, plans and problems of government can travel to the people at the same time as the ideas, desires and misunderstandings of the people can travel to government. This is the job of the new TANU" (quoted in Bienen 1970: 165–166). TANU's role in this regard became particularly important after the 1967 Arusha Declaration which promoted rural development through cooperatives, increased accumulation of human capital, nationalization of industry, and wage restraints on urban workers.

In contrast, nondemocratic regimes without institutions find it significantly more difficult to promote economic growth. Without institutions to serve as a conduit of information, investments by both public and private agents are likely to be less efficient. In addition, without institutions, entrepreneurs face higher risks of expropriation and lower returns. These risks emanate from both groups within society and the state. When legislatures and parties do not exist to provide institution-alized mechanisms for domestic groups to express their grievances, entrepreneurs may face higher risks in the form of strikes and protests. Because semiautonomous legislative parties indicate some limitations (even if self-imposed) on executive power, their absence can result in greater insecurity on the part of investors. Domestic owners of capital in Ecuador, for example, protested against the military dictatorship under General Rodriguez Lara even though it was willing to enact policies in their interests precisely for this reason: "Without access to decision making although other economic policies clearly were benefi-cial to industrialists, the regime had shown that it could impose policies that capitalists were unable to shape or stop. Despite official rhetoric, there were no guarantees that their interests were secure" (Neuhouser 1996: 646–647).

Do nominally democratic institutions, then, shed light on the orig-inal puzzle: explaining outcomes under Park and Mobutu? Both Park and Mobutu changed their institutional arrangements during their long years of rule. For the few years when Park closed the legislature, the economy grew on average 4.22 percent. For most of his tenure, how-ever, Park allowed for nominally democratic institutions, and average growth was over 9 percent. Mobutu's record, however, appears mixed. Beginning in 1967, Mobutu governed with the Popular Movement of the Revolution for over twenty years. During this period, average growth was a paltry 0.88 percent. Yet when Mobutu finally ended the one-party system in 1990, growth rates turned negative, with an aver-age of −4.84. Part of the reason for this downturn was the increase in insurgent activity culminating in Mobutu's overthrow in 1997. To iso-late the effect of institutions from other factors influencing economic performance, then, regression analysis is necessary.

5.3 ALTERNATIVE THEORETICAL FRAMEWORKS

The politics of economic development has been examined through a variety of lenses. Literatures on single-party regimes, state autonomy, and ideological commitment offer alternative explanations and predic-tions about economic growth under dictatorships. Before turning to the empirical results that will speak to these theories, I provide a brief summary of these alternative claims.

5.3.1 Mobilization Power of Single-Party Regimes

For late developing countries, the state was supposed to be the leader of efforts to catch up with the developed world. The state would not only correct for traditional market failures but also coordinate investment and allocate resources to eliminate bottlenecks in production (Gerschenkron 1962, Hirschman 1970, Murphy et al. 1989, Rosenstein-Rodan 1943).

Before centrally planned economies under communism stagnated, the regime party was supposed to be the state's instrument to make the "big push" and lead countries into the modern era (Apter 1965, Huntington 1970). As Kalyvas observes, the single party "represent[ed] the efforts of leaders of 'more modern' social forces to suppress 'more backward' social forces on the way to modernity" (Kalyvas 1999: 328).

The official party would be useful for the project of development in a number of ways. First, the party would serve as a corporatist form in which interest groups could have their interests heard and in which they could be persuaded to moderate their demands for consumption. In Mexico, for example, a direct Political Agreement in addition to informal links between the PRI and the umbrella organization encompassing most major unions, the *Congreso del Trabajo*, enabled the regime to claim the support of almost 80 percent of the unionized labor force. In this case, the party could claim to represent the interests of workers but also "persuade" them to cooperate with the needs of the state's plans for development. Second, hegemonic parties directly would carry out the regime's plans for directing investment and labor. Party members were expected to "play an active entrepreneurial role in the formation of new ideas, in the establishment of a network of communication for those ideas, and in the linking of the public and the leadership in such a way that power is generated, mobilized and directed" (Apter 1965: 186). Indeed, as Kenyatta's and Nyerere's statements illustrate, Lenin's invention was copied throughout the developing world for precisely these reasons.

The power of the single party to serve as a conduit of information and more importantly, to mobilize resources led both public officials and scholars to believe that single-party states would experience rapid economic growth. The Soviet Union's rapid recovery from war and industrialization only seemed to confirm this expectation. The conclusion, then, would be to expect that single-party states would experience the highest rates of economic growth.

5.3.2 State Autonomy

The fall of communism and exposure of the failures of centralized planning, however, cast doubt on the utility of regime parties in facilitating development. In addition, recognition of the East Asian "miracle" led to the emergence of a new theoretical paradigm. Scholars of economies in the region argue that rapid growth was possible because governments were able to insulate themselves from interest group pressures for redistributive policies that ultimately hurt growth of the overall economy. In this account, special interests are pernicious in that they lobby for policies that provide only selective benefits and harm the collective good. Because public officials are at risk of being "captured" by special interests, the state can intervene effectively in the economy only by insulating itself against these groups and developing its own goals and modes of operation. In this regard, authoritarian states have advantages over democratic ones as Haggard (1990: 262) points out:

> Since authoritarian political arrangements give political elites autonomy from distributionist pressures, they increase the government's ability to extract resources, provide public goods, and impose the short-term costs associated with efficient economic adjustment. Weak legislatures that limit the representative role of parties, the corporatist organization of interest groups, and recourse to coercion in the face of resistance should all expand governments' freedom to maneuver on economic policy.

In a similar vein, advocates of "embedded autonomy" argue that the complete separation of policy-makers from society would result in inefficiencies due to informational asymmetries and rent-seeking by unchecked bureaucrats. Therefore, the state should have the autonomy to act but should remain connected to society.

The conditions under which embedded autonomy exists are fairly specific. As Evans (1989: 575) explains: "[E]mbedded autonomy depends on the existence of a project shared by a highly developed bureaucratic apparatus with interventive capacity built on historical experience and a relatively organized set of private actors who can provide useful intelligence and a possibility of decentralized implementation." Yet the types of constructive links between the state and society that facilitate growth are not thought to occur through institutions such as legislatures and parties. As a result, the state autonomy literature leads to an empirical prediction of rapid growth for noninstitutionalized dictatorships.

5.3.3   Importance of Noninstitutionalized Factors

The claim that countries such as South Korea grew because the state developed bureaucratic autonomy and established meritocratic means of advancement whereas states such as Zaire did not only begs the question of why Park and his successors chose to establish this type of institutional apparatus, whereas Mobutu did not. Arguably, the motives and preferences of rulers may explain this difference – especially in dictatorships where rulers face few institutional constraints on behavior. So in contrast to Mobutu, Park may have had a developmental outlook, prioritizing economic development due to the exigencies of nation-building or of catching up to developed countries.

The goal of economic development sometimes is accompanied by concern about political development. Some dictators clearly view their regimes as necessary, but transitory, periods for improving the political and economic climate of their countries. President Ernesto Geisel, for example, gave a speech before the Brazilian cabinet in 1974, describing the improvement in economic conditions over the past ten years that was a result of the military's prioritization of development. In addition, he explained: " ... In regard to domestic politics, we shall welcome sincere movements toward gradual but sure democratic progress, expanding honest and mutually respectful dialogue and encouraging more participation from responsible elites and from the people in general ... " (quoted in Loveman and Davies 1989: 232).

As Geisel went on to clarify: "One must not accuse this doctrine of being antidemocratic when ... it is essentially aiming at perfecting, in realistic terms, democratic practices and adapting them in a way better suited to the characteristics of our people and to the current stage of the social and political revolution of the country ... " (quoted in Loveman and Davies 1989: 232–233). President Francisco Morales Bermudez in Peru similarly emphasized how "tutelary" rule would proceed in stages: "... our revolution cannot be imposed by blood and fire... ... the most acute problem which a movement such as ours has to face is how to carry out profound structural change while still guaranteeing personal freedom. The solution we have found is gradualism" (quoted in Loveman and Davies 1989: 261).

As the words of both Geisel and Morales Bermudez show, however, some dictators appear to be "enlightened" in that they seek both to improve economic conditions and to gradually reintroduce democratic institutions. They may even view the two goals as linked, using institutions, such as legislatures and political parties, to facilitate economic growth. As a result, our empirical methods must sort out the confounding effects of institutions and motives.

In the next section, I examine the effect of nominally democratic institutions on economic growth using a conventional linear regression model and then a Heckman selection model to take into account the possible importance of unobservable factors such as motives.

5.4 INSTITUTIONS AND ECONOMIC GROWTH

The analysis employs cross-sectional time-series data to exploit the variation in institutions and growth rates across both countries and years. This variation is evident in a comparison between dictatorships with and without institutions. Dictatorships without institutions experienced average growth of 3.32 percent (standard deviation = 7.01; $N = 314$), whereas those with a single institution grew on average 4.44 percent (s.d. = 7.74; $N = 450$). The average growth rate of broadened dictatorships is 4.61 percent (s.d. = 7.35; $N = 523$). The differences in average growth rates across institutional arrangements are small, whereas the standard deviations are relatively large. As a result, it seems that institutions under dictatorship do not have a significant impact on economic growth. The assumption, however, is that the conditions of regimes that have institutions match exactly the conditions of those regimes that do not.

Another alternative is to exploit the variation in institutional arrangements within the spell of a single regime. Consider, for example, the nineteen-year regime of Mathieu Kérékou in Benin. He steadily institutionalized after initially governing without institutions for several years. Without institutions, average growth was 1.74 percent. With a legislature and a single party, Benin's economy experienced average growth of 3.57 percent. Once he allowed for multiple legislature parties, for the one year in which data exist, growth was 1.22 percent. For the before-after approach, the sample includes only those dictatorships that changed institutions, and the effect of institutions is measured as the difference between the average growth of regimes before and after the introduction of institutions. Without institutions, these dictatorships grew on average 3.93 percent (s.d. = 6.22; $N = 263$). Once they became narrow dictatorships, their average growth rate was 3.97 percent (s.d. = 8.20; $N = 559$), whereas under a full set of institutions, average growth was 4.68 percent (s.d. = 7.28; $N = 398$). Here the differences-in-means are even smaller than in the with-without comparison, indicating little significant effect of institutions on economic performance. The assumption of this approach, however, is that conditions over time have not changed. Because both the with-without and the before-after approaches make strong assumptions about the randomness of outside conditions, regression analysis is necessary to determine the effect of institutions.

5.4.1 Model Specification

Output is modeled as a function of productive inputs:

$$Y = AK^{\alpha}L^{\beta},$$

where K stands for capital stock, L for labor in productive activities, and A for the degree of technical knowledge in the economy. α and β denote the relative importance of capital and labor, respectively, in production. From this production function comes the reduced-form growth equation (i subscript suppressed):

$$\frac{\Delta Y_t}{Y_t} = \frac{\Delta A_t}{A_t} + \alpha \frac{\Delta K_t}{K_t} + \beta \frac{\Delta L_t}{L_t} + \epsilon.$$

$\Delta A_t / A_t$, or technical progress, is treated as a constant, whereas α and β are the estimates of the efficiency with which capital and labor are used to produce output.

Specifications of reduced-form growth models, however, are the subject of controversy. Everything from government spending to war has exhibited some significant correlation to growth although the robustness of results is suspect (Levine and Renelt 1992, Sala-I-Martin 1997). After testing the effect of institutions on growth in a barebones model, I control for a variety of economic and political factors. The rationale for their inclusion and their measurement are discussed below.

5.4.2 Data

The dependent variable is *Growth of total output* (PPP dollars) as constructed from Penn World Table's (version 6.1) figures for per capita income and population growth. For the postwar sample of dictatorships, the data series covers 102 countries for the period 1951 to 2000.

As in the previous chapter, the independent variable of primary interest is *Institutions*, coded 2 if the dictatorship has a legislature with multiple political parties (i.e., broadened dictatorship), 1 if the regime party controls all legislative seats (i.e., narrow dictatorship), and 0 if either parties are not allowed within the assembly or the legislature is closed (e.g., noninstitutionalized dictatorship).

In the barebones model, growth of output is determined by growth of two productive inputs, *Capital stock growth* and *Labor force growth*. Both variables are constructed with Penn World Tables data with missing values of the former filled by imputation (details are in Przeworski et al. 2000). Both factors are expected to have a positive effect on the growth of output.

In addition to labor and physical capital, human capital is also an essential component for growth (Mankiw et al. 1992; although see Benhabib and Spiegel 1994 and Pritchett 2001 for dissenting views). The variable *Education growth* measures the annual rate of growth of the cumulative years of education of the average member of the labor force. Like the other factors of production, increases in human capital are expected to lead to increases in income growth.

Initial conditions are an important determinant of growth rates. Classical growth theory predicts that poor countries should grow faster than wealthy ones, leading to zero long-term growth and consequently, convergence in levels of income. In contrast, endogenous growth models predict that impoverished countries will find it difficult to catch up with wealthier states. The differing theories, however, are in agreement about the importance of initial levels of wealth in determining rates of return to capital and subsequent output growth. As a proxy for initial conditions, *Per capita income* is included.

Government spending may be an important determinant of growth although there are conflicting theories of its predicted effect. On the one hand, too much government intervention in the economy may crowd out private investment, leading to a potential decline in growth. In addition, governments may misallocate resources to projects that do not facilitate development. On the other hand, the state has an important role to play in overcoming coordination failures common to underdeveloped economies (Gerschenkron 1962, Grossman 1990, Hirschman 1970). To the extent that public resources are spent on correcting market failures, higher government expenditures may lead to higher growth (Cheibub and Przeworski 1997, Ram 1986). Consequently, the annual change in the central government's share of GDP is included to capture these effects.

International trade allows countries to capitalize on their comparative advantages. State can develop specializations and achieve growth of output and income by trading their products with each other. The East Asian miracles, for example, have demonstrated how export-oriented production can serve as an engine of growth (Haggard 1990, World Bank 1993). In addition to the evidence from particular cases, cross-national analysis reveals a link between trade and growth (Frankel and Romer 1999; for a dissenting view, see Edwards 1993). To capture the effects of trade on growth, the annual change in a country's exports and imports as a percentage of nominal GDP is included. *Trade growth* is expected to have a positive sign.

Participation in agreements with the International Monetary Fund may affect countries' development trajectories. The conditionality of loans may force governments to eliminate wasteful spending with positive effects for growth. In the effort to trim budgets, however, governments may allocate fewer resources to education and infrastructure – the inputs needed for growth. Khan (1990) and Conway (1994) find that IMF programs have no negative effects on growth. Vreeland (2003: 122), however, shows that countries under IMF agreement have growth rates that on average are 1.5 percent lower than if they had not been under agreement. To control for the impact of IMF agreements, *IMF program*, a dummy variable coded 1 for the country-years when there was an IMF agreement in force, and 0 otherwise, is included. Based on Vreeland's findings, the effect of IMF programs on growth is expected to be negative.

War, whether internal or interstate, is probably the most significant political factor affecting economic growth. Conflict leads to immediate destruction of infrastructure, diversion of public expenditures to nonproductive activities, and dissaving on the part of private investors (Collier 1999). *War*, a dummy variable indicating whether a civil or interstate war is occurring within a country's own territory, is expected to have a negative coefficient.

The type of dictatorship also may determine the commitment and ability of authoritarian governments to promote economic development. Many military leaders seize power during times of economic crisis on the grounds that they can better promote the "national interest" than corrupt civilian politicians (Brooker 2000). Furthermore, the armed forces under military regimes may be used to facilitate development. Under Suharto, for example, the Indonesian army was involved in nearly one-fifth of all economic activity. As a result, growth may be higher in military regimes. The dummy variables, *Military dictator* and *Monarch*, indicate the types of authoritarian regime, with civilian dictatorships forming the residual category.

Table 5.1 shows descriptive statistics for these variables that will be used in reduced-form growth regressions. All of the independent variables are lagged by one year except for *IMF program*, *War*, *Military dictator*, and *Monarch*. Because a number of the economic control variables come from the World Bank with data coverage commencing no earlier than 1960, their inclusion reduces the size of the sample.

5.4.3   Effect of Institutions: Results from Random Effects Models

Table 5.2 shows the results of the reduced-form growth regressions when country heterogeneity is accounted for by the use of random effects models. Column 1 in the table shows the results of the barebones model: the regression of annual rate of growth of per capita income

TABLE 5.1. *Descriptive Statistics of Variables in Economic Growth Analysis*

Variable	Mean	Standard Deviation	Minimum	Maximum	Cases
Total income growth$_t$	4.272	7.700	−59.274	80.577	2702
Institutions$_{t-1}$	0.979	0.817	0	2	4443
Capital stock growth$_{t-1}$	7.354	14.469	−72.266	139.389	2452
Labor force growth$_{t-1}$	2.254	1.835	−32.447	22.780	2412
Education growth$_{t-1}$	4.912	9.417	−33.333	303.448	1734
Per capita income$_{t-1}$/1000	2.836	2.546	0.281	24.939	2763
Government expenditure growth$_{t-1}$	0.196	3.339	−32.840	32.527	2679
Trade growth$_{t-1}$	0.697	9.724	−98.982	82.147	2679
IMF program$_t$	0.248	0.432	0	1	4439
War$_t$	0.106	0.308	0	1	4588
Military dictator$_t$	0.344	0.475	0	1	4588
Monarch$_t$	0.147	0.354	0	1	4588

on institutions, controlling for the growth rates of capital stock and labor force. The coefficient on *Institutions* is positive and statistically significant even after controlling for observable conditions related to capital and labor.

Column 2 of Table 5.2 shows the results after inclusion of other political control variables: IMF agreement, conflict, and the type of dictator. In this model, the growth of capital stock has a positive effect on the growth of income, whereas participation in IMF programs lowers growth by almost 1 percent. As expected, conflict has the most devastating impact on the economy; interstate or civil war reduces growth by over 2 percent in a given year. Military dictators are not more likely than other types of rulers to have the motives or capacity to promote development but monarchs do. Furthermore, the positive and statistically significant coefficient of *Monarch* is not an artifact of the natural resource wealth of many contemporary monarchies. Because growth data are missing for the monarchies of the Persian Gulf, of the six countries that have experienced royal rule that are included in the sample, only one (Iran under the Shah) has significant resource wealth. Indeed, substitution of an indicator of natural resources for *Monarch* shows no effect of resources alone on growth of output. Finally, the positive and significant impact of *Institutions* remains even after inclusion of various political control variables that have

TABLE 5.2. *Effect of Institutions on Economic Growth*

	Column 1	Column 2	Column 3
Institutions$_{t-1}$	0.381**	0.476**	0.473**
	(0.188)	(0.211)	(0.214)
Capital stock growth$_{t-1}$	0.058***	0.052***	0.059***
	(0.015)	(0.051)	(0.019)
Labor force growth$_{t-1}$	0.095	0.112	0.150
	(0.088)	(0.085)	(0.101)
Education growth$_{t-1}$			−0.021
			(0.013)
Per capita income$_{t-1}$			−0.045
			(0.071)
Gov't expend. growth$_{t-1}$			−0.025
			(0.132)
Trade growth$_{t-1}$			0.024
			(0.023)
IMF program$_t$		−0.890***	−1.103***
		(0.324)	(0.338)
War$_t$		−2.118***	−1.869***
		(0.579)	(0.623)
Military dictator$_t$		0.180	0.183
		(0.352)	(0.372)
Monarch$_t$		1.535**	1.260*
		(0.644)	(0.671)
Constant	3.467***	3.686***	3.901***
	(0.354)	(0.491)	(0.569)
N	2069	2069	1565

Standard errors in parentheses.
*** $p < 0.01$; ** $p < 0.05$; * $p < 0.10$.

measurable effects themselves. A one-step increase in the degree of institutionalization leads to a 0.48-percent increase in the growth of total output.

The last column in Table 5.2 provides the results in a smaller sample due to the inclusion of additional economic control variables: education, per capita income, government consumption, and trade openness. Of the battery of economic controls, only increases in capital stock continue to exert significant positive effects on growth of output. The magnitude and significance of the effect of conflict remains strong, whereas the results concerning IMF programs are consistent with those in Vreeland's (2003) study. *Institutions* continues to have a positive impact on growth.

5.4.4 Effect of Institutions: Results from Heckman Selection Model

Determining the effects of political institutions on economic growth is difficult for a number of reasons. Economic development is a process of indeterminate duration, obfuscating the precise effect of institutions (Pritchett 2000). In addition, political and economic processes clearly have simultaneous impacts, and many factors that determine growth, including institutions, are endogenous (Przeworski 2005).

The literature on the developmental state points to the significance of one of these problems. In the contrast between Park and Mobutu, institutions do clearly have an explanatory role: countries such as South Korea grew because the state developed bureaucratic autonomy and established meritocratic means of advancement, whereas states such as Zaire did not. But the assertion only begs the question of why Park and his successors chose to establish this type of institutional apparatus, whereas Mobutu did not.

The difference, ultimately, may be due to motivations. So in contrast to Mobutu or Ferdinand Marcos of the Philippines, who sought only to pilfer from their national coffers, some authoritarian rulers, such as Park and Lee Kuan Yew in Singapore, have a developmental outlook to which their countries' miraculous growth is sometimes attributed. Similarly, for some dictators the goal of economic development is accompanied by concerns over the creation of efficacious political institutions. They may even view the two goals as linked, using institutions, such as legislatures and political parties, to facilitate economic growth.

Methods that take into account of only observable conditions, however, run squarely into the problem of unobserved heterogeneity among dictators. There are observable systematic reasons for why dictators have institutions, but the dictators with "enlightened" motives show that unobservable conditions also may influence both decisions to allow for somewhat pluralist institutions and to prioritize economic growth. In other words, dictators who allow multiple parties to operate within a legislature may be "unusual" or "selective" in that they are the rulers who care about economic development as well. If true, the effects of these unobservable motives must be separated from the effects of institutions to determine the true effect of institutions on growth.

Achen (1986) notes that the effects of selection bias can be avoided in regression analysis if and only if the unobserved factors influencing selection are uncorrelated with the unobserved factors influencing outcomes. This condition holds only if the decision to have institutions and the decision to prioritize economic growth are made independently. In other words, methods that rely on observable factors will yield unbiased estimates only if dictators never have "tutelary" motives.

Because dictators may vary in their motives, with some "enlightened" more than others, a selection model can determine the extent to which the decision to institutionalize and to facilitate economic growth are linked. Heckman's two-step selection model is one way of modeling this relationship (Heckman 1979). It consists of first estimating

$$Pr(\text{Institutions}_{it} = j) = \alpha Z_{it} + v_{it},$$

where i stands for country, t for year, and $j = 0, 1, 2$, where j stands for the degree of institutionalization. Z is a vector of exogenous independent variables. In this case, the first-stage selection equation is modeled using the ordered probit analysis from Chapter 3. The model produces inverse Mill ratios, λ_{itj}, which serve as a proxy for v_{it}, or those unobserved factors (such as motives) that influence the development of political institutions and growth of income. λ_{itj} is included in the second-stage performance equation along with X_{it}, a vector of independent variables affecting the outcome of interest:

$$Y_{itj} = \gamma_j X_{itj} + \theta_j \lambda_{itj} + \epsilon_{itj}.$$

This equation, then, is estimated separately for each j subsample. For example, for the subsample, $j = 0$, or dictatorships without institutions, we obtain an unbiased estimate of γ_0 due to the inclusion of λ_{it0}. The estimate, $\widehat{\gamma}_0$, is then applied to the entire sample to create $\widehat{Y}_{it0} = \widehat{\gamma}_0 X_{it}$. For each observation, $\widehat{Y}_{it0}$ tells us what the value of Y would have been in that country-year had $j = 0$ or had the dictatorship had no institutions. The average of all the values of $\widehat{Y}_{it0}$ is simply the average of these counterfactual observations, or the "average value of Y had all observations existed under no institutions." The procedure is repeated for $j = 1$ and $j = 2$, producing average values of Y had all observations existed under those degrees of institutionalization, respectively.

TABLE 5.3. *Heckman Second-Stage Growth Model*

	No Institutions	Single Institution	Multiple Institutions
Capital stock growth$_{t-1}$	−0.005	0.115***	0.071***
	(0.022)	(0.035)	(0.024)
Labor force growth$_{t-1}$	0.049	−0.064	0.682***
	(0.138)	(0.194)	(0.247)
IMF program$_t$	−0.606	−0.256	−0.595
	(0.711)	(0.827)	(0.559)
War$_t$	−2.746**	−0.739	−0.513
	(1.067)	(1.447)	(0.938)
Military dictator$_t$	−0.114	−1.116	0.619
	(1.231)	(1.042)	(0.796)
Monarch$_t$	2.033	−0.122	−2.002
	(1.648)	(5.386)	(1.957)
λ	−0.808	0.863	1.033
	(1.130)	(1.331)	(1.086)
Constant	3.820**	4.931**	4.032**
	(1.788)	(2.008)	(1.827)
N	513	368	412
$\widehat{Y}$	3.445	4.794	6.119
Standard deviation	(1.060)	(1.652)	(1.728)

Standard errors in parentheses except for the numbers in parentheses in the last row.
*** $p < 0.001$; ** $p < 0.01$; * $p < 0.05$.

Table 5.3 provides the second-stage regressions of the Heckman model for the specification used in Column 2 of Table 5.2. Recall that λ_{itj}, which was generated by the first-stage ordered probit model of institutions, serves as a proxy for those unobserved factors (such as motives) that influence the development of political institutions and growth of income. As such, it serves as an instrument for *Institutions*.

At the bottom of the first column in Table 5.3 is the predicted average rate of growth of all dictatorships in the sample (1,293 observations) if they all had been noninstitutionalized.[1] This average is calculated by using the coefficients displayed in this first column.

---

[1] Even though both this model and that in Column 2 of Table 5.2 have the same specification, the former includes fewer observations due to missing data in the first-stage institutions model.

Similarly, at the bottom of Column 2, 4.79 percent is the predicted averaged growth rate of all dictatorships if they had a regime party and a legislature. The difference in growth under a narrowly institutionalized dictatorship and a noninstitutionalized regime is 1.35 percent and statistically significant (standard error of the difference is 0.055). Finally, the highest average growth would have occurred under dictatorships with a full panoply of legislative and partisan institutions. Had all dictatorships been fully institutionalized with multiple parties within a legislature, their total outputs would have grown an average of 6.12 percent. Again, the differences in predicted average growth rates between broadened dictatorships and other regime forms are statistically significant. Allowing into the legislature parties other than the one representing the regime is correlated with a 1.33 percent increase in growth (standard error of the difference is 0.066). Once the conditions under which institutions exist are taken into account and control variables included, the selection-corrected averages across the table show that institutionalized regimes grow faster than their noninstitutionalized counterparts.

5.4.5   Conclusion

The analysis in the chapter provides evidence that dictatorships with nominally democratic institutions experience better economic performance in terms of the growth of total output. The impact of institutions remains strong even after including a variety of economic and political control variables and using econometric models that handle the endogeneity of institutions. Whether institutions are treated as an exogenous factor or as endogenous to unobservable motives that also may influence economic development, they exhibit a substantive effect on the growth rates of nondemocracies.

Before reviewing the substantive findings, one note, pertaining to claims made in previous chapters, is in order. Recall that the theory about institutionalization in Chapter 3 rests on the claim that policy concessions occur within institutions. Dictators face different severity of threat and need for cooperation. These conditions motivate their concessions to the potential opposition in terms of policy and rents. Rents may be distributed in a variety of ways, but policy concessions, I argue, are best organized with parties within legislatures. In this claim,

I differ with much of the extant literature on nondemocracies that claims that legislatures and parties are used only for the distribution of patronage.

Yet the fact that broadened dictatorships experience higher rates of growth potentially confirms that institutions are being used to facilitate policy concessions and not rents. If dictatorial legislatures and parties are only to lower the costs of exchanging support for the dictator for spoils to domestic groups, then rent-seeking should be highest in broadened dictatorships. Yet several studies show rent-seeking to be detrimental to growth (Bardhan 1997, Mauro 1995), in which case we should have observed lower growth under institutionalized dictatorships. This, however, is not the case. Consequently, the correlation between institutions and growth indirectly supports the notion that dictatorial legislatures and parties serve as more than just patronage machines but are the arena in which policy compromises emerge.

In showing that a panoply of legislative parties are compatible with economic development, the findings speak to a variety of work related to modernization and state autonomy. Because dictatorships that allows for multiple political parties experience higher economic development, it is clear that the single party is not always in the vanguard of modernization. The poor economic performance of single-party states may be due to several reasons. It may be that constricting pluralism has ill effects on the amount of information that government officials have in formulating and implementing policy. It also may be the case that private agents are reluctant to invest in productive activities because a single party cannot guarantee political stability or the credibility of its commitments. Finally, that single-party states experience lower growth than broadened dictatorships may be due to an overly centralized economy that produces bad policies and in turn, bad incentives for owners of capital and labor (Ericson 1991). Because so many regime parties in the developing world emerged in emulation of the Leninist model and adopted its ideological and economic trappings as well, it is difficult to parse out the independent effects of single parties and of centralized economic systems on development.

Yet the results also show that broadened dictatorships experience higher growth that noninstitutionalized regimes. A correlation between noninstitutionalization and type of economic system is unlikely, lending credence to the importance of institutions in accounting for growth.

To the extent that the paucity of nominally democratic institutions allows for state autonomy, the results confirm a point that has been made in the voluminous literature on regime type and growth: the autonomy of the executive in dictatorships is harmful for growth. The results speak to the literature on state autonomy, questioning whether the links between state and society must always be corrosive.

The findings here are more in line with more recent work that stresses the economic benefits of more inclusive regimes (Bueno de Mesquita et al. 2003, McGuire and Olson 1996, Olson 1993). The general idea is that a broader inclusion of society and its interests within the regime facilitates better economic performance. The mechanisms underlying this correlation are as yet unclear. One possibility is that when outside groups have some access to decision-making – even if limited – they may be more willing to make costly and longer term investments because these institutions constitute somewhat of a commitment that, even if not entirely credible, is better than nothing. Another possibility is that institutions facilitate the flow of information between the regime and domestic groups so that resources are mobilized and allocated more efficiently. Finally, it may be that because institutions provide a forum in which the requests of domestic groups can be made, those demands are not likely to be made in the street. Future work lies in determining which mechanisms allow for institutions under dictatorship to improve economic performance.

6

Institutions and the Survival of Dictators

6.1 INTRODUCTION

Some dictators rule so long that they are feared even after their deaths, whereas others fall almost immediately. Sobhuza II reigned over Swaziland sixty-two years; Haile Selassie of Ethiopia ruled for forty-seven years. Even those without royal blood can hold onto power for ages: Kim Il Sung died in 1994 after forty-seven years in power. Even in death he remains the Eternal Leader. Yet for every Kim Il Sung, there is a Léon Cantave, the first of many who tried to take power in 1957 in Haiti: he lasted five days. Why do some dictators survive for decades, whereas others fall soon after taking power?

The force of tradition or legitimacy from religious or other sources may play a role in the survival of some rulers, particularly monarchs. But, then again, it was not enough to save Libya's King Idriss, Egypt's King Fuad II, or Iraq's King Faisal II from being deposed in military coups. Similarly, charismatic or personalistic leadership is frequently evoked to explain the maintenance of power in sub-Saharan Africa (Bratton and Van de Walle 1997; Jackson and Rosberg 1982, 1984). Yet, along with Southeast Asia and the Middle East and North Africa, this region has one of the highest turnover rates of dictatorial rulers.

Alternatively, the long tenure of some dictators is attributed to their overwhelming monopoly of force. It is certainly true that many long-standing dictators headed some of the most repressive regimes on Earth: Stalin remained in power for thirty-one years and Mao ruled over China for thirty-three years; each was responsible for millions of deaths. Yet life under short-lived dictators can be equally brutal. Within three years, over two million Cambodians perished in Pol Pot's killing fields. In addition, sometimes dictators survive in power by relaxing repression and establishing a material basis for consent. "Goulash communism" in Hungary kept Janos Kadar in power for thirty-two years, whereas Lee Kuan Yew brought the "Second Industrial Revolution" to Singapore and remained in office for thirty-one years.

We know that for any ruler, dictatorial or democratic, the ability to navigate among various political forces and to build crucial coalitions is important for the maintenance of power (Bueno de Mesquita et al. 2003). But although democratic leaders have properly constituted institutions and rules by which they can establish coalitions, the channels through which dictators consolidate support over time remain opaque. The issue to be examined here, then, is whether nominally democratic institutions can help authoritarian rulers maintain coalitions and survive in power.

Dictators face two types of threats to their rule: those that emerge from within the ruling elite and those that come from outsiders within society. Dictators establish smaller institutions, such as consultative councils, juntas, and political bureaus, as a first institutional trench against threats from the ruling elite. But when dictators need to neutralize threats from larger groups within society and solicit the cooperation of outsiders, they rely on nominally democratic institutions, such as legislatures and political parties. Dictators who are more dependent on outsiders and face stronger opposition must institutionalize significantly, whereas those rulers who have little need for cooperation and face weak opposition institutionalize little or not at all. But because the institutions we observe are supposed to be rulers' best responses to the conditions they face, absent unforeseen events, we should not observe that institutionalized rulers survive significantly longer in power than their uninstitutionalized counterparts. Conditioning on exogenous factors, then, institutions should not have a significant impact on the survival of dictators. If they do, then the account of institutional formation in Chapter 3 requires revision.

To test this argument, I proceed as follows. First, I review the arguments made in earlier chapters about the challenges dictators face and their institutional responses. Then, I draw implications for the survival of dictators that are tested using event history analysis for all postwar authoritarian rulers. The chapter ends with a brief conclusion.

6.2 MANAGING POLITICAL SURVIVAL

Dictators leave power in many different ways. Some die quietly in their sleep, to be succeeded by their sons or other hand-picked successors. Many monarchs leave power in this way, though Kim Il Sung and Hafez Assad prove that royal blood is not necessary to carry out familial succession. Some are forced into political oblivion under the formal rules of dictatorship: the case in point being Mexican presidents (Casteñeda 2000).

Some are overthrown by a popular revolution, like Mohammad Reza Pahlevi, or forced to flee under an imminent threat of one, like Ferdinand Marcos. Some are removed by a decision of their closest collaborators: this was the normal *modus operandi* of communist regimes after the death of Stalin. Some may also be killed by some of their most trusted lieutenants. Park in South Korea was assassinated by the head of his own intelligence services; several African dictators, most recently Laurent Kabila in the Democratic Republic of Congo, were shot by their own bodyguards. When Garcia Marquez's dictator in *The Autumn of the Patriarch* checks several times that all doors and windows to his palace are bolted from the inside or when Rafael Trujillo in Vargas Llosa's *The Feast of the Goat* orders to kill his closest confidant, they appear paranoid. But if so many dictators are paranoid, it is for good reasons: their enemies are many, both within the ruling elite and among outsiders in society.

As proof that dictators have much to fear from those within their own ruling coterie, one need only look at who succeeds whom. Monarchs are often threatened by their family members, who are the only people legitimately qualified to succeed them: approximately seven of ten monarchs who did not die on the throne were overthrown by their kin. In 1995, for example, Sheikh Hamad bin Khalifa al-Thani of Qatar, the forty-five-year-old son of the ruling emir, Sheikh Khalifa, ousted his father, who was vacationing in Switzerland. Military dictators, in turn, have mainly other military to fear. In Guatemala, power changed hands between various military factions thirteen times

TABLE 6.1. *Replacement of Dictators by Type*

Type of Current Dictator	Type of Successor				
	Monarch	Military	Civilian	Democrat	Total
Monarch	24	6	4	1	35
Military	0	100	46	58	204
Civilian	2	60	158	33	253
Total	26	166	208	92	491

since World War II. Even after devising explicit rules of alternation for the presidency of the junta prior to the 1976 coup, the heads of the service branches in Argentina violated them as General Viola ousted General Videla only to be deposed by General Galtieri. Finally, civilian dictators must fear almost everyone: the military, leaders of their own party who are only too eager to replace them, as well as democrats. Recall the table from from Chapter 1, showing who replaces whom (Table 6.1).

The table shows the type of dictator governing in a given year and his successor's type. Included are authoritarian leaders who exited from power due to ouster or natural death. In almost 19 percent of cases, authoritarian rulers step down to usher in democracy. But usually, they are succeeded by other dictators of their own type.

As a result, consultative councils, juntas, and political bureaus are the first institutional trench for dictators. These smaller institutions neutralize threats from within the ruling elite. But their efforts to co-opt the ruling class are not always successful, as demonstrated by the fates of Park, Kabila, and many others. Therefore, we should not expect dictators to retain power forever, even if they are able to perfectly co-opt outsiders through their second institutional trench: legislatures and parties.

Legislatures and parties are designed to co-opt larger segments of society rather than the ruling elite. Assemblies serve as a controlled forum in which groups make their demands and negotiate with the regime over limited policy concessions. Parties provide a system for career advancement and the distribution of spoils. Together, these institutions provide the means through which authoritarian leaders can offer policy and material concessions to maintain coalitions when conditions dictate their necessity. Dictators forge compromises and consequently, have institutions when they need the cooperation of outsiders and when the potential opposition is strong.

Through a variety of means, dictators are able to observe and determine with some accuracy the conditions under which they need these institutions. One of the primary roles of the secret police, for example, is to provide information about the extent of support for and dissent against the regime. Infamous examples of their work abound. The *Stasi* kept files on six million East Germans or almost one-third of the population. Operation Condor formalized intelligence-sharing among the United States and military regimes in Argentina, Brazil, Bolivia, Chile, Paraguay, and Uruguay in the 1970s (Dingis 2004). In Paraguay alone, over five tons of reports and photos were collected during General Stroessner's thirty-five-year-rule. Certainly the security apparatus plays an active role in repression, but its information-gathering function is just as important.

Electoral contests, even if seemingly fraudulent, also provide information to the regime. For example, when Leopold Senghor ran in Senegal's first presidential election after independence, his *Union Populaire Senegalaise* (UPS) was able to insure that he received almost unanimous acclaim from voters. Two elections later, he could claim only 82.2 percent of votes. After stepping down, his hand-picked successor, Abdou Diouf, also garnered increasingly smaller vote shares: from 84.2 percent in 1983 to 73.2 percent in 1988 and finally, 58.4 percent in 1993. Even if incumbents manage to cajole and steal enough votes to obtain a majority, slowly declining vote shares in successive elections may convey a number of important pieces of information for the regime. First, these successive results may indicate diminishing support within the electorate. Second, they demonstrate the increasing inability of the regime to intimidate ordinary citizens into acquiescing in public displays of support. Moreover, electoral contests may display the opposition's ability to unite, providing rulers with information about its strength. In Kenya, for example, Jomo Kenyatta and his successor, Daniel Arap Moi, won successive elections in Kenya in part due to the inability of opposition parties to support a single challenger (Kasara 2005). Elections, then, provide a variety of information that allows the regime to assess the strength of the potential opposition in society – even if the signal is somewhat noisy due to attempts at manipulation and fraud.

As for the degree to which dictators may need the cooperation of others, the problem of observation is much simpler. Based on the type of economy, for example, autocrats can determine how much incentive they need to provide to citizens to engage in productive activity – the profits of which may be taxed. If a country derives most of its revenues from the sale of natural resources, then authoritarian incumbents need little cooperation from the private sector and labor in generating revenue. As discussed in Chapter 2, the case of the military government in Ecuador demonstrates the opposite case: when enclave industries do not dominate the economy, rulers must solicit the cooperation of entrepreneurs and workers to insure a productive economy. Alternatively, consider a country at war or one facing "systemic vulnerability" (Doner et al. 2005). In this case, a ruler needs to recruit soldiers and resources to defend the country. In all of these situations, then, rulers should be able to determine the degree to which they must seek the cooperation of groups outside the ruling elite because these conditions are exogenous and observable.

With institutions such as secret police and elections, many dictators can uncover with some accuracy the strength of the potential opposition so they can determine the degree of concessions necessary to neutralize dissent.[1] Given a country's economic structure and geopolitical position, authoritarian rulers can gauge how much they depend on larger groups within society. With this information, nondemocratic leaders are in a good position to determine the optimal degree of institutionalization. If few opponents to their rule exist and little help from outsiders is necessary, dictators will make few or no concessions and consequently, will not govern with legislatures or parties. If the incumbent must confront strong opposition and solicit cooperation, he must make more significant compromises on policy, which can be done only through institutions.

If the theory accurately characterizes institutionalization under dictatorship, then absent any exogenous shocks, the likelihood of survival for dictators both with and without institutions should not be

---

[1] Notable exceptions do exist because citizens have incentives for "preference falsification" (Kuran 1991). Kamiński (1999), for example, discusses the Polish case in which both the Communist government and Solidarity overestimated the degree of support for the former, leading to unexpected electoral results in 1989.

significantly different because the absence or presence of institutions is an optimal response to the degree of threat that dictators face and the amount of cooperation they need. In other words, dictators who face weak opposition, need little cooperation, and institutionalize little should survive in power for as long as rulers who institutionalize more as a response to stronger opposition and greater dependence on outside groups. Conversely, a strong, positive impact of institutions on tenure would suggest either that some dictators mistakenly are underinstitutionalizing or that institutionalization carries positive externalities for the tenure of dictators.

6.3 IMPACT OF INSTITUTIONS ON SURVIVAL

To determine the effect of legislative parties on the political survival of authoritarian rulers, I use event history analysis. A brief description of the model reveals the advantages of using this approach to analyze the question at hand.

6.3.1 Event History Analysis

Event history analysis is concerned with analyzing the time to the occurrence of an event. Consider, then, that while a dictator is in power, he exists in some state σ_0. While in this state, he may govern with or without institutions. Once the dictator loses power, however, he transitions to a new state σ_1. The transition in states, or the loss of political power, is the *event* of primary interest.

Let T be a random variable for duration of the risk period for this event occurring. The hazard rate, $h(t)$, then, expresses the instantaneous risk of the event occurring at time t. More formally, the hazard rate $h(t)$ is given as

$$h(t) = \lim_{t \to 0} \frac{P(t + \Delta t > T \geq t | T \geq t)}{\Delta t},$$

where $P(t + \Delta t > T \geq t | T \geq t)$ indicates the probability that the event occurs during the time interval $(t, t + \Delta t)$ given that the event has not yet occurred prior to time t. In other words, modeling $h(t)$ allows us to determine the likelihood that a dictator will lose power at some time t given that he has been in office up until that point in time. And because we are interested in whether institutions affect the incumbent's ability to remain in power, we model the hazard rate as a function of covariates, x_i, which include institutions:

$$h(t) = f(x_i) + \epsilon_i,$$

where i indicates individual dictators.

We can model this relationship with parametric event history models. The idea is similar to that of linear regression: we determine the effect of covariates (i.e., institutions) on an event (i.e., likelihood of losing power). The main difference, however, is that although in linear regression the residuals are assumed to be distributed normally, parametric models substitute the normality assumption with more appropriate distributional assumptions. If we think that an event has an instantaneous chance of occurring that is constant over time, then an exponential model is appropriate. If the likelihood of the event is monotonically increasing or decreasing with time, a Weibull model is preferred. A U-shaped likelihood calls for either a log-normal or a log-logistic model. The choice depends both on theoretical considerations and on results from diagnostic tests.[2]

Event history models are sometimes referred to as survival or duration models because determining the likelihood of an event or transition from state σ_0 to σ_1 (the dictator losing office) also implies the likelihood of remaining in the original state σ_0 (the incumbent surviving in power).

In fact, during the time period under analysis here, not all dictators lose power. For authoritarian rulers who survive in power as of 2002, they remain in the original state σ_0 and therefore do not experience the event of interest while they are under observation. These cases are right-censored observations in that we do not know if and when the event of interest – loss of power – occurs after the period of analysis. Obviously, these types of dictators should be distinguished from those who actually lose office while under observation. Event history

---

[2] It is possible to determine the effect of covariates on the survival or failure of dictators through semiparametric models, such as the Cox proportional hazards model. In the Cox model, because no distributional assumptions are made, estimation requires that there be at least two observations for every time period. Because the data on dictators frequently do not satisfy this requirement, I use parametric models whose distributional assumptions allow for more efficient estimation.

models conveniently take into consideration both types of observations in estimating the effects of covariates on the likelihood of the event occurring.

6.3.2 Data

The period under observation begins in 1946 or the year of independence for countries previously under colonial rule and ends in 2002. The unit of analysis is the individual dictator. Adhering to the country-year format of the data used in previous chapters, I identify the ruler governing as of December 31 in any given year and country. As a result, the sample consists of 558 dictators: 49 monarchs, 228 military rulers, and 281 civilian dictators. Some dictators in the sample have multiple spells, that is, reappear after losing power. There are twelve such cases, notably Pierre Buyoya in Burundi, Oswaldo Lopez Arellano in Honduras, Ne Win in Burma, and Wladyslaw Gomulka in Poland. They reappear as dictators, in contrast to the 7 dictators during this period who returned to power as democrats (e.g., Mathieu Kérékou in Benin, Olusegun Obasanjo in Nigeria, and Victor Paz Estenssoro in Bolivia). Each spell, however, is treated as if belonging to a new effective head of government.

The dependent variable is *Age*, or the number of years the autocrat has been in power.[3] Seventy-seven dictators begin the period of observation having already been in power for more than one year. Several of them are African leaders, such as Seretse Khama in Botswana and Felix Houphouet-Boigny in Cote d'Ivoire, who became president a few years before the end of colonial rule. Other rulers from countries that had long been independent were already in power for anywhere from two (e.g., General Salvador Castaneda Castro in El Salvador) to forty-eight years (e.g., King Sobhuza II in Swaziland) before the period of observation begins. None of these observations, however, are left-censored because the number of years they have been in power at the start date of the study is known.

Almost one-third are right-censored observations for one of two reasons. Eighty-one rulers were still in power as of the end of 2002. As discussed earlier, because during the period of observation we do not

---

[3] In the duration models, the dependent variable is the log of *Age*.

TABLE 6.2. *Life Table of Dictators in the Sample* [a,b,c]

Years	Enter	Censored	At Risk	Exited	Survival Rate	Hazard Rate
0.0–3.0	558	34	541	171	1.0000 (0.000)	0.1231 (0.009)
3.0–6.1	353	34	336	83	0.6839 (0.020)	0.0924 (0.010)
6.1–9.1	236	16	228	29	0.5150 (0.022)	0.0445 (0.008)
9.1–12.2	191	18	182	31	0.4495 (0.022)	0.0610 (0.011)
12.2–15.3	142	16	134	18	0.3729 (0.022)	0.0472 (0.011)
15.3–18.3	108	11	102	13	0.3228 (0.022)	0.0444 (0.012)
18.3–21.4	84	10	79	14	0.2819 (0.022)	0.0638 (0.017)
21.4–24.4	60	6	57	5	0.2319 (0.022)	0.0301 (0.013)
24.4–27.4	49	8	45	5	0.2116 (0.022)	0.0386 (0.017)
27.4–30.5	36	2	35	0	0.1881 (0.022)	0.0000 (0.000)
30.5–33.5	34	4	32	7	0.1881 (0.022)	0.0805 (0.030)
33.5–36.6	23	6	20	3	0.1469 (0.022)	0.0532 (0.031)
36.6–39.6	14	3	12	2	0.1249 (0.022)	0.0570 (0.040)
39.6–42.7	9	3	7	0	0.1049 (0.023)	0.0000 (0.000)
42.7–45.8	6	1	5	1	0.1049 (0.023)	0.0656 (0.065)
45.8–48.8	4	2	3	0	0.0858 (0.025)	0.0000 (0.000)
48.8–51.8	2	0	2	1	0.0858 (0.025)	0.2186 (0.206)
51.8–54.9	1	0	1	0	0.0429 (0.033)	0.0000 (0.000)
54.9–58.0	1	0	1	0	0.0429 (0.033)	0.0000 (0.000)
58.0–61.0	1	1	0	0	0.0429 (0.033)	0.0000 (0.000)

[a] Number of observations in stratum = 558
[b] Number of observations exiting = 383
[c] Number of observations censored = 175

observe the event of interest, their loss of power, these observations are treated differently. The remaining dictators are right-censored because they died while in office. Therefore, we do not know when they would have exited office had they not died. Because it is not always clear whether rulers have died naturally or "accidentally," all cases of death are treated similarly. Table 6.2 provides an actuarial table for the sample of dictators.

Based on the sample of 558 dictators, Table 6.2 provides nonparametric likelihoods of survival and failure (i.e., exit from office) without the effect of any covariates.[4] Almost one-third of all authoritarian rulers fall from power within three years. The long-surviving dictator is Sohuza II at 61 years. But these long-lasting dictators are rare;

---

[4] The life table is computed by the method of Cutler and Ederer (1958). See Greene (1998) for details.

median survival time is five years, whereas the average is just over nine years.

To determine the effect of institutions on the likelihood of maintain office, however, we must turn to parametric models. For this analysis, the dependent variable is the duration of rulers' tenure in power measured in calendar years. Results of the model indicate the effect of covariates on the likelihood of remaining in power.

Institutions is the independent variable of primary interest. To remind, the variable is ordinal with a value of 0 indicating the absence of either an assembly or of legislative parties, 1 if all legislative seats are held by the regime party, and 2 signifying multiple political parties operating within an assembly. Because dictators are thought to be able to perceive threats to their rule emanating from society and use institutions to neutralize this threat, the observed institutions should not account for the variance in survival among leaders. In other words, the effect of institutions on dictators' tenures should be statistically insignificant.

The assumption that dictators want to remain in office is seen as generally unproblematic except in the case of military rulers. Upon seizing power, military officials frequently announce their intention to act as only "arbitrators " or "guardians, " implying temporary rule until immediate crises are resolved (Nordlinger 1977, Perlmutter 1977). Even if they do prefer to cling to power, military rulers may step down in the interests of preserving the integrity of the military itself – especially if politicization and factionalization of the armed forces has been a problem in the past (Biglaiser 2002). Indeed, Geddes (1999) finds evidence that the tenure of military regimes is significantly shorter than that of other types of dictatorships – a finding she ascribes to their unique motives. As a result, the dummy variable *Military dictator* is included as a control variable. Military rulers are expected to be more likely to leave office voluntarily. Because the variable is coded 1 for all military rulers and 0 otherwise, the expectation is for its coefficient to have a negative sign.

Threats to dictators emanate from both the ruling elite and society at large. To assess whether the potential opposition within society still poses a threat to dictators' tenures even after institutionalization, it is necessary to control for the threat that stems from the elite. To some extent, the type of dictator captures the source of these threats because monarchs often are replaced by their own family members while generals are ousted by their colleagues in uniform. More directly, however, past experience with elite infighting may indicate a greater threat from the elite in the current period. Past successful coups demonstrate that elites have been willing to intervene and overthrow the leader in the past, which also may be a sign of the willingness and ability to do so again. To examine the effect of past instability resulting from elite machinations, the variable *Turnover by coup* is included. *Turnover by coup* is the rate of coups overthrowing effective heads of government per year in the life of a political regime, lagged by one year. The variable is constructed by aggregating the accumulated number of coups within a country divided by the length of dictatorial spell.[5] The value of the variable spikes upward with each additional coup, capturing the imminent threat of elites when there is a history of frequent coups. But after each coup, the value of *Turnover by coup* declines (because it is divided by the increasing age of the regime), reflecting the gradual consolidation of power achieved by incumbents over time (Bienen and Van de Walle 1991). The impact of past instability due to elite-led coups is expected to have a negative effect on the survival of dictators.

In addition, conflict, whether civil or interstate, is likely to affect the tenure of dictators. Either because war engenders bad outcomes such as the destruction of life and property or because opposing combatants are trying to remove the ruler, armed conflict has a negative impact on the political survival of rulers (Bueno de Mesquita and Siverson 1995, Chiozza and Goemans 2004). To capture this possibility, *War*, a dummy variable coded 1 if a country is experiencing hostilities with either an internal or external combatant and 0 otherwise, is included. The coefficient on the variable is expected to be negative.

Neutralizing threats to their rule requires control over territory. Dictators in larger countries may experience more difficulty in maintaining such control. They must spread resources, both coercive and co-optative, over a larger territory. In addition, the likelihood that some areas may remain beyond the control of the center is higher because a larger land mass requires greater infrastructure. *Land*, then, indicates the country's area in square kilometers and is expected to have a negative effect on tenure length.

---

[5] The use of coups as an indicator of elite-led threats is due to the fact that, by definition, coups are quick seizures of power by a small group.

TABLE 6.3. *Descriptive Statistics of Variables in Event History Analysis*

Variable	Mean	Standard Deviation	Minimum	Maximum	Cases
Age_t	10.441	9.406	1	61	4588
$Institutions_t$	0.972	0.818	0	2	4559
$Military\ dictator_t$	0.344	0.475	0	1	4588
$Turnover\ by\ coups_{t-1}$	0.067	0.158	0	3	4414
War_t	0.106	0.308	0	1	4588
$Land_t\ /100,000$	6.367	12.390	0.003	93.275	3653
Per capita $income_{t-1}\ /1,000$	2.741	3.521	0.218	43.806	3958

Economic development also may have an impact on the political survival of rulers. Londregan and Poole (1990) find that many low-income countries appear to be caught in a coup trap in which leadership instability becomes the norm. Yet high levels of economic development do not necessarily guarantee stability for dictatorial rulers. Pointing to the high correlation between income and democracy, some proponents of modernization theory (e.g., Boix and Stokes 2003, Lipset 1959) claim that economic development has a causal impact on the likelihood of transitions from dictatorship to democracy.[6] In this case, autocratic leaders in wealthy countries face the likelihood of being overthrown by democratic forces. To control for the effect of development on political stability within dictatorships, included is *Per capita income* (lagged by one year) which indicates the previous year's per capita income in PPP dollars as measured by Maddison (2003). Due to the countervailing influences of income on the political stability of authoritarian regimes, the expected effect of income on the tenure of dictatorial leaders is not clear.

Table 6.3 provides descriptive statistics for all variables used in the analysis.

6.3.3 Impact of Institutions on Survival

Because the addition of control variables changes the sample size, Table 6.4 shows results from three different specifications. The first

[6] In a dissenting view, Przeworski et al. (2000) find that although income helps democracy survive, it does not lead to democratic transitions.

column includes just the primary independent variable of interest, *Institutions*. Column 2 shows the results after inclusion of all the control variables that do not alter significantly the size of the sample. The model shown in the last column includes all the independent variables discussed above. The size of the sample reduces considerably because *Land* is not available before 1960 and *Per capita income* is missing for smaller countries.

At the bottom of each column are listed the Akaike information criteria (AIC) for four different parametric models. The AIC is defined as

$$2lnL + 2(k + c),$$

where L is log-likelihood, k is the number of covariates, and c is the number of model-specific distributional parameters. For each specification, the log-logistic and log-normal parameterizations have the lowest AIC values, indicating their goodness of fit (Box-Steffensmeier and Jones 2004: 44). Because both models produce similar coefficients, the results from the log-logistic model are shown in Table 6.4 due to ease of interpretation. Under this distributional assumption, $E(t_j|x_j) = \exp(\beta_0 + \beta_k x_j)$. Consequently, $\beta_k > 0$ indicates that increases in x_j increase the likelihood of survival, whereas $\beta_k < 0$ signifies a negative effect on tenure.

The results show that only the type of dictatorship and involvement in conflict have significant effects on the political survival of dictators. Consistent with Geddes' (1999) findings, military leaders are less likely to survive in power while conflict also curtails the tenure of autocrats. The results in Column 2 indicate that, all else being equal, military dictators survive half as long as nonmilitary rulers [exp(−0.665)], whereas wartime dictators survive two-thirds as long as rulers governing in times of peace [exp(−0.410)]. A military dictator at war can expect to survive in power on average for 3.8 years while his civilian counterpart not engaged in hostilities will survive for 11.1 years.

In comparison, the threat posed by elites, as indicated by the rate of leadership turnover by coup, does not have a statistically significant impact on political survival. Similarly, neither the size of the territory nor the level of development affect the likelihood of falling from power.

Most importantly, for all specifications, the coefficient on *Institutions* is not significantly different from zero. Dictators with institutions on average do not survive longer than those without legislative parties, suggesting that most authoritarian incumbents are able to perceive with

TABLE 6.4. *Effect of Institutions on Political Survival of Dictators*

	Log-Logistic Models		
	Model 1	Model 2	Model 3
Constant	1.877***	2.406***	2.217***
	(0.089)	(0.127)	(0.141)
Institutions$_t$	0.122	−0.025	−0.019
	(0.073)	(0.078)	(0.078)
Military$_t$		−0.665***	−0.485***
		(0.146)	(0.142)
War$_t$		−0.410**	−0.345*
		(0.186)	(0.185)
Turnover by coup$_{t-1}$		0.194	−0.008
		(0.338)	(0.329)
Land$_t$			−0.003
			(0.005)
Per capita income$_{t-1}$			0.002
			(0.024)
λ	0.136***	0.125***	0.147***
	(0.009)	(0.008)	(0.010)
p	1.206***	1.263***	1.425***
	(0.066)	(0.069)	(0.076)
Log-likelihood	−1333.018	−1255.555	−1102.542
AIC	2672.036	2523.110	2223.084
AIC – Exponential	2722.066	2552.784	2227.840
AIC – Weibull	2708.530	2550.114	2229.772
AIC – Log-normal	2672.036	2523.110	2223.084
No. country-years	4559	4389	3237
No. dictators	552	523	386
Median survival time	7.362***	7.972***	6.812***
	(0.480)	(0.518)	(0.443)

Standard errors in parentheses.
*** $p < 0.01$; ** $p < 0.05$; * $p < 0.10$.

some accuracy the threats germinating within society and to respond with the appropriate degree of institutionalization.

6.4 CONCLUSION

The results from the event history analysis – that legislative and partisan arrangements do not affect the tenure of dictators – are null findings. One interpretation is that because these results show no statistical correlation between institutions and tenure in office, legislative and partisan arrangements seem not to be useful in maintaining coalitions necessary for the political survival of dictators. If institutions do not facilitate the survival of dictators, they are likely not instruments of co-optation.

In the context of the account of dictatorial institutions that has been presented so far, however, another interpretation of the null findings is possible. The results, in fact, potentially constitute additional empirical confirmation for the theoretical claims advanced here. They suggest that most dictators accurately perceive the threats they face and their needs for cooperation. In response, they make enough concessions in the form of rents and policies through institutions to insure that their tenures remain secure. Leaders requiring little cooperation and facing weak threats to their rule offer little in the way of concessions and build few institutions. Rulers who need more cooperation and confront stronger potential opposition must engage in more significant compromises as reflected by a greater degree of institutionalization. And because observed institutions reflect a best response on the part of both types of dictators, these institutions do not advantage or disadvantage any of them in terms of tenure in power.

In spite of "statistically insignificant" effects of institutions on tenure, it is still possible to understand legislative and partisan arrangements as promoting the survival of autocrats. Consider what would happen if dictators were to err – because of misinformation, idiosyncratic beliefs, or hubris. They would underinstitutionalize, and their tenures would be cut short. This is one way of interpreting the events that transpired under the military government in Ecuador (discussed in Chapter 2). The leaders of the coup, having received some initial support and believing that domestic entrepreneurs and urban workers would support them given that they stood to be beneficiaries of the junta's reform program, made a mistake in closing the legislature and banning partisan activity. As a result, the groups that should have supported the regime (i.e., the entrepreneurs and workers) led the opposition to the dictatorship before the government could enact most of its reforms. Had the military government made concessions to these groups through institutions, it might have survived in power longer. Although we cannot observe this counterfactual, some accounts of events in Ecuador, most notably Neuhouser's (1996), strongly suggest this distinct possibility. Consequently, it is possible to conclude that institutions affect the political survival of autocrats because without them, these incumbents would not be able to co-opt potential opposition and maintain the coalitions necessary to remain in power as long as those rulers who need not make concessions.

7

Conclusion

If parties do not compete and legislatures do not legislate, then what do these institutions do under dictatorship? This question naturally emerges if we adopt the typical view of dictatorial institutions as mere "window-dressing." Yet this understanding of nondemocratic legislatures and parties makes little sense in light of neo-institutionalist approaches that pervade the study of other political structures and events. For one, we think that institutions, in general, are not randomly generated phenomena but rather are purposely constructed to further the goals of political actors, whether they are to solve particular problems that prevent the fruition of more efficient outcomes, to solidify distributional power, to survive in office, or to achieve whatever else. Actors use institutions to realize their goals but are constrained by the types of action available to them and by the goals and actions of others. As a result, institutions are the product of strategic behavior on the part of political actors. But this standard notion of institutions runs counter to the idea that dictatorial institutions are "window dressing." If assemblies and parties are mere ornamentation under dictatorship, then what explains the variation in the presence and absence of these institutions? Are we to assume that such variation is determined only by the capriciousness of individual leaders rather than by the strategic logic that governs the functioning of other types of institutions?

Moreover, if this exceptional treatment of dictatorial institutions seems unwarranted, then there is no reason not to extend the institutionalist agenda that has pervaded the study of democracies to the study of nondemocracies. On this point, a large literature on regime parties emerged early, but there is no reason to think that other institutions, such as legislature, party systems, and elections, do not also play important roles in authoritarian regimes. This book, along with other recent work in the study of nondemocracies, is intended as a contribution in this vein.

The argument here is that for autocratic rulers, institutions help in addressing two basic dilemmas of governance. First, dictators must secure their position in power, neutralizing any threats to their rule. Second, nondemocratic incumbents must solicit the cooperation of outsiders to insure that individuals have incentives to engage in productive activities. The degree to which these constraints bind dictators, however, varies. Those autocrats who face weak opposition and can govern without the cooperation of outsiders need not make concessions. Dictators who confront a strong opposition and rely on citizens for the maintenance of political and economic security must make policy compromises and distribute rents. Otherwise, they risk internal upheaval and stagnation.

Yet to forge policy compromises with the potential opposition, authoritarian leaders need institutions. Legislatures and regime parties serve as a controlled institutionalized channel through which outside groups can make their demands and incumbents can make concessions without appearing to cave into popular protest. Dictators may need to allow for parties to form with some autonomy from the regime. Participation within a legislature keeps these parties encapsulated within the system.

Participation within these institutions signals the potential opposition's acceptance of dictatorial concessions. For some outside groups, the perks and privileges that stem from collaboration are enough to induce participation within these institutions. But even those groups who are committed to regime change may participate in institutions if they offer the chance to influence government decisions, even if in limited policy realms. The benefits that outside groups gain from participation are real even if potentially fleeting.

Several observable implications flow from this account of institutionalization. The first implication is that policies should vary across differently organized regimes. The policy outcomes in institutionalized dictatorships should reflect compromise between the dictator and outside groups in contrast to policies in uninstitutionalized regimes that can be unilaterally determined by the ruler. Because we do not have data on the policy preferences of rulers and of legislative parties under authoritarianism, it is difficult to test this argument directly. But with a few additional assumptions, a test of the effects of institutions on government expenditures and rights policies provides some evidence in support of this idea. A variety of civil rights are better protected under institutionalized regime, reflecting the fact that legislatures are the forum in which autocrats organize concessions on these policies. In addition, rulers with nominally democratic institutions spend less on the armed forces, suggesting that they must allocate resources to priorities other than guaranteeing their own security. The cross-national data reveal no correlation between institutions and social spending, however, leaving unclear what these other priorities may be. Alternatively, government expenditures – of any kind, including those on education, health, and welfare – may be subject to distributional battles and as a result, poor proxies of public goods. If this is the case, then institutions may have no effect because members or parties within the legislature do not have unified policy preferences and a bargain with the dictator cannot be reached. Yet the evidence regarding civil liberties and military spending suggests that legislative and partisan arrangements are instrumental in the construction of policy compromises between the regime and the potential opposition.

If policies differ across institutionalized regimes, then outcomes must differ as well. In particular, institutionalized dictatorships should provide a political environment more conducive to economic development than noninstitutionalized regimes. Legislatures and parties help maintain political stability by serving as a repository for popular demands that could have been made on the street. Their presence also may produce a degree of stability in policy-making. Although these institutions can not completely constrain incumbents, they can raise the costs of arbitrary policy switches. Finally, assemblies and parties facilitate transparency because they serve as a forum in which regimes announce their plans and outside groups make their preferences known. Through these mechanisms, institutions help create an environment that is more conducive to investment in productive activities. As the evidence shows, the result is higher economic growth in more institutionalized dictatorships.

Finally, institutions and the survival of dictators are linked, but perhaps not in the most obvious way. If dictators are able to perceive with accuracy the problems of governance they face and to use institutions as a strategic response, then the observed political survival of rulers with and without institutions should not differ significantly. Dictators who do not need the cooperation of outside groups and who do not face strong opposition should not institutionalize, whereas those who are dependent on their citizens and who encounter strong resistance must govern with institutions. In either case, rulers choose the degree of institutionalization as an answer that is commensurate to the problems of governance that they face. Having neutralized threats to their rule with appropriate institutional responses, they should survive in power for similarly long periods of time. In support of this claim, the evidence shows that during the postwar period, dictators with and without institutions do not have statistically significant differences in tenure. Yet institutions help some dictators maintain power: those that need them to solicit cooperation and neutralize threats to their rule would not have been able to survive as long as they did without them.

Although the evidence for these implications lends support to this account of legislatures and parties in nondemocratic states, two rival hypotheses merit consideration. The first competing claim regards institutionalization as evidence of dictatorial power rather than weakness. Dictators may allow for legislative parties not when they must bow in the face of opposition challenges but when they are strong enough to pursue a strategy of divide and rule. The result will be a political arena crowded with multiple parties, each with its own interests, allowing the dictator to "rise above partisanship" and achieve his own ends. In Jordan, for example, King Hussein may have ceded control over religious and educational matters to the Muslim Brotherhood in an attempt to discredit the group. Anticipating that the Brotherhood would propose policies that would displease secular Jordanians, the king made policy concessions with an eye toward strengthening his position in the long run. This case suggests that greater institutionalization may not be the result of a weakened dictator forced to grant more policy concessions but rather a ruler with the upper hand when dealing with the opposition.

Although it is plausible that the strength of dictatorial power motivates increasing pluralism within a legislature, the aggregate findings presented in Chapter 3 portray a different story. The quantitative evidence indicates that it is only when dictators need the help of others to govern and face strong challenges to their rule that they govern with institutions. Although the proxies to capture these factors are far from perfect, they do confirm that it is under conditions of "weakness" that nondemocratic rulers have legislative and partisan institutions.

On this question, another piece of evidence to consider is the effect of institutions on policies. If multiple legislative parties are really just indicative of a strong dictator presiding over an inchoate, fractured opposition, then policies within noninstitutionalized regimes should resemble policies of institutionalized regimes: dictators would be able to unilaterally impose their preferences – in the former because they face no negotiating partner and in the latter because they manage to manipulate and rise above the fractious opposition. Yet this is not the case. Significant differences in government spending occur across differently organized dictatorships. Those regimes with a higher degree of institutionalization have lower military spending, suggesting that institutions press rulers to alter their spending priorities. In addition, more institutionalized dictatorships have more liberalized policies on civil rights. If institutionalization is driven by dictatorial strength, we should not observe the aggregate empirical patterns in policies that are evident in the cross-national data.

The account of institutionalization here, however, is consistent with the notion of divide and rule. The decision to institutionalize on the part of the dictator is driven by conditions of weakness, but the existence of legislatures and parties, then, can lead to growing dictatorial power. Incumbents, in fact, institutionalize for precisely this reason: they want to co-opt the potential opposition in an attempt to broaden their bases of support and increase their power relative to other political actors. The authority to grant legalized status provides rulers with a way to divide the opposition into "insiders" – the parties allowed to compete in elections and occupy seats in the legislature – and "outsiders" or those who are banned from participating in the political arena (Lust-Okar 2005). Yet for those groups that agree to involve themselves in the constructed institutional space, the dictator must follow through on his promises of concessions. Otherwise, outside groups may withdraw and the institutional edifice designed to facilitate his rule may crumble.

The second point to consider is that although dictatorial institutions may be correlated with certain policies and outcomes, they may not be causal. The correlation between institutions and greater political and civil rights, for example, may be evidence of one of two underlying processes: either institutions "cause" liberalization in that without them the regimes would be more restrictive or some underlying factor is driving both liberalization of institutions and individual rights.

In this account, underlying conditions do drive both the decision to make policy concessions and to institutionalize. The formal model in Chapter 3 demonstrates this point most precisely. The exogenous factors motivating concessions and hence, institutionalization include the dictator's need for cooperation and the strength of the potential opposition. These conditions confronting rulers influence their decision to make concessions – whether they are in the form of rents or policy. For these policy concessions to materialize, however, dictators need institutions. Without a forum in which to forge policy compromises, dictators would not be able to make policy concessions without losing face. So without a need for cooperation or a strong opposition, incumbents would not want to make concessions. Without institutions, they cannot make policy concessions. Institutions, then, are "causal" along with the exogenous conditions that dictators face. As a result, the differences in policies and outcomes we observe are in part due to institutional differences among dictatorships.

Although the "correlation, not causation" critique is a standard one of quantitative analysis, it has wider theoretical implications in this context. The question is: if legislatures and parties "cause" various policies and outcomes under dictatorship, are their causal processes similar to those of democratic assemblies and parties? For example, if assemblies under dictatorship allow for outside groups to negotiate with the government and influence certain realms of policy-making, then how are nondemocratic legislatures different from democratic ones? In this case, we might think that dictatorships with nominally democratic institutions are semidemocratic: "democratic" because the presence of dictatorial institutions means that incumbents are not free to unilaterally enact their policy preferences and determine outcomes and "semidemocratic" because these institutions do not perfectly constrain incumbents.

We must be cautious, however, of ascribing the same characteristics to dictatorial institutions that happen to bear the same names as democratic ones. Under democracy, institutions are central to understanding how state power is constrained and credible commitments by the state are possible. Constraints and the credibility of commitments are related because the commitments of the executive (as the personification of state power) cannot be credible unless he is constrained either through delegation of authority for making decisions in the first place or punishment for reneging on commitments (Sánchez-Cuenca 1998). But for these constraints on the executive to be truly binding, the executive must accept the legitimacy of institutional constraints and more importantly, constraining institutions must have the means by which they can defend their prerogatives. To ask, then, whether legislatures and parties make some dictatorships more "democratic" is to ask whether these institutions in nondemocracies serve as real constraints on executive power.

First is the question of whether the executive accepts the legitimacy of the institutional constraints that bind him. In democracies, political parties influence decision-making, legislatures legislate – all resulting in the inability of democratic leaders to unilaterally implement their preferred policies. Yet we can think that democratic chief executives comply with the rules of this process because they view the participation of other institutions in decision-making as standard and intrinsic to the democratic process.

Consider whether this is the case with autocrats. If a dictator compromises with the legislature over civil liberties, for example, he does not do so because he recognizes the legislature as a political actor with legitimate and equal claims to making policy. He makes policy concessions out of concern for the consequences of not doing so: that outside groups might air their grievances on the street and precipitate his downfall. Holmes's (1995: 111) characterization of Bodin's advice to absolutist kings in France precisely captures the motivation of contemporary autocrats in governing with institutions: "A prudent sovereign will relinquish some of his power voluntarily when he learns . . . that limitations placed upon his caprice markedly increase his capacity to govern and to achieve his steady aims." The dictator governs with these institutions not because he views their participation as legitimate but because he finds them to be a convenient means by which he can deal with potential opposition.

The second question is whether legislatures and parties have the power to defend their place in the decision-making process. In a democracy, if the executive were to circumvent or eliminate the parliament, such a move would prompt a response. There are rules by which the executive would be punished for such actions (e.g., electoral sanctions, rulings by an independent judiciary, and impeachment by the legislature) and these punishments are certain to be carried out. Consider what happens in dictatorships. If an autocrat closes the legislature, he faces outside groups that may protest their exclusion. But there is little that the legislature, or any other institution, can do. There are no procedures by which these institutions or citizens can remove the dictator. Although protests sometimes lead to the fall of authoritarian leaders, they do not always. The contrast, then, is that in dictatorships, the punishment of executives for such institutional encroachments is neither rule-bound nor certain.

One result is that dictatorial rulers, even in the presence of institutions, retain much power to shape political institutions to fulfill their own goals. Although authoritarian rulers govern with institutions when necessary, they do not acknowledge the legitimacy of other institutions in determining policies. As a result, when conditions change such that they no longer need institutions to neutralize opposition and co-opt outsiders, dictators can abolish these institutions. Because these institutions have no means by which to challenge such moves, in the end, they do not constrain autocrats in the same way that institutions constrain democratic rulers. Nor can these institutions signify a completely credible commitment on the part of autocratic leaders.

This distinction in the nature of democratic and dictatorial legislatures and parties, however, has implications for policy-makers and scholars who are interested in fostering democratic transitions. The common perception is that the establishment of multiparty competition for legislative seats in authoritarian regimes indicate greater liberalization and possible preparatory steps for democracy. Incumbents are assumed to be against greater institutionalization so the presence of additional legislative parties is interpreted as a sign that the opposition is gaining strength at the expense of the regime. In addition, participation in these institutions should help citizens build a civic culture steeped in participation, deliberation, and tolerance.

Yet it seems more likely that these institutions will not pave the way toward democracy. For one, participation in nominally democratic institutions involves playing in a rigged game, making it less likely that groups learn the virtues of a civic culture. Second, and most importantly, dictatorial institutions aid in the political survival of those dictators who need to make concessions. Studies of electoral authoritarianism similarly make this point. Indeed, authoritarian incumbents appear to be aware of the need for and the use of institutions to preserve their power. In describing the motivation for political reforms in Qatar, for example, Weaver (2000: 61) observes: "Sheikh Hamad's reforms also grew out of his desire to perpetuate the al-Thani dynasty. If he wanted one of his sons or grandsons to assume the throne in a changing world, he had to begin sharing power." So although the benefits of participation in these institutions are real, they do not necessarily include an increasing likelihood of democracy. In fact, to the extent that dictatorial legislatures and parties help incumbents address problems of governance, they would appear to make democratic transitions even less likely.

8

Codebook of Variables

Age
Years in power of the current effective head of government. Compiled from Banks (various years), Beck et al. (2000), Beinen and Van de Walle (1991), Lentz (1994), and Zarate (2001).

British colony
Coded 1 for every year in countries that were British colonies any time after 1918 and 0 otherwise. Updated from Przeworski et al. (2000) with Banks (various years).

Capital stock growth
Growth of capital stock (annual percentage). Source is Przeworski et al. (2000).

Civilian dictator
Coded 1 if the effective head of government is neither a member of the armed forces nor a monarch and 0 otherwise. Compiled from Banks (various years), Beck et al. (2000), Beinen and Van de Walle (1991), Lentz (1994), and Zarate (2001).

Dependent population
Nonworking young and old population (as percentage of total population). Constructed by adding "Population ages 0-14 (percent of total)" [SP.POP.0014.TO.ZS] and "Population ages 15-64 (percent of total)" [SP.POP.1564.IN.ZS] from World Bank (2004).

Education growth
Growth of cumulative years of education of the average member of
the labor force (annual rate). Source is Przeworski et al. (2000).

Ethnic polarization
Degree of polarization among a country's ethnic groups. Calculated as
$1-\sum(0.5 - p_i)^2 * p_i/0.25$ where p_i is the share of the population that
belongs to ethnic group i, as defined and measured in Fearon (2003).

Government expenditure growth
Annual change in government share of real GDP. Constructed as the
difference in the current and previous years' values of "Government
share of CGDP" [CG] from Heston et al. (2002) (i.e., Penn World
Table 6.1).

IMF program
Coded as 1 for the years a conditioned IMF agreement is in force
and 0 otherwise. The types of IMF agreements included are Stand-
by Arrangements, Extended Fund Facility, and Structural Adjustment
Facility, Enhanced Structural Adjustment Facility (Poverty Reduction
and Growth Facility after 1999). Source is Vreeland (2007).

Income inequality
Gini coefficient of gross incomes. Constructed by extending the value
of a country-year observation for five additional years after the original observation unless a new value is observed for all high quality
observations recorded in Deininger and Squire (1996).

Inherited parties
Number of political parties dictator inherits from his predecessor.
Coded 2 if multiple political parties exist, 1 if only the regime party exists, and 0 if all political parties are banned. If a dictator's predecessor
changed the number of parties allowed during the course of his tenure,
then *Inherited parties* takes the value which constitutes the largest
share of country-year observations during his tenure. If democratic
rule preceded a dictator, *Inherited parties* is coded as 2. Note that this
variable is distinct from *Institutions* in that it codes the number of
parties that exist rather than the number of parties that occupy seats
within the legislature. Compiled from Akhavi (1994), Amawi (1994),
Ashford (1961), Banks (1996), Barros (2002), Deiner (1982), Di Tella
(2004), Engel (1999), Grotz (1999), Hartlyn (1989), Hodgkin (1961),

Jalal (1995), Janda (2000), Keller (1988), Kramer (1994), Krennerich (1999, 2005a, 2005b), Landau (1994), Lawson (1994), Lentz (1994), Léon-Roesch and Ortiz (2005), Lewis (1980), Lewis and Sagar (1992), McDonald and Ruhl (1989), Moore (1965), Morris (1984), Mortimer and Hoadley (1985), Nicholls (1979), Nohlen and Pachano (2005), Olson and Simon (1982), Przeworski et al. (2007), Raina (1990), Rasanayagam (2003), Robins (2004), Römer (1999), Saikal (2004), Sanders (1992), Simon (1994), SSHL-UCSD (2000), Stroux (1999), Suter and Nohlen (2005), Suwannathat-Pian (1995), Trouillot (1990), Ulc (1982), Van Praagh (1996), Walter (1993), Whelpton (2005), White (1973), Wyatt (2003), and Yamada (1985).

Institutions
Number of political parties in the legislature under dictatorship. Coded 2 if the dictatorship has a legislature with multiple political parties, 1 if the regime party controls all seats within the legislature, and 0 if either parties are not allowed in the legislature or the legislature is closed. Compiled from Akhavi (1994), Amawi (1994), Ashford (1961), Banks (1996), Barros (2002), Deiner (1982), Di Tella (2004), Engel (1999), Grotz (1999), Hartlyn (1989), Hodgkin (1961), Jalal (1995), Janda (2000), Keller (1988), Kramer (1994), Krennerich (1999, 2005a, 2005b), Landau (1994), Lawson (1994), Lentz (1994), Léon-Roesch and Ortiz (2005), Lewis (1980), Lewis and Sagar (1992), McDonald and Ruhl (1989), Moore (1965), Morris (1984), Mortimer and Hoadley (1985), Nicholls (1979), Nohlen and Pachano (2005), Olson and Simon (1982), Przeworski et al. (2007), Raina (1990), Rasanayagam (2003), Robins (2004), Romer (1999), Saikal (2004), Sanders (1992), Simon (1994), SSHL-UCSD (2000), Stroux (1999), Suter and Nohlen (2005), Suwannathat-Pian (1995), Trouillot (1990), Ulc (1982), Van Praagh (1996), Walter (1993), Whelpton (2005), White (1973), Wyatt (2003), and Yamada (1985).

Labor force growth
Growth of labor force (annual percentage). Source is Przeworski et al. (2000).

Land
Land area (square km). Source is World Bank (2004) [AG.LND. TOTL.K2].

Leadership changes
Number of changes of the effective head of government accumulated during the life of a political regime (as classified by Przeworski et al. 2000 and Cheibub and Gandhi 2004). Compiled from Banks (various years), Beck et al. (2000), Beinen and Van de Walle (1991), Lentz (1994), and Zarate (2001).

Military dictator
Coded 1 if the effective head of government is or ever was a member of the military by profession, and 0 if otherwise. Retired members of the military are coded as 1 because the shedding of a uniform is not enough to indicate the civilian character of a leader. In addition, rulers who come to power as head of guerilla movements are not considered as military. Compiled from Banks (various years), Beck et al. (2000), Beinen and Van de Walle (1991), Lentz (1994), and Zarate (2001).

Military spending
Central government expenditures on the armed forces (as percentage of GNP). Compiled from Stockholm International Peace Research Institute (various years).

Monarch
Coded 1 if the effective head of government is of hereditary royalty and 0 otherwise. To qualify as a monarch, the effective head must meet two criteria: (1) rule under a title, such as kings, emirs, sultans, and (2) have been preceded or succeeded by a relative. Part (1) means that Khama in Botswana, Mutesa in Uganda, Souvanna Phouma in Laos, Mohammed Daud in Afghanistan, and Sihanouk in Cambodia do not qualify as monarchs because they abdicated their places in the royal line to rule as heads of republics. Part (2) means that self-proclaimed royalty such as Bokassa in the Central African Republic are not monarchs. Compiled from Banks (various years) and Lentz (1994).

Open economy
Total trade (as percentage of GDP). Source is "Exports plus imports (as a share of CGDP)" [OPENC] from Heston et al. (2006) (i.e., Penn World Table 6.2).

Other democracies
Percentage of democratic regimes (as classified by Przeworski et al.

2000 and Cheibub and Gandhi 2004) in the current year (other than the regime under consideration) in the world. Updated from Przeworski et al. (2000) with Cheibub and Gandhi (2004).

Per capita income
Real GDP per capita. Source is "Real GDP per capita" [RGDPCH] from Heston et al. (2002) (i.e., Penn World Table 6.1) for analyses in Chapters 4 and 5 and from Maddison (2003) for analyses in Chapter 6.

Press freedom
Coded 0 if press is clearly free and the news media are capable of functioning as an arena of political competition; 1 if press freedom is compromised by corruption or unofficial influence, but the news media are still capable of functioning as an arena of political competition; 2 if the press is not directly controlled by the government but is not capable of functioning as an arena of political competition or debate; 3 if the press is directly controlled by the government or strictly censored. Source is Van Belle (1997).

Purges
Number of systematic eliminations by jailing or execution of political opposition within the ranks of the regime or the opposition. Source is [V62 S17F5] from Banks (1996) .

Resources
Mineral resource endowment of countries. Coded 1 if the average ratio of mineral exports (including oil) to exports exceeds 50 percent and 0 otherwise. Compiled from International Monetary Fund (1999) and World Bank (2000).

Riots
Number of violent demonstrations or clashes of more than 100 citizens involving the use of physical force. Source is [V63 S17F6] from Banks (1996).

Social spending
Government expenditure on education, health, and social security and welfare (as percentage of GDP). Constructed by adding "Education," "Health," and "Social security and welfare" from International Monetary Fund (2003).

Speech freedom
Extent to which freedoms of speech and press are affected by government censorship, including ownership of media outlets. Coded 2 if no censorship, 1 if some censorship, and 0 if complete censorship. Source is Cingranelli and Richards (2004).

Total income growth
Growth of real GDP (annual rate). Constructed by adding annual rate of growth of per capita income [RGDPCH] and annual rate of growth of population [created from POP] from Heston et al. (2002) (i.e., Penn World Table 6.1).

Trade growth
Annual change in total trade's share of GDP. Constructed as the difference in the current and previous years' values of "Exports plus imports (as a share of CGDP)" [OPENC] from Heston et al. (2002) (i.e., Penn World Table 6.1).

Turnover by coup
Rate of coups overthrowing effective head of government per year of life of a political regime [as classified by Przeworski et al. (2000) and Cheibub and Gandhi (2004)]. Calculated as the accumulated count of successful coups over the duration of a political regime divided by the age of the regime. Information on coups was compiled from Banks (1996), Lentz (1994), and Przeworski et al. (2007).

War
Coded 1 if any type of war (extrastate, interstate, or civil) was fought in a country in a given year and 0 otherwise. Singer and Small (1994) updated with Sarkees and Schafer (2000).

Workers' rights
Extent to which workers enjoy internationally recognized rights at work, including freedom of association in the workplace, collective bargaining with employers, prohibition on the use of forced labor, minimum age for child employment, and acceptable conditions of work related to minimum wages, hours of work, and occupation health and safety. Coded as 2 for fully protected rights, 1 for somewhat restricted rights, and 0 for severely restricted rights. Source is Cingranelli and Richards (2004).

Bibliography

Acemoglu, Daron, and James Robinson. 2006. *Economic Origins of Dictatorship and Democracy*. New York: Cambridge University Press.

Achen, Christopher. 1986. *The Statistical Analysis of Quasi-Experiments*. Berkeley: University of California Press.

Akhavi, Shahrough. 1994. "Iran." In Frank Tachau (ed.), In *Political Parties of the Middle East and North Africa*. Westport, CT: Greenwood Press. pp. 133–173.

Aldrich, John. 1995. *Why Parties? The Origin and Transformation of Political Parties in America*. Chicago: University of Chicago Press.

Amawi, Abla. 1994. "Jordan." In Frank Tachau (ed.), *Political Parties of the Middle East and North Africa*. Westport, CT: Greenwood Press. pp. 259–296.

Apter, David. 1965. *The Politics of Modernization*. Chicago: University of Chicago Press.

Arendt, Hannah. 1951. *The Origins of Totalitarianism*. New York: Harcourt Brace Jovanovich.

Aron, Janine. 2000. "Growth and Institutions: A Review of Evidence." *World Bank Research Observer* 15: 99–136.

Ashford, Douglas. 1961. *Political Change in Morocco*. Princeton, NJ: Princeton University Press.

Ashford, Douglas. 1964. *Perspectives of a Moroccan Nationalist*. Totowa, NJ: Bedminster Press.

Avelino, George, David Brown, and Wendy Hunter. 2005. "The Effects of Capital Mobility, Trade Openness, and Democracy on Social Spending in Latin America, 1980–1999." *American Journal of Political Science* 49, 3: 625–641.

Baehr, Peter, and Melvin Richter. 2004. "Introduction." In Peter Baehr and Melvin Richter (eds.), *Dictatorship in History and Theory: Bonapartism,*

Caesarism, and Totalitarianism. New York: Cambridge University Press. pp. 1–28.

Banks, Arthur. 1996. *Cross-National Time-Series Data Archive.* Binghamton, NY: Center for Social Analysis, State University of New York at Binghamton. Electronic Format.

Banks, Arthur, Alan Day, and Thomas Muller. Various years. *Political Handbook of the World.* Binghamton, NY: Center for Social Analysis, State University of New York at Binghamton.

Bardhan, Pranab. 1997. "Corruption and Development: A Review of Issues." *Journal of Economic Literature* 35, 3: 1320–1346.

Barros, Robert. 2002. *Constitutionalism and Dictatorship: Pinochet, the Junta, and the 1980 Constitution.* New York: Cambridge University Press.

Beck, Nathaniel. 1992. "Comparing Dynamic Specifications: The Case of Presidential Approval." *Political Analysis* 3: 51–87.

Beck, Nathaniel, David Epstein, Simon Jackman, and Sharon O'Halloran. 2001. "Alternative Models of Dynamics in Binary Time-Series-Cross-Section Models: The Example of State Failure." Prepared for the Annual Meeting of the Society for Political Methodology, Emory University, Atlanta, GA, July 19–21, 2001.

Beck, Thorsten, George Clarke, Alberto Groff, Philip Keefer, and Patrick Walsh. 2000. *The Database of Political Institutions.* Washington D.C.: World Bank. Electronic Format.

Becker, Gary. 1983. "A Theory of Competition Among Pressure Groups for Political Influence." *Quarterly Journal of Economics* 98, 3: 371–400.

Belkin, Aaron, and Evan Schofer. 2003. "Toward a Structural Understanding of Coup Risk." *Journal of Conflict Resolution* 47, 5: 594–620.

Ben Barka, Mehdi. 1999. *Écrits Politiques, 1957–1965.* Paris: Éditions Syllepse.

Benhabib, Jess, and Mark Spiegel. 1994. "The Role of Human Capital in Economic Development: Evidence from Aggregate Cross-Country Data." *Journal of Monetary Economics* 34: 143–173.

Bertocchi, Graziella and Michael Spagat. 2001. "The Politics of Co-optation." *Journal of Comparative Economics* 29: 591–607.

Bienen, Henry. 1970. *Tanzania: Party Transformation and Economic Development.* Princeton, NJ: Princeton University Press.

Bienen, Henry, and Nicolas Van de Walle. 1991. *Of Time and Power: Leadership Duration in the Modern World.* Stanford, CA: Stanford University Press.

Biglaiser, Glen. 2002. *Guardians of the Nation?* Notre Dame, IN: University of Notre Dame Press.

Binder, Leonard. 1964. *Iran: Political Development in a Changing Society.* Berkeley: University of California Press.

Blaydes, Lisa. 2006. "Electoral Budget Cycles under Authoritarianism: Economic Opportunism in Mubarak's Egypt." Prepared for the Annual

Meeting of the Midwest Political Science Association, Chicago, IL, April 19–22, 2006.

Bligh, Alexander. 1984. *From Prince to King: Royal Succession in the House of Saud in the Twentieth Century*. New York: New York University Press.

Bobbio, Norberto. 1989. *Democracy and Dictatorship: The Nature and Limits of State Power*. Minneapolis: University of Minnesota Press.

Boix, Carles, and Susan Stokes. 2003. "Endogenous Democratization." *World Politics* 55, 4: 517–549.

Bourqia, Rahma. 1999. "The Cultural Legacy of Power in Morocco." In Rahma Bourqia and Susan Gilson Miller (eds.), *In the Shadow of the Sultan: Culture, Power, and Politics in Morocco*. Cambridge, MA: Harvard University Press. pp. 243–258.

Box-Steffensmeier, Janet and Bradford Jones. 2004. *Event History Modeling: A Guide for Social Scientists*. New York: Cambridge University Press.

Bratton, Michael, and Nicolas Van de Walle. 1997. *Democratic Experiments in Africa: Regime Transitions in Comparative Perspective*. New York: Cambridge University Press.

Brooker, Paul. 1995. *Twentieth-Century Dictatorships: the Ideological One Party States*. New York: New York University Press.

Brooker, Paul. 2000. *Non-Democratic Regimes: Theory, Government, and Politics*. New York: St. Martin's Press.

Brown, David. 1999. "Reading, Writing, and Regime Type: Democracy's Impact on Primary School Enrollment." *Political Research Quarterly* 52, 4: 681–707

Brown, David, and Wendy Hunter. 2004. "Democracy and Human Capital Formation: Education Spending in Latin America, 1980–1997." *Comparative Political Studies* 37, 7: 842–864.

Brown, Nathan. 2002. *Constitutions in a Nonconstitutional World: Arab Basic Laws and the Prospects for Accountable Government*. Albany: State University of New York Press.

Brownlee, Jason. 2007. *Authoritarianism in an Age of Democratization*. New York: Cambridge University Press.

Bueno de Mesquita, Bruce, and Randolph Siverson. 1995. "War and the Survival of Political Leaders: A Comparative Study of Regime Types and Political Accountability." *American Political Science Review* 89, 4: 841–855.

Bueno de Mesquita, Bruce, James Morrow, Randolph Siverson, and Alastair Smith. 2003. *The Logic of Survival*. Cambridge, MA: MIT Press.

Cameron, David. 1978. "The Expansion of the Public Economy: A Comparative Analysis." *American Political Science Review* 72: 1243–1261.

Cardoso, Fernando Henrique. 1979. "On the Characterization of Authoritarian Regimes in Latin America." In David Collier (ed.), *The New Authoritarianism in Latin America*. pp. 33–60.

Cardoso, Fernando Henrique, and Enzo Faletto. 1978. *Dependency and Development in Latin America*. Berkeley: University of California Press.

Castañeda, Jorge. 2000. *Perpetuating Power: How Mexican Presidents Were Chosen*. New York: The New Press.

Chehabi, H. E., and Juan Linz. 1998. (eds.) *Sultanistic Regimes*. Baltimore, MD: Johns Hopkins University Press.

Cheibub, José Antonio, and Jennifer Gandhi. 2004. "Classifying Political Regimes: An Update and an Extention." American Political Science Association Annual Meeting, Chicago, IL. September 2–5, 2004.

Cheibub, José Antonio, and Adam Przeworski. 1997. "Government Spending and Economic Growth under Democracy and Dictatorship." In Albert Breton et al. (eds.), *Understanding Democracy: Economic and Political Perspectives*. Cambridge: Cambridge University Press. pp. 107–124.

Chiozza, Giacomo, and H. E. Goemans. 2004. "International Conflict and the Tenure of Leaders: Is War Still Ex Post Inefficient?" *American Journal of Political Science* 48, 3: 604–619.

Cingranelli, David, and David Richards. 2004. *The Cingranelli-Richards (CIRI) Human Rights Database*. http://ciri.binghamton.edu.

Collier, David. (ed.) 1980. *The New Authoritarianism in Latin America*. Princeton, NJ: Princeton University Press.

Collier, David, and Robert Adcock. 1999. "Democracy and Dichotomies: A Pragmatic Approach to Choices about Concepts." *Annual Review of Political Science* 2: 537–565.

Collier, Paul. 1998. "The Political Economy of Ethnicity." In Boris Pleskovic and Joseph Stiglitz (eds.), *Proceedings of the Annual World Bank Conference on Development Economics*. Washington D.C.: World Bank.

Collier, Ruth Berins. 1982. *Regimes in Tropical Africa: Changing Forms of Supremacy, 1945–1975*. Berkeley: University of California Press.

Collier, Ruth Berins. 1999. *Paths Toward Democracy*. New York: Cambridge University Press.

Colton, Timothy. 1979. *Commissars, Commanders, and Civilian Authority: The Structure of Soviet Military Politics*. Cambridge, MA: Harvard University Press.

Conaghan, Catherine. 1988. *Restructuring Domination: Industrialists and the State in Ecuador*. Pittsburgh, PA: University of Pittsburgh Press.

Conway, Patrick. 1994. "IMF Lending Programs: Partipation and Impact." *Journal of Development Economics* 45: 365–391.

Cox, Gary W. 1987. "Efficient Secret: The Cabinet and the Development of Political Parties in Victorian England." Cambridge: Cambridge University Press.

Crystal, Jill. 1990. *Oil and Politics in the Gulf: Rulers and Merchants in Kuwait and Qatar*. New York: Cambridge University Press.

Cutler, Sydney, and Fred Ederer. 1958. "Maximum Utilization of the Life Table Method in Analyzing Survival." *Journal of Chronic Diseases* 8, 6: 699–712.

Davenport, Christian. 1996. "Constitutional Promises and Repressive Reality: A Cross-National Time-Series Investigation of Why Political and Civil Liberties Are Suppressed." *Journal of Politics* 58, 3: 627–654.

Davenport, Christian. 1998. "Liberalizing Event or Lethal Episode? An Empirical Assessment of How National Elections Affect the Suppression of Political and Civil Liberties." *Social Science Quarterly* 79, 2: 321–340.

Davis, David, and Michael Ward. 1990. "They Dance Alone: Deaths and the Disappeared in Contemporary Chile." *Journal of Conflict Resolution* 34: 449–475.

De Schweinitz, Karl, Jr. 1964. *Industrialization and Democracy: Economic Necessities and Political Possibilities*. Glencoe: The Free Press.

Deiner, John. 1982. "Argentina." In Robert Alexander (ed.), *Political Parties of the Americas: Canada, Latin America, and the West Indies, Volume 1*. Westport, CT: Greenwood Press. pp. 52–89.

Deininger, K., and Lyn Squire. 1996. "A New Dataset Measuring Income Inequality." *World Bank Economic Review* 10: 565–591.

Diamond, Larry. 2002. "Thinking About Hybrid Regimes." *Journal of Democracy* 13, 2: 21–35.

Diaz, Ramona. 2003. *Imelda*. Film (103 minutes). Unico Entertainment.

Dinges, John. 2004. *The Condor Years*. New York: The New Press.

Di Tella, Torcuato. 2004. *History of Political Parties in Twentieth Century Latin America*. Piscataway, NJ: Transaction.

Doner, Richard, Bryan Ritchie, and Dan Slater. 2005. "Systemic Vulnerabilities and the Origins of Developmental States: Northeast and Southeast Asia in Comparative Perspective." *International Organization* 59: 327–361.

The Economist. "Cleared out." September 24, 1998.

Edwards, Sebastian. 1993. "Openness, Trade Liberalization, and Growth in Developing Countries." *Journal of Economic Literature* 31, 3: 1358–1393.

Britannica Book of the Year, 2001. *Statistical Info on Countries*. Online. Encyclopaedia Britannica Online. http://search.eb.com Downloaded 2001.

Engel, Ulf. 1999. "South Africa." In Dieter Nohlen, Michael Krennerich, and Bernhard Thibaut (eds.), *Elections in Africa*. New York: Oxford University Press. pp. 817–842.

Ericson, Richard. 1991. "The Classical Soviet-Type Economy: Nature of the System and Implications for Reform." *Journal of Economic Perspectives* 5, 4: 11–27.

Evans, Peter. 1989. "Predatory, Developmental, and Other Apparatuses: A Comparative Analysis of the Third World State." *Sociological Forum* 4, 4: 561–582.

Evans, Peter. 1995. *Embedded Autonomy*. Princeton, NJ: Princeton University Press.

Fearon, James. 1993. "Ethnic and Cultural Diversity by Country." *Journal of Economic Growth* 8, 2: 195–222.

Fearon, James. 1994. "Domestic Political Audiences and the Escalation of International Disputes." *American Political Science Review* 88, 3: 577–592.

Fearon, James. 2003. "Ethnic and Cultural Diversity by Country." *Journal of Economic Growth* 8, 2: 195–222.

Finer, Samuel. 1988. *The Man on Horseback: The Role of the Military in Politics*. Boulder, CO: Westview Press.

Fitch, John Samuel. 1977. *The Miltiary Coup d'Etat as a Political Process: Ecuador, 1948–1966*. Baltimore, MD: Johns Hopkins University Press.

Fontana, Andres Miguel. 1987. "Political Decision-Making by a Military Corporation: Argentina 1976–1983." Ph.D. Dissertation. Department of Political Science, University of Texas – Austin.

Frankel, Jeffrey, and David Romer. 1999. "Does Trade Cause Growth?" *American Economic Review* 89, 3: 379–399.

Franzese, Robert, Jr. 2002. *Macroeconomic Policies of Developed Democracies*. New York: Cambridge University Press.

Friedrich, Carl, and Zbigniew Brzezinski. 1965. *Totalitarian Dictatorship and Autocracy*. New York: Praeger.

Galor, Oded, and Omer Moav. "Das Human-Kapital: A Theory of the Demise of the Class Structure." *Review of Economic Studies* 73, 1: 85–117.

Gandhi, Jennifer, and Wonik Kim. 2005. "Cooptation and Coercion of Workers under Dictatorship." Presented at the Annual Meeting of the Midwest Political Science Association, Chicago, IL, April 7–10, 2005.

Gandhi, Jennifer, and Melissa Schwartzberg. 2004. "The Logic and Legitimacy of Hereditary Succession." Presented at the Midwest Political Science Association Conference, Chicago, IL, April 15–18, 2004.

Gandhi, Jennifer, Joseph Gochal, and Sebastian Saiegh. 2003. "Governments' Legislative Defeats Under Dictatorship." Presented at the Midwest Political Science Association Conference, Chicago, IL, April 3–6, 2003.

Garciá Márquez, Gabriel. 1976. *The Autumn of the Patriarch*. New York: Harper & Row.

Garrett, Geoffrey. 1998. *Partisan Politics in the Global Economy*. New York: Cambridge University Press.

Gasiorowski, Mark. 1995. "Economic Crisis and Political Regime Change: An Event History Analysis." *American Political Science Review* 89, 4: 882–897.

Geddes, Barbara. 1999. "What Do We Know about Democratization after Twenty Years?" *Annual Review of Political Science* 2: 115–144.

Gerschenkron, Alexander. 1962. *Economic Backwardness in Historical Perspective*. Cambridge, MA: Belknap.

Gershenson, Dmitriy, and Herschel Grossman. 2001. "Cooptation and Repression in the Soviet Union." *Economics and Politics* 13, 1: 31–47.

Gershovich, Moshe. 2000. *French Military Rule in Morocco: Colonialism and Its Consequences*. London: Frank Cass.

Gertzel, Cherry. 1966. "Parliament in Independent Kenya." *Parliamentary Affairs* 19, 4: 486–504.

Ginkel, John, and Alastair Smith. 1999. "So You Say You Want a Revolution: A Game Theoretic Explanation of Revolution in Repressive Regimes." *Journal of Conflict Revolution* 43, 3: 291–316.

Greene, William. 1998. *Econometric Analysis.* 3rd edition. Upper Saddle River, NJ: Prentice Hall.

Greif, Avner, Paul Milgrom, and Barry Weingast. 1994. "Coordination, Commitment and Enforcement: The Case of the Merchant Guild." *Journal of Political Economy* 102, 41: 745–776.

Grossman, Gene. 1990. "Promoting New Industrial Activities: A Survey of Recent Arguments and Evidence." *OECD Economic Studies* 14: 87–126.

Grossman, Herschel. 1999. "Kleptocracy and Revolutions." *Oxford Economic Papers* 51: 267–283.

Grotz, Florian. 1999. "Burkina Faso." In Dieter Nohlen, Michael Krennerich, and Bernhard Thibaut (eds.), *Elections in Africa.* New York: Oxford University Press. pp. 123–152.

Gupta, Sanjeev, Luiz de Mello, and Raju Sharan. 2001. "Corruption and Military Spending." *European Journal of Political Economy* 17: 749–777.

Gurr, Ted. 1970. *Why Men Rebel.* Princeton, NJ: Princeton University Press.

Habibi, Nader. 1994. "Budgetary Policy and Political Liberty: A Cross-Sectional Analysis." *World Development* 22, 4: 579–586.

Haggard, Stephen. 1990. *Pathways from the Periphery: The Politics of Growth in the Newly Industrializing Countries.* Ithaca, NY: Cornell University Press.

Haggard, Stephan, and Robert Kaufman. 1995. *The Political Economy of Democratic Transitions.* Princeton, NJ: Princeton University Press.

Hartlyn, Jonathan. 1989. "Colombia: The Politics of Violence and Accommodation." In Larry Diamond, Juan J. Linz, and Seymour Martin Lipset (eds.), *Democracy in Developing Countries: Latin America, Volume Four.* Boulder, CO: Lynne Rienner. pp. 291–334.

Hassan II. 1978. *The Challenge: The Memoirs of King Hassan II of Morocco.* Translated by Anthony Rhodes. London: Macmillan.

Havel, Vaclav. 1985. "The Power of the Powerless." In John Keane (ed.), *The Power of the Powerless: Citizens against the State in Central-eastern Europe.* John Keane (ed.), Armonk, NY: M.E. Sharpe. pp. 23–96.

Heckman, James. 1979. "Sample Selection Bias as a Specification Error." *Econometrica* 47: 153–161.

Hellman, Joel S. 1998. "Winners Take All: The Politics of Partial Reform in Postcommunist Transitions." *World Politics* 50, 2: 203–234.

Henderson, Conway. 1991. "Conditions Affecting the Use of Political Repression." *Journal of Conflict Resolution* 35, 1: 120–142.

Herb, Michael. 1999. *All in the Family: Absolutism, Revolution, and Democracy in the Middle Eastern Monarchies.* Albany: State University of New York Press.

Hermet, Guy, Richard Rose, and Alain Rouquié. 1978. *Elections without Choice.* New York: John Wiley & Sons.

Heston, Alan, Robert Summers, and Bettina Aten. 2002. Penn World Table Version 6.1, Center for International Comparisons at the University of Pennsylvania (CICUP).

Heston, Alan, Robert Summers, and Bettina Aten. 2006. Penn World Table Version 6.2, Center for International Comparisons of Production, Income and Prices at the University of Pennsylvania.

Hibbs, Douglas, Jr. 1973. *Mass Political Violence*. New York: Wiley.

Hidrobo, Jorge. 1993. *Power and Industrialization in Ecuador*. Boulder, CO: Westview.

Hirschman, Albert. 1970. *A Bias for Hope: Essays on Development and Latin America*. New Haven, CT: Yale University Press.

Hodgkin, Thomas. 1961. *African Political Parties*. Baltimore, MD: Penguin Books.

Holmes, Stephen. 1995. *Passions and Constraint: On the Theory of Liberal Democracy*. Chicago: University of Chicago Press.

Holmes, Stephen. 2003. "Lineages of the Rule of Law." In José Maria Maravall and Adam Przeworski (eds.), *Democracy and the Rule of Law*. Cambridge: Cambridge University Press.

Howard, Marc Morjé, and Philip Roessler. 2006. "Liberalizing Electoral Outcomes in Competitive Authoritarian Regimes." *American Journal of Political Science* 50, 2: 365–381.

Huntington, Samuel. 1968. *Political Order in Changing Societies*. New Haven, CT: Yale University Press.

Huntington, Samuel. 1970. Social and Institutional Dynamics of One-Party Systems. In Samuel Huntington and C. Moore (eds.), *Authoritarian Politics in Modern Society: The Dynamics of Established One-Party Systems*, New York: Basic Books. pp. 3–47.

Im, Hyug Baeg. 1987. "The Rise of Bureaucratic Authoritarianism in South Korea." *World Politics* 39, 2: 231–257.

International Monetary Fund. Various years. *Government Finance Statistics Yearbooks*. Washington, D.C.: International Monetary Fund.

International Monetary Fund. May 1999. *World Economic Outlook*. Washington D.C.: International Monetary Fund.

International Monetary Fund. 2003. *Government Finance Statistics Yearbook, 2003*. Washington D.C.: IMF.

Isaacs, Anita. 1993. *Military Rule and Transition in Ecuador, 1972–92*. Pittsburgh, PA: University of Pittsburgh Press.

Ismael, Jacqueline. 1993. *Kuwait: Dependency and Class in a Rentier State*. Gainesville: University Press of Florida.

Jackson, Robert, and Carl Rosberg. 1982. *Personal Rule in Black Africa: Prince, Autocrat, Prophet, Tyrant*. Berkeley: University of California Press.

Jackson, Robert, and Carl Rosberg. 1984. "Personal Rule: Theory and Practice in Africa." *Comparative Politics* 16, 4: 421–442.

Jalal, Ayesha. 1995. *Democracy and Authoritarianism in South Asia.* New York: Cambridge University Press.

Janda, Kenneth. "Peru: The Party System in 1950–1956." In *Political Parties: A Cross-National Survey.* http://janda.org/icpp/ICPP1980/Book/PART2/3-SouthAmerica/37-Peru/Peru50-62.htm (downloaded October 21, 2007)

Jodice, D., and D. L. Taylor. 1983. *World Handbook of Social and Political Indicators.* New Haven: Yale University Press.

Kalyvas, Stathis. 1999. The Decay and Breakdown of Communist One-Party Systems. *Annual Review of Political Science* 2: 323–343.

Kamiński, Antoni. 1992. *An Institutional Theory of Communist Regimes: Design, Function, and Breakdown.* San Francisco, CA: ICS Press.

Kamiński, Marek. 1999. "How Communism Could Have Been Saved: Formal Analysis of Electoral Bargaining in Poland in 1989." *Public Choice* 98: 83–109.

Kapuścinski, Ryszard. 1983. *The Emperor: Downfall of an Autocrat.* San Diego, CA: Harcourt Brace Jovanovich.

Karl, Terry Lynn. 1997. *The Paradox of Plenty: Oil Booms and Petro-States.* Berkeley: University of California Press.

Kasara, Kimuli. 2005. "A Prize Too Large to Share: Opposition Coalitions and the Kenyan Presidency, 1991–2002." Department of Political Science, Stanford University, Unpublished manuscript.

Kaufman, Robert, and Alex Seguro-Ubiergo. 2001. "Globalization, Domestic Politics, and Social Spending in Latin America: A Time-Series Cross-Section Analysis, 1973–97." *World Politics* 53: 553–587.

Keller, Edmond. 1988. *Revolutionary Ethiopia: From Empire to People's Republic.* Bloomington: Indiana University Press.

Kelsen, Hans. 1945. *General Theory of Law and State.* Cambridge, MA: Harvard University Press.

Khan, Mohsin. 1990. "The Macroeconomic Effects of Fund-Supported Adjustment Programs." *IMF Staff Papers* 37: 195–231.

Khuri, Fuad, and Gerald Obermeyer. 1974. "The Social Bases for Military Intervention in the Middle East." In Catherine McArdle Kelleher (ed.), *Political-Military Systems: Comparative Perspectives.* London: Sage. pp. 55–85.

Kim, Chong Lim, Joel Barkan, llter Turan, and Malcolm Jewell. 1983. *The Legislative Connection: The Politics of Representation in Kenya, Korea, and Turkey.* Durham, NC: Duke University Press.

Kirkpatrick, Jeane. 1979. "Dictatorships and Double Standards." *Commentary* November: 34–45.

Knight, Jack. 1992. *Institutions and Social Conflict.* New York: Cambridge University Press.

Kolkowicz, Roman. 1967. *The Soviet Military and the Communist Party.* Princeton, NJ: Princeton University Press.

Kramer, Robert. 1994. "Sudan." In Frank Tachau (ed.), *Political Parties of the Middle East and North Africa*. Westport, CT: Greenwood Press. pp. 476–499.

Krennerich, Michael. 1999. "Ghana." In Dieter Nohlen, Michael Krennerich, and Bernhard Thibaut (eds.), *Elections in Africa*. New York: Oxford University Press. pp. 423–446.

Krennerich, Michael. 2005a. "El Salvador." In Dieter Nohlen (ed.), *Elections in the Americas: A Data Handbook, Volume 1*. Oxford: Oxford University Press. pp. 269–299.

Krennerich, Michael. 2005b. "Nicaragua." In Dieter Nohlen (ed.), *Elections in the Americas: A Data Handbook, Volume 1*. Oxford: Oxford University Press. pp. 479–510.

Kuran, Timur. 1991. "Now out of Never: The Element of Surprise in the East European Revolution of 1989." *World Politics* 44, 1: 7–48.

La Porta, Rafael, Florencio Lopez-de-Silanes, Andrei Shleifer, and Robert Vishny. 1998. "Law and Finance." *Journal of Political Economy* 106, 6: 1113–1155.

Lai, Brian, and Dan Slater. 2006. "Institutions of the Offensive: Domestic Sources of Dispute Initiation in Authoritarian Regimes, 1950–1992." *American Journal of Political Science* 50, 1: 113–126.

Lake, David, and Matthew Baum. 2001. "The Invisible Hand of Democracy: Political Control and the Provision of Public Services." *Comparative Political Studies* 34, 6: 587–621.

Landau, Jacob. 1994. "Turkey." In Frank Tachau (ed.), *In Political Parties of the Middle East and North Africa*. Westport, CT: Greenwood Press. pp. 549–610.

Lawson, Fred. 1994. "Syria." In Frank Tachau (ed.), *In Political Parties of the Middle East and North Africa*. Westport, CT: Greenwood Press. pp. 500–529.

Lehoucq, Fabrice. 2003. "Electoral Fraud: Causes, Types, and Consequences." *Annual Review of Political Science* 6: 233–256.

Leksykon Pan'stw S'wiata 1993–1994. 1993. Warsaw: Real Press.

Lenin, Vladimir. 1965 [1921]. "Preliminary Draft Resolution of the Tenth Congress of the R.C.P. on the Syndicalist and Anarchist Deviation in our Party." In *Lenin: Collected Works*. Moscow: Progress Publishers.

Lentz III, Harris. 1994. *Heads of States and Governments: A Worldwide Encyclopedia of over 2,300 Leaders, 1945–1992*. Jefferson, NC: McFarland and Company.

Léon-Roesch, Marta, and Richard Ortiz Ortiz. 2005. "Paraguay." In Dieter Nohlen (ed.), *Elections in the Americas: A Data Handbook, Volume 2*. Oxford: Oxford University Press. pp. 411–444.

Levi, Margaret. 1988. *Of Rule and Revenue*. Berkeley: University of California Press.

Levine, Ross, and David Renelt. 1992. "A Sensitivity Analysis of Cross-Country Regressions." *American Economic Review* 82, 4: 942–963.

Levitsky, Steven, and Lucan A. Way. 2002. "The Rise of Competitive Authoritarianism." *Journal of Democracy* 13, 2: 51–65.

Lewis, Paul. 1980. *Paraguay under Stroessner*. Chapel Hill: University of North Carolina Press.

Lewis, D. S, and S. J. Sagar. 1992. *Political Parties of Asia and the Pacific: A Reference Guide*. London: Longman.

Lichbach, Mark. 1987. "Deterrence or Escalation? The Puzzle of Aggregate Studies of Repression and Dissent." *Journal of Conflict Resolution* 31, 2: 266–297.

Lindberg, Staffan. 2006. "Tragic Protest: Why Do Opposition Parties Boycott Elections?" In Andreas Schedler (ed.), *Electoral Authoritarianism*. Boulder, CO: Lynne Rienner Publishers. pp. 149–163.

Lindert, Peter. 2004. *Growing Public: Social Spending and Economic Growth since the Eighteenth Century*. New York: Cambridge University Press.

Linz, Juan. 1970. "An Authoritarian Regime: Spain." In Erik Allardt and Stein Rokkan (eds.), *Mass Politics*. New York: The Free Press.

Linz, Juan, and Alfred Stepan. 1996. *Problems of Democratic Transition and Consolidation*. Baltimore, MD: Johns Hopkins University Press.

Lipset, Seymour Martin. 1959. "Some Social Requisites of Democracy: Economic Development and Political Legitimacy." *American Political Science Review* 53, 1: 69–105.

Londregan, John, and Keith Poole. 1990. "Poverty, the Coup Trap, and the Seizure of Executive Power." *World Politics* 42, 2: 151–183.

Loveman, Brian, and Thomas M. Davies, Jr. 1989. *The Politics of Antipolitics: The Military in Latin America*. Lincoln: University of Nebraska Press.

Lucas, Russell. 2005. *Institutions and the Politics of Survival in Jordan: Domestic Responses to External Challenges, 1988–2001*. Albany: State University of New York Press.

Luciani, Giacomo. 1987. "Allocation vs. Production States: A Theoretical Framework." In H. Beblawi and G. Luciani (eds.), *The Rentier State*. London: Croom Helm.

Lust-Okar, Ellen, and Amaney Ahmad Jamal. 2002. "Rulers and Rules: Reassessing the Influence of Regime Type on Electoral Law Formation." *Comparative Political Studies* 35, 3: 337–366.

Lust-Okar, Ellen. 2005. *Structuring Conflict in the Arab World: Incumbents, Opponents, and Institutions*. New York: Cambridge University Press.

Machiavelli, Niccolò. 1950. "The Discourses." In *The Prince and the Discourses*. New York: Random House.

Maddison, Angus. 2003. *The World Economy: Historical Statistics*. Paris: OECD.

Magaloni, Beatriz. 2006. *Voting for Autocracy: Hegemonic Party Survival and Its Demise in Mexico*. New York: Cambridge University Press.

Mankiw, N. G., P. Romer, and D. Weil. 1992. "A Contribution to the Empirics of Economic Growth." *Quarterly Journal of Economics* 107: 407–438.

Marx, Karl. 1994. [1869]. *The Eighteenth Brumaire of Louis Bonaparte*. New York: International.

McCormick, John. 2004. "From Constitutional Technique to Caesarist Ploy: Carl Schmitt on Dictatorship, Liberalism, and Emergency Powers." In Peter Baehr and Melvin Richter (eds.), *Dictatorship in History and Theory: Bonapartism, Caesarism, and Totalitarianism*. New York: Cambridge University Press. pp. 197–220.

McDonald, Ronald, and J. Mark Ruhl. 1989. *Party Politics and Elections in Latin America*. Boulder, CO: Westview Press.

McGuire, Martin, and Mancur Olson. 1996. "The Economics of Autocracy and Majority Rule: The Invisible Hand and the Use of Force." *Journal of Economic Literature* 34: 72–96.

McKinlay, R. D., and A. S. Cohan. 1975. "A Comparative Analysis of the Political and Economic Performance of Military and Civilian Regimes." *Comparative Politics* 8: 1–30.

McKinlay, R. D., and A. S. Cohan. 1976. "Performance and Instability in Military and Nonmilitary Regime Systems." *American Political Science Review* 70, 3: 850–864.

Mezey, Michael. 1983. "The Functions of Legislatures in the Third World." *Legislative Studies Quarterly* 8, 4: 511–550.

Michels, Robert. 1949. *Political Parties*. Glencoe, IL: The Free Press.

Middlebrook, Kevin. 1995. *Paradox of Revolution: Labor, the State, and Authoritarianism in Mexico*. Baltimore, MD: Johns Hopkins University Press.

Milgrom, Paul, Douglass North, and Barry Weingast. 1990. "The Role of Institutions in the Revival of Trade: The Medieval Law Merchant, Private Judges, and the Champagne Fairs." *Economics and Politics* 2: 1–23.

Mitchell, Neil, and James McCormick. 1988. "Economic and Political Explanations of Human Rights Violations." *World Politics* 40: 476–498.

Montesquieu. 1995. *De l'Esprit des lois*. Paris: Gallimard.

Moore, Barrington, Jr. 1966. *Social Origins of Dictatorship and Democracy*. Boston, MA: Beacon Press.

Moore, Clement. 1965. *Tunisia since Independence: The Dynamics of One-Party Government*. Berkeley: University of California Press.

Moore, Pete. 2004. *Doing Business in the Middle East: Politics and Economic Crisis in Jordan and Kuwait*. New York: Cambridge University Press.

Moore, Will. 1998. "Repression and Dissent: Substitution, Context, and Timing." *American Journal of Political Science* 42, 3: 851–873.

Morris, James. 1984. *Honduras: Caudillo Politics and Military Rule*. Boulder, CO: Westview Press.

Mortimer, Rex, and J. Stephen Hoadley. 1985. "Indonesia." In Haruhiro Fukui (ed.), *Political Parties of Asia and the Pacific, Volume 1*. Westport, CT: Greenwood Press. pp. 379–384.

Munck, Gerardo L., and Jay Verkuilen. 2002. "Conceptualizing and Measuring Democracy: Evaluating Alternative Indices." *Comparative Political Studies* 35, 1: 5–34.

Murphy, Kevin, Andrei Shleifer, and Robert Vishny. 1989. "Industrialization and the Big Push." *Journal of Political Economy* 97: 1003–1026.

Musolf, Lloyd, and Joel Smith, eds. 1979. *Legislatures in Development.* Durham, NC: Duke University Press.

Ndikumana, Leonce, and James Boyce. 1998. "Congo's Odious Debt: External Borrowing and Capital Flight in Zaire." *Development and Change* 29, 2: 195–217.

Neuhouser, Kevin. 1996. "Limits on Authoritarian Imposition of Policy: Failed Ecuadoran Military Populism in Comparative Perspective." *Comparative Political Studies* 29, 6: 635–659.

Nicholls, David. 1979. *From Dessalines to Duvalier: Race, Colour and National Independence in Haiti.* London: Cambridge University Press.

Nicolet, Claude. 2004. "Dictatorship in Rome." In Peter Baehr and Melvin Richter (eds.), *Dictatorship in History and Theory: Bonapartism, Caesarism, and Totalitarianism.* New York: Cambridge University Press. pp. 263–278.

Nohlen, Dieter, and Simon Pachano. 2005. "Ecuador." In Dieter Nohlen (ed.), *Elections in the Americas: A Data Handbook, Volume 2.* Oxford: Oxford University Press. pp. 365–410.

Nordlinger, Eric. 1977. *Soldiers in Politics: Military Coups and Governments.* Englewood Cliffs, NJ: Prentice Hall.

North, Douglass, and Robert Paul Thomas. 1973. *The Rise of the Western World.* New York: Cambridge University Press.

North, Douglass, and Barry Weingast. 1989. "Constitutions and Commitment: The Evolution of Institutions Governing Public Choice in Seventeenth-Century England." *Journal of Economic History* 49, 4: 803–832.

O'Donnell, Guillermo. 1979. *Modernization and Bureaucratic-Authoritarianism: Studies in South American Politics.* Berkeley, CA: Institute of International Studies.

O'Donnell, Guillermo, and Philippe Schmitter. 1986. *Transitions from Authoritarian Rule: Tentative Conclusions about Uncertain Democracies.* Baltimore: Johns Hopkins University Press.

Olson, Mancur. 1993. "Democracy, Dictatorship, and Development." *American Political Science Review* 87, 3: 567–576.

Olson, David, and Maurice Simon. 1982. "The Institutional Development of a Minimal Parliament: The Case of the Polish Sejm." In Daniel Nelson and Stephen White (eds.), *Communist Legislatures in Comparative Perspective.* Albany: State University of New York Press. pp. 47–84.

Peceny, Mark, Caroline Beer, and Shannon Sanchez-Terry. 2002. "Dictatorial Peace?" *American Political Science Review* 96, 1: 15–26.

Pennell, C.R. 2003. *Morocco: From Empire to Independence.* Oxford: Oneworld.

Perlmutter, Amos. 1977. *The Military and Politics in Modern Times: On Professionals, Pretorians, and Revolutionary Soldiers.* New Haven, CT: Yale University Press.

Poe, Steven, and C. Neal Tate. 1994. "Repression of Human Rights to Personal Integrity in the 1980s: A Global Analysis." *American Political Science Review* 88, 4: 853–872.

Pritchett, Lant. 2000. "Understanding Patterns of Economic Growth: Search for Hills among Plateaus, Mountains, and Plains." *World Bank Economic Review* 14: 221–250.

Pritchett, Lant. 2001. "Where Has All the Education Gone?" *World Bank Economic Review* 15, 3: 367–391.

Przeworski, Adam. 1991. *Democracy and the Market: Political and Economic Reforms in Eastern Europe and Latin America.* New York: Cambridge University Press.

Przeworski, Adam. 1999. "Minimalist Conception of Democracy: A Defense." In Ian Shapiro and Casiano Hacker-Cordón, (eds.), *Democracy's Value.* New York: Cambridge University Press. pp. 23–55.

Przeworski, Adam. 2005. "Is the Science of Comparative Politics Possible?" In Carlos Boix and Susan Stokes (eds.), *Oxford Handbook of Comparative Politics.* New York: Oxford University Press.

Przeworski, Adam, Michael Alvarez, Jose Antonio Cheibub, and Fernando Limongi. 2000. *Democracy and Development: Political Institutions and Well-Being in the World, 1950–1990.* New York: Cambridge University Press.

Przeworski, Adam, Tamar Asadurian, Carolina Curvale, Sunny Kaniyathu, and Anjali Thomas. 2007. *The PACKT Data Set.* New York: Department of Politics, New York University. Electronic Format.

Przeworski, Adam, and Fernando Limongi. 1993. "Political Regimes and Economic Growth." *Journal of Economic Perspectives* 7, 3: 51–69.

Raina, Peter. 1990. "Elections in Poland." In Robert K. Furtak (ed.), *Elections in Socialist States.* Hertfordshire, UK: Harvester Wheatsheaf.

Ram, Rati. 1986. "Government Size and Economic Growth: A New Framework and Some Evidence from Cross-Section and Time-Series Data." *American Economic Review* 76, 1: 191–203.

Ramseyer, J. Mark, and Frances Rosenbluth. 1995. *The Politics of Oligarchy: Institutional Choice in Imperial Japan.* New York: Cambridge University Press.

Rasanayagam, Angelo. 2003. *Afghanistan: A Modern History.* London: I. B. Tauris.

Rasler, Karen. 1986. "War Accommodation and Violence in the United States, 1890–1970." *American Political Science Review* 80, 3: 921–945.

Reiter, Dan, and Allan C. Stam III. 1998. "Democracy, War Initiation, and Victory." *American Political Science Review* 92, 2: 377–389.

Remmer, Karen. 1978. "Evaluating the Policy Impact of Military Regimes in Latin America." *Latin American Research Review* 13, 2: 39–54.

Risse, Thomas, Stephen Ropp, and Kathryn Sikkink. (eds.) 1999. *The Power of Human Rights: International Norms and Domestic Change.* New York: Cambridge University Press.

Robins, Philip. 2004. *A History of Jordan.* New York: Cambridge University Press.

Rodrik, Dani. 1995. "Getting Interventions Right: How South Korea and Taiwan Grew Rich." *Economic Policy* 10, 1: 55–107.

Rodrik, Dani. 1998. "Why Do More Open Economies Have Bigger Governments?" *Journal of Political Economy* 106, 5: 997–1032.

Rolicki, Janusz. 1990. *Edward Gierek: Przerwana Dekada.* Warsaw: Wydawnictwo FAKT.

Römer, Manuela. 1999. "Chad." In Dieter Nohlen, Michael Krennerich, and Bernhard Thibaut (eds.), *Elections in Africa.* New York: Oxford University Press. pp. 221–242.

Rouquié, Alain. 1987. *The Military and the State in Latin America.* Berkeley: University of California Press.

Rousseau, Jean-Jacques. 1987. "On the Social Contract." In Donald Cress (ed. and trans.), *The Basic Political Writings.* Indianapolis, IN: Hackett.

Rosenstein-Rodan, P. N. 1943. "Problems of Industrialization of Eastern and South-eastern Europe." *Economic Journal* 53: 202–211.

Ross, Michael. 2001. "Does Oil Hinder Democracy?" *World Politics* 53: 325–361.

Rudra, Nita. 2002. "Globalization and the Decline of the Welfare State in Less-Developed Countries." *International Organization* 56, 2: 411–445.

Saikal, Amin. 2004. *Modern Afghanistan: A History of Struggle and Survival.* London: I. B. Tauris.

Sala-I-Martin, Xavier. 1997. "I Just Ran Two Million Regressions." *American Economic Review, Papers and Proceedings* 87: 178–183.

Salisbury, Harrison. 1992. *The New Emperors: China in the Era of Mao and Deng.* Boston: Little, Brown.

Sánchez-Cuenca, Ignacio. 1998. "Institutional Commitments and Democracy." *Archives Européennes de Sociologie.* 39: 78–109.

Sanders, Alan. 1992. "Mongolia's New Constitution: Blueprint for Democracy." *Asian Survey* 32, 6: 506–520.

Sarkees, Meredith Reid, and Phil Schafer. 2000. "The Correlates of War Data on War: an Update to 1997." *Conflict Management and Peace Science* 18, 1: 123–144.

Schedler, Andreas. 2002. "The Menu of Manipulation." *Journal of Democracy* 13, 2: 36–50.

Schedler, Andreas. 2006. *Electoral Authoriansim: The Dynamics of Unfree Competition.* Boulder, CO: Lynne Rienner.

Schodt, David. 1987. *Ecuador: An Andean Enigma.* Boulder, CO: Westview Press.

Schumpeter, Joseph. 1976. *Capitalism, Socialism, and Democracy.* New York: Allen & Unwin.

Schwedler, Jillian. 2006. "Faith in Moderation: Islamist Parties in Jordan and Yemen. New York: Cambridge University Press.

Short, Philip. 2000. *Mao: A Life.* New York: Henry Holt.

Sikkink, Kathryn, Steve Ropp, and Thomas Risse-Kappen, eds. 1999. *The Power of Human Rights.* New York: Cambridge University Press.

Simon, Reeva. 1994. "Iraq." In Frank Tachau (ed.), *Political Parties of the Middle East and North Africa.* Westport, CT: Greenwood Press. pp. 174–197.

Singer, J. David, and Melvin Small. 1994. *Correlates of War Extra-State Database.* http://www.umich.edu/~cowproj/dataset.html. Downloaded in 2001.

Slater, Dan. 2003. "Iron Cage in an Iron Fist: Authoritarian Institutions and the Personalization of Power in Malaysia." *Comparative Politics* 36, 1: 81–101.

Smith, Benjamin. 2004. "Oil Wealth and Regime Survival in the Developing World, 1960–1999." *American Journal of Political Science* 48, 2: 232–246.

Smith, Benjamin. 2005. "Life of the Party: The Origins of Regime Breakdown and Persistence under Single-Party Rule." *World Politics* 57, 3: 421–451.

Social Sciences and Humanities Library (SSHL), University of California – San Diego. 2000. *Latin American Election Statistics: Colombia: Elections and Events 1940–1954.* http://sshl.ucsd.edu/collections/las/colombia/1940.html (downloaded October 21, 2007).

Social Sciences and Humanities Library (SSHL), University of California – San Diego. 2000. *Latin American Election Statistics: Dominican Republic: Elections and Events 1963–1969.* http://sshl.ucsd.edu/collections/las/dominicanrepublic/1963.html (downloaded October 27, 2007).

Social Sciences and Humanities Library (SSHL), University of California – San Diego. 2000. *Latin American Election Statistics: El Salvador: Elections and Events 1934–1960.* http://dodgson.ucsd.edu/las/elsal/1934–1960.html (downloaded October 21, 2007).

Social Sciences and Humanities Library (SSHL), University of California – San Diego. 2000. *Latin American Election Statistics: Guatemala: Elections and Events 1951–1960.* http://sshl.ucsd.edu/collections/las/guatemala/1951.html (downloaded October 21, 2007).

Social Sciences and Humanities Library (SSHL), University of California – San Diego. 2000. *Latin American Election Statistics: Honduras: Elections and Events 1902–1947.* http://sshl.ucsd.edu/collections/las/honduras/1902.html (downloaded October 21, 2007).

Social Sciences and Humanities Library (SSHL), University of California – San Diego. 2000. *Latin American Election Statistics: Honduras: Elections and*

Events 1948–1979. http://sshl.ucsd.edu/collections/las/honduras/1948.html (downloaded October 21, 2007).

Social Sciences and Humanities Library (SSHL), University of California – San Diego. 2000. *Latin American Election Statistics: Nicaragua: Elections and Events 1937–1970*. http://sshl.ucsd.edu/collections/las/nicaragua/1937.html (downloaded October 21, 2007).

Social Sciences and Humanities Library (SSHL), University of California – San Diego. 2000. *Latin American Election Statistics: Nicaragua: Elections and Events 1971–1982*. http://sshl.ucsd.edu/collections/las/nicaragua/1971.html (downloaded October 21, 2007).

Social Sciences and Humanities Library (SSHL), University of California – San Diego. 2000. *Latin American Election Statistics: Panama: Elections and Events 1931–1980*. http://sshl.ucsd.edu/collections/las/panama/1931.html (downloaded October 21, 2007).

Stasavage, David. 2005. "Democracy and Education Spending in Africa." *American Journal of Political Science* 49, 2: 343–358.

Stepan, Alfred. 1971. *The Military in Politics: Changing Patterns in Brazil*. Princeton, NJ: Princeton University Press.

Stockholm International Peace Research Institute. Various years. *Yearbook of World Armament and Disarmament*. Stockholm: Author.

Stohl, Michael, David Carleton, George Lopez, and Stephen Samuels. 1986. "State Violation of Human Rights: Issues and Problems of Measurement." *Human Rights Quarterly* 8, 4: 592–606.

Stroux, Daniel. 1999. "Togo." In Dieter Nohlen, Michael Krennerich, and Bernhard Thibaut (eds.), *Elections in Africa*. New York: Oxford University Press. pp. 891–909.

Stultz, Newell M. 1970. "The National Assembly in the Politics of Kenya." In Allan Kornberg and Lloyd Musolf (eds.), *Legislatures in Developmental Perspective*. Durham, NC: Duke University Press. pp. 303–333.

Summers, Robert, and Alan Heston. 1991. The Penn World Table (Mark 5): An Expanded Set of International Comparisons 1950–1988. *Quarterly Journal of Economics* 106, 2: 327–368.

Suter, Jan, and Dieter Nohlen. 2005. "Cuba." In Dieter Nohlen (ed.), *Elections in the Americas: A Data Handbook. Volume 1*. Oxford: Oxford University Press. pp. 195–222.

Suwannathat-Pian, Kobkua. 1995. *Thailand's Durable Premier: Phibun through Three Decades 1932–1957*. Kuala Lampur: Oxford University Press.

Svolik, Milan. 2007. "Power-sharing and Leadership Dynamics in Authoritarian Regimes." Chicago, IL: Presented at the American Political Science Association Annual Meeting, August 30–September 2, 2007.

Swearingen, Will D. 1987. "Morocco's Agricultural Crisis." In *The Political Economy of Morocco*, edited by I. William Zartman. New York: Praeger. pp. 159–172.

Taylor, Charles Lewis and David A. Jodice. 1983. *World Handbook of Political and Social Indicators*. New Haven, CT: Yale University Press.

Trouillot, Michel-Rolph. 1990. *Haiti: State against Nation*. New York: Monthly Review Press.

Tucker, Robert. 1961. "Towards a Comparative Politics of Movement-Regimes." *American Political Science Review* 55, 2: 281–289.

Ulc, Otto. 1982. "Legislative Politics in Czechoslovakia." In Daniel Nelson and Stephen White (eds.), *Communist Legislatures in Comparative Perspective*. Albany: State University of New York Press. pp. 111–124.

USAID. n.d. *A Decade of Change: Profiles of USAID Assistance to Europe and Eurasia*, Washington D.C.: USAID.

Valenzuela, Samuel. 1991. "Labor Movements and Political Systems: A Conceptual and Typological Analysis." Manuscript.

Valenzuela, Samuel. 1992. "Labour Movements and Political Systems: Some Variations." In *The Future of Labour Movements*, edited by Marino Regini. London: Sage. pp. 53–101.

Vanneman, Peter. 1977. *The Supreme Soviet: Politics and the Legislative Process in the Soviet Political System*. Durham, NC: Duke University Press.

Vargas Llosa, Mario. 2001. *The Feast of the Goat*. New York: Farrar, Straus, and Giroux.

Van Belle, Douglas. 1997. "Press Freedom and the Democratic Peace." *Journal of Peace Research*. 34: 405–414.

Van Praagh, David. 1996. *Thailand's Struggle for Democracy: The Life and Times of M.R. Seni Pramoj*. New York: Holmes & Meier.

Von Beyme, Klaus. 2000. *Parliamentary Democracy: Democratization, Destabilization, Reconsolidation, 1789–1999*. New York: St. Martin's Press.

Vreeland, James. 2003. *The IMF and Economic Development*. New York: Cambridge University Press.

Vreeland, James. 2007. *The International Monetary Fund: Politics of Conditional Lending*. New York: Routledge.

Vreeland, James. 2008. "Political Institutions and Human Rights: Why Dictatorships Enter into the United Nations Convention Against Torture." *International Organization* 62, 1: 65–101.

Walter, Knut. 1993. *The Regime of Anastasio Somoza 1936–1956*. Chapel Hill: University of North Carolina Press.

Wantchekon, Leonard. 2002. "Why Do Resource Abundant Countries Have Authoritarian Governments?" *Journal of African Finance and Economic Development* 5, 2: 57–77.

Waterbury, John. 1970. *The Commander of the Faithful: The Moroccan Political Elite – A Study in Segmented Politics*. New York: Columbia University Press.

Weaver, Mary Anne. 2000. "Letter from Qatar: Democracy by Decree." *The New Yorker* November 20: 54–61.

Weede, Erich. 1996. "Political Regime Type and Variation in Economic Growth Rate." *Constitutional Political Economy* 7, 3: 167–176.

Welch, Claude, Jr. 1974. "Personalism and Corporatism in African Armies." In *Political-Military Systems: Comparative Perspectives*, edited by Catherine McArdle Kelleher. London: Sage. pp. 125–145.

Whelpton, John. 2005. *A History of Nepal*. New York: Cambridge University Press.

White, Alastair. 1973. *El Salvador*. London: Ernest Benn Ltd.

Wintrobe, Ronald. 1998. *The Political Economy of Dictatorship*. New York: Cambridge University Press.

World Bank. 1993. *The East Asian Miracle*. Oxford: Oxford University Press.

World Bank. 2000. *World Development Indicators 2000*. Washington, D.C.: World Bank. CD-ROM.

World Bank. 2004. *World Development Indicators 2004*. Washington, D.C.: World Bank. CD-ROM.

Wright, Joseph. 2008. "Do Authoritarian Institutions Constrain? How Legislatures Impact Economic Growth and Investment." *American Journal of Political Science*. 52, 2: 322–343.

Wyatt, David K. 2003. *Thailand: A Short History*. New Haven: Yale University Press.

Yamada, Tatsuo. 1985. "China." In Haruhiro Fukui (ed.), *Political Parties of Asia and the Pacific. Volume 1*. Westport, CT: Greenwood Press. pp. 153–163.

Zárate, Roberto Ortiz de. "World Political Leaders." http://www.terra.es/personal2/monolith/00index.htm, downloaded 2001.

Zartman, I. William. 1964a. *Destiny of a Dynasty: The Search for Institutions in Morocco's Developing Society*. Columbia: University of South Carolina Press.

Zartman, I. William. 1964b. *Morocco: Problems of New Power*. New York: Atherton Press.

Zolberg, Aristide. 1969. *One-Party Government in the Ivory Coast*. Princeton, NJ: Princeton University Press.

Zuk, Gary, and William Thompson. 1982. "The Post-Coup Military Spending Question: A Pooled Cross-Sectional Time-Series Analysis." *American Political Science Review* 76, 1: 60–74.

Author Index

Subject Index